Jim Harrison

Twayne's United States Authors Series

Frank Day, General Editor

Clemson University

TUSAS 664

JIM HARRISON
Gary Isaacs Photography

Jim Harrison

Edward C. Reilly
Arkansas State University

Twayne Publishers
An Imprint of Simon & Schuster Macmillan
New York

Prentice Hall International
London • Mexico City • New Delhi • Singapore • Sydney • Toronto

Twayne's United States Authors Series No. 664

Jim Harrison
Edward C. Reilly

Twayne Publishers
An Imprint of Simon & Schuster Macmillan
1633 Broadway
New York, New York 10019-6785

Library of Congress Cataloging-in-Publication Data

Reilly, Edward C.
   Jim Harrison / Edward C. Reilly
      p. cm. — (Twayne's United States authors seres ; TUSAS 664)
   Includes bibliographical references and index.
   ISBN 0-8057-3978-5 (alk. paper)
   1. Harrison, Jim, 1937– —Criticism and interpretation.
2. Michigan—In literature. I. Title. II. Series.
PS3558.A67Z87 1996
818'.5409-dc20   95-45851
                                                                        CIP

The paper used in this publication meets the minimum requirements of American National Standard for Information Sciences—Permanence of Paper for Printed Library Materials. ANSI Z3948–1984. ∞™

10 9 8 7 6 5 4 3 2 1 (hc)

Printed in the United States of America

To the New Irish Kids on the Block
Skyler Aaron Malone
Austin Arlin Johanning

And in Memoriam
Francis Robert Reilly Sr.
Helen Patricia Fisher Reilly
Maureen Elizabeth Craven
Rosemary Reilly O'Brien

Contents

CONTENTS

Preface

My interest in Jim Harrison and his works began with "The Spoof Is in the Putting," a humorous book review of *Warlock* that appeared in the *Memphis Commercial Appeal* and featured an intriguing picture of the burly, mustachioed author in a short-sleeved Hawaiian shirt, arms folded, standing ankle-deep in snow. I read *Warlock* and rollicked in its humor, and then I read *Farmer*, *A Good Day to Die*, and the others. While the works shared some similarities, each was remarkably different and layered in meaning. They were all, in the main, enjoyable. Harrison is a consummate artist with a great deal of creative energy. He has published six novels, nine novellas, ten books of poetry, one book of nonfiction, not to mention book reviews, magazine articles, and screenplays.

Considering how long he has been writing, how many works he has produced, and the quality of his opus, scholarly attention and critical analyses have been scant. The sprinkling of critical articles should presage the deluge to come. Until then, book reviews, magazine and newspaper articles, interviews, and particularly his *Esquire* columns entitled "The Raw and the Cooked" and his essays reprinted in *Just before Dark* provide a basis for understanding Harrison's life, ideas, and works. I augmented my research with three interviews: a telephone chat with Dan Gerber, Harrison's longtime friend; an interview with John Harrison, Jim's older brother who is director of libraries at the University of Arkansas, where Jim's private papers are kept; and a two-day interview in Lake Leelanau with the author himself. Jim took me on treks around Harrison country—namely, Dick's Pour House, the Blue Bird Tavern, and Lake Michigan—in December snows, or at least I thought it was snow until, with his puckish humor, Jim assured me, "No, it isn't snow. It's lake effect. That's what the local TV weathermen call it."

Certain biographical facts shaped and changed Harrison's life and ultimately influenced his writings. They include, to mention a few, his family ties and Scandinavian heritages; hunting and fishing; being blinded in his left eye; years of being on the road; the deaths of his father and younger sister; and returning to his Michigan roots. John Harrison said that his brother's friendships with Dan Gerber, Tom McGuane, Russell Chatham, and Guy de la Valdene are central to his life; in this study, I try to explain their importance. Using interviews and Harrison's essays, I also discuss Harrison's views on greed, ecology, game laws, hunting and fishing, and Native Americans, all of which are equally central to his life and color his writings.

I analyze each of Harrison's novels and novellas, focusing on characters, settings, conflicts, themes, styles, and techniques. Because of the lack of criticism, I preface these discussions with book reviews to provide some general views about each work. I also emphasize similarities and differences between the work discussed and others. In analyzing Harrison's poetry, I discuss his poetic techniques and themes and look at similarities and differences between his poetry and his fiction.

While this study was intellectually stimulating and enjoyable, the layers of meaning in Harrison's fiction and poetry made it difficult and challenging as well. If I have revealed some of these layers, others await discovery, and I leave this formidable task to other scholars and Harrison aficionados.

Acknowledgments

For permission to quote from Jim Harrison's works, I thank the following:

From *Plain Song* by Jim Harrison. Copyright © 1965 by Jim Harrison. All rights reserved. Reprinted by permission of W. W. Norton Company.

From *Locations* by Jim Harrison. Copyright © 1968 by Jim Harrison. All rights reserved. Reprinted by permission of W. W. Norton Company.

From *Wolf: A False Memoir* by Jim Harrison. Copyright © 1971, 1981, 1989 by Jim Harrison. All rights reserved. Reprinted by permission of Simon & Schuster.

From *Outlyer and Ghazals* by Jim Harrison. Copyright © 1971 by Jim Harrison. All rights reserved. Reprinted by permission of Simon & Schuster.

From *A Good Day to Die* by Jim Harrison. Copyright © 1973, 1981, 1989 by Jim Harrison. All rights reserved. Reprinted by permission of Simon & Schuster.

From *Letters to Yesenin and Returning to Earth* by Jim Harrison. Copyright © 1973, 1977, 1979, 1981 by Jim Harrison. All rights reserved. Reprinted by permission of Dell Publishing Company, Inc.

From *Farmer* by Jim Harrison. Copyright © 1976, 1980, 1989 by Jim Harrison. All rights reserved. Reprinted by permission of Viking Press.

From *Legends of the Fall* by Jim Harrison. Copyright © 1979, 1980, 1982, 1989 by Jim Harrison. All rights reserved. Reprinted by permission of Dell Publishing Company, Inc.

From *Warlock* by Jim Harrison. Copyright © 1981, 1982 by Jim Harrison. All rights reserved. Reprinted by permission of Dell Publishing Company, Inc.

From *Selected and New Poems, 1961–1981* by Jim Harrison. Copyright © 1981, 1982 by Jim Harrison. All rights reserved. Reprinted by permission of Dell Publishing Company, Inc.

From *Sundog* by Jim Harrison. Copyright © 1984, 1991 by Jim
      Harrison. All rights reserved. Reprinted by permission
      of E. P. Dutton, Inc.

From *Dalva* by Jim Harrison. Copyright © 1988, 1989 by Jim
      Harrison. All rights reserved. Reprinted by permission
      of Washington Square Press.

From *The Theory and Practice of Rivers and New Poems* by Jim Harrison.
      Copyright © 1989 by Jim Harrison. All rights reserved.
      Reprinted by permission of Clark City Press.

From *The Woman Lit by Fireflies* by Jim Harrison. Copyright © 1990 by
      Jim Harrison. All rights reserved. Reprinted by permis-
      sion of Houghton Mifflin Company.

From *Just before Dark: Collected Nonfiction* by Jim Harrison. Copyright
      © 1991, 1992 by Jim Harrison. All rights reserved.
      Reprinted by permission of Clark City Press.

From *Julip* by Jim Harrison. Copyright © 1994 by Jim Harrison. All
      rights reserved. Reprinted by permission of Houghton
      Mifflin Company.

Although connotatively acknowledgments can never go wide enough or
deep enough, I would like to acknowledge and personally thank:

John Harrison for the interview, for the personal, often humorous
insights into Jim's life, and for the giant chocolate chip cookie he bought
me after lunch.

Rebecca Newth Harrison for her comments about and insights into
Jim's life and writings and for making Jim's papers available.

Dan Gerber for the telephone interview and for his insights and anecdotes about Jim.

Joyce Harrington Bahle for coordinating dates, times, and reservations for my interview with Jim.

Frank Day at Clemson University for agreeing again to be my in-field
editor for this book.

Mark Zadrozny at Twayne Publishers, who sent me several articles
about Jim Harrison.

Carol Sue Johnson, who once again agreed to be my typist despite my
propensity for changing paragraphs and even pages and who manages to
keep my endnote numbers in sequence.

Rush Nash, fellow friend and rascal.

Bob, Marie, and Jayson Ivey for their hospitality in Ruidoso, New Mexico, during the summer of 1993 and Christmas 1995 because I needed the mountains and the laughs.

The three Raggedies—Cathy, Byron, and Barrett.

And finally, Jim Harrison, to whom I can only say thanks, thanks, thanks, thanks—for the two-day interview, for the gourmet meal, for your writings, and for explaining the mystery of lake effect.

Chronology

1937 James Thomas Harrison born 11 December in Grayling, Michigan, to Winfield Sprague and Norma Olivia Wahlgren Harrison.

1940 Family moves to Reed City, Michigan.

1945 Harrison accidentally blinded in his left eye.

1952–1956 Attends Haslett Rural High School. Hitchhikes to California in 1956.

1960 Marries Linda May King. Earns B.A. degree, Michigan State University. Daughter Jamie born 21 May.

1962 Father and sister Judith killed in an automobile accident.

1965 Earns M.A. degree, Michigan State University (master's thesis: "The Natural History of Some Poems"). Becomes assistant professor of English, State University of New York at Stony Brook. *Plain Song* is published.

1967–1969 Receives National Endowment for the Arts grants. Purchases Lake Leelanau farm.

1969 Awarded a Guggenheim fellowship. *Walking* is published.

1971 Daughter Anna born 6 April. *Wolf: A False Memoir* and *Outlyers and Ghazals* are published.

1973 *A Good Day to Die* and *Letters to Yesenin* are published.

1975 *Farmer* is published.

1977 *Returning to Earth* is published.

1979 *Legends of the Fall* is published.

1981 *Warlock* and *Selected and New Poems, 1961–1981* are published.

1984 *Sundog* is published.

1988 *Dalva* is published.

1989 *The Theory and Practice of Rivers and New Poems* is published.

1990 *The Woman Lit by Fireflies* is published. *Revenge* (film) is released.

1991 *Just before Dark: Collected Nonfiction* is published.

1994 *Julip* is published. *Wolf* (film) is released (not based on *Wolf: A False Memoir*).

1995 *Legends of the Fall* (film) is released.

Chapter One

"Where I Feel the Best in the World": Harrison's Life and Times

Believing that he could not be an artist in Michigan, Jim Harrison hitch-hiked to California when he was 19; he would also live in Boston and New York, searching for the right setting: "I was at the age," says Harrison, "when you think all your problems are geographical and if you can only get to the right setting, you'll begin writing. Of course, you never do."[1] But Harrison's ties to Michigan were strong, his roots in Michigan fixed. Eventually and inexorably, he returned there: "It's where I feel the best in the world. It's the only place I've ever been able to write—I've never been able to write in transit."[2] He has admitted that he tried writing for "two months at a hotel in Los Angeles, at the Sunset Marquis. It was just terrifying. . . . The writing was worthless" (Stocking 1977, 21). He added, however, that the hotel guests on either side of him at the swimming pool were interesting—"Kinky of Kinky Friedman and the Texas Jew Boys and Harry Reems, the star of *Deep Throat*" (21). Jim Harrison now does all his living and writing in Michigan, either at his farm in Lake Leelanau or at his cabin on a two-track near Grand Marais in the Upper Peninsula.

"I Grew up within That Framework"

James Thomas Harrison was born on 11 December 1937 in Grayling, Michigan, to Winfield Sprague and Norma Wahlgren Harrison; he was the second of five children, who included his older brother John, a younger brother David, and two younger sisters, Mary and Judith. After working as a librarian at Harvard and Yale, John Harrison is now the director of libraries at the University of Arkansas in Fayetteville. According to John, David is affiliated with the University of Washington in Seattle, where he is a consultant on water resources and specializes in grant writing.[3] Mary, a court social worker, lives in Big Rapids, Michigan, and Judith died in 1962.

The Harrison family moved to Reed City when Jim was three and lived there until he was twelve. When Winfield Harrison took a state agricul-

1

tural agent position, the family moved to Haslett, near Lansing. It was in Reed City, however, in 1945, that Jim Harrison was blinded in his left eye. While having his first sexual experience, his girl playmate "rammed me in the face with a broken beaker. It was in a big wooded lot in Reed City behind the hospital. We were fooling around doing something. So I went and hid under a porch. You know, the usual thing. It wasn't pretty. The glass was sticking out of the eyeball."[4] Because the family had no insurance, Harrison had to save almost $2,000 for an eye operation, which failed. Years later he said, "The doctor took all the money, so I have lots of reasons to be anti-doctors and anti-lawyers" ("Lake").

Was Jim an interesting or unusual child? Not according to him: "I was basically an obnoxious child. . . . I don't think I was the least bit creative at all. I was a different sort. . . . And I didn't have particularly good grades" (Stocking 1977, 21). When they were quite young, their father often took John and Jim to Reed City's public library, introducing them to the world of books and words. In addition, both boys played football for Haslett Rural Agricultural High School. Jim spoke fondly about playing next to his big brother John, who was a senior when Jim was a sophomore. John played left tackle, and Jim played left guard (a pulling guard) on offense and middle linebacker on defense. Jim added that he was "not very good," "just okay." He believes that football is a "terrible sport, frankly," because it knocks the "shit out of so many people": "Like my sinus operation. They did a CAT scan, and they said, 'What happened to you?' And I said, 'Well, when I was 18—it was the last year before face masks—I got my face crushed playing football.' It obviously had not been set correctly, and that caused years of discomfort . . . all for that stupid sport" ("Lake").[5]

Even though his parents were Congregationalists, Harrison claimed he was saved at a Baptist evangelistic service. "Between 14 and 15," he confesses, "I was a passionate Baptist preacher . . . just in little churches. And I was president of the Bible Club, champion Bible whiz kid. But it didn't last very long."[6] According to one source, Harrison's reconversion occurred in a fire tower when he was 16 and working as a waiter at Rocky Mountain Park: "This girl just took me up there and started giving me kisses and everything, and took off her trousers. . . . And I said, '*Holy shit, is this ever fun.*' So that sort of loosened up the religion bit."[7] Similar reconversions happen to Swanson in *Wolf*, to Strang in *Sundog*, and to B.D. in *Brown Dog*. In a recent edition of the biographical work *Contemporary Authors*, Harrison lists his religious preference as "Zennist" (Ross,), a choice influenced by his longtime friend and fellow writer Dan Gerber.

At Haslett Rural Agricultural High School, both John and Jim Harrison were influenced by Bernice Smith, who taught English and was in charge of the school library. According to John, "There were 30 people in my class, and there were 50 or 60 in Jim's. So it was real small, and she recognized that we were *word* people. . . . We read the *Nation* and *Saturday Review* when we were in high school because she gave them to us. And we worked in the library for her because nobody else wanted to or was willing" ("John Harrison"). When he was a sophomore, Jim wanted to be a writer because he thought that would be an interesting life and because, as he admitted, "I was so romantic I squeaked" (Skwira, 17). Although he wanted to be a novelist, Harrison could only write poems, because "I had an attention span something like Richard Nixon's, very brief; poetry is a young man's form in a sense."[8] He said that initially he wanted to be a painter, because he was "caught up in the aftershocks of being a dead-end romantic . . . and because, when I was 18 and working on farms and stuff, I wanted to be like Van Gogh, Lord Byron, and Gauguin. They were my heroes." Harrison realized, however, that he had no talent for art and decided that the "next best thing was to be a poet" ("Lake"). He wrote poetry until his thirties, when he wrote his first novel, *Wolf: A False Memoir*.

When he was 19, Harrison decided he wanted to see the Pacific Ocean and find the right setting, so he hitchhiked to California. Although he had very little money for the trip, he knew if he needed more he could always stop and work on a farm bucking hay bales, digging ditches, mending fences—work he had done while growing up. Later, when he had saved up $90, he decided to leave Michigan again, travel to New York, and live in what he called "Green-witch" Village. Along with his favorite books—the King James Bible, Joyce's *Finnegans Wake*, Faulkner's *The Sound and the Fury*, Rimbaud's *Illuminations*, and Dostoyevsky's *Notes from the Underground*—he took his $20 typewriter, a 17th birthday present from his father.[9] In his late twenties, Harrison returned to Michigan and ended up staying.

Before and between these sojourns, Harrison had been enrolled at Michigan State University, where his brother John was working on his degree. As an undergraduate, Harrison would enroll and then drop out: "I couldn't stand college. . . . Of all the writers I admired, like Sherwood Anderson, Faulkner, Hemingway, I didn't notice any B.A.'s attached to their names. . . . None. Hart Crane, Rimbaud, Garcia Lorca. Where are the B.A.'s?" (Skwira, 17). Fortunately, every time Harrison returned to Michigan State, the official in the scholarship office kept giving him a scholarship, out of sympathy for Harrison's "desire to be an author" (Ross, 227). Harrison said that during his years at Michigan State he never took a creative writing course. Although he met Tom McGuane at Michigan State, they did not become close friends until much later, or as McGuane has said, "Jim and I were quite competitive in college in certain ways. . . . We were kind of like two old roosters who walked around each other."[10] It was also at Michigan State that Harrison met and became friends with Dan Gerber.

Of his undergraduate days Harrison said warmly, "The only thing that got me through college is that I fell in love and got married" (Skwira, 17). He married Linda May King in October 1960, and they have been married ever since. Actually, they had first met when he was 16 and she was 14: "I saw her walking up a sidewalk in riding clothes and thought she looked nifty. That's actually true" (Bohy, 11). Harrison also laughingly recalled that when he and Linda started seeing each other seriously when he returned to Michigan, her father came home one day and said to Linda's mother, "Your daughter's dating a Mexican" ("Lake").

If Harrison's undergraduate years were sporadic, he describes his M.A. years as "hideous": "I sort of flunked out of the M.A. program" (Ross, 227). To support his family, Harrison worked as a carpenter, a well digger, and a block mason. One time when he was laying blocks for a house, the delivery truck could not get close enough to the excavation: "I had to wheelbarrow 1,200 cement blocks for about seventy yards, load them and unload them. It was a cold, icy, early November day, and it took me about nine hours to do it. That day I manhandled thirty-five tons worth of cement blocks and that was for two and half dollars an hour" (Fergus 1988, 59). Before he started laying blocks, Harrison could type, but after block laying for two years he could only type using one finger; block laying "stretches all those tendons, and your hands thicken and you don't have that dexterity. I know an old man that's been a block layer all his life, and his hands are like clubs" ("Lake").

It was during his block mason days that Harrison was persuaded to complete a master's degree, especially after W. W. Norton Company published his *Plain Song* in 1965. Herbert Weisinger had been Harrison's professor in comparative literature at Michigan State, and Harrison has praised him as "the smartest man I know." As Harrison told it: "Weisinger wrote me a note and said, look, this is not too neat. You can't forever be a block layer, right? So he said if I wrote a long essay on how I wrote this book of poems he could wrangle it so I could get my master's"

(Skwira, 18). His 1965 master's thesis, "The Natural History of Some Poems," is included in *Just before Dark: Collected Nonfiction*.

When Weisinger became the chair of the English Department at State University of New York at Stony Brook, he persuaded Harrison to come teach there. Harrison taught for almost two years. He has candidly admitted that he hated teaching, not only because it interfered with his writing but also because, "when you're a writer in a university, you're a freak, sort of a town clown. I feel much less isolated here [on the farm] than at a university."[11] Harrison said that a university teaching position is most enticing when a writer is neither famous nor making much money: "The hardest thing was during our poorest years when I got offers to be the poet in residence at some place. . . . I remember about five years ago this university had offered me $80,000 to come be the writer in residence. I thought, 'My God, that's quite a draw!' But I wrote back and said, 'Thank you, but someone has to stand on the outside'" ("Lake").

In 1967 the Harrisons moved back to Michigan and bought a nine-acre farm for $18,000 in Lake Leelanau. Because they had moved about four times before, Jamie, who was six, asked if they would have to move again. Harrison replied no. "We never did. I wanted to a couple of times but said, 'Well, no, I'm not going to. That's not right'" ("Lake"). The Harrison house, barn, and granary nestle among rolling, wooded hills, and near the drive is an easy-to-read sign: DO NOT ENTER THIS DRIVEWAY UNLESS YOU HAVE CALLED FIRST. THIS MEANS YOU. Joyce Harrington Bahle, Harrison's secretary, explains that she decided to post the sign after Harrison became well known and people would stop by at any hour of the day or night, not only to talk but especially to party.

Like Jim Harrison himself, the house is prepossessing, comfortably worn, and unpretentious. There is a spaciously comfortable living room with a fireplace, ample windows, built-in bookcases, chairs, tables, a sofa, a coffee table laden with books, and Russell Chatham's paintings on the walls. Dogs and cats sprawl on the floor and the furniture; as John Harrison laughingly exaggerates: "You look on the furniture, and there's a dog on every one of them—on every easy chair or sofa or anything. It's just totally tolerated. Nobody thinks twice about that. There's an animal wherever you sit, and you just sit with the animal. And the animals are highly tolerant." From the bookcase holding numerous cookbooks to the two Jenn-Air stoves, the Harrison kitchen also mirrors Linda and Jim's interior decorating and culinary tastes. Indeed, the kitchen is the usual gathering place for both family and guests, who sit in the countertop-high director's chairs that flank the butcher block–topped island down the center of the kitchen. The Harrison kitchen is an especially important gathering place in the fall when Russell Chatham and Guy de la Valdene visit for the hunting and the "fattening." According to Jim Fergus: "An enormous portion of the day is devoted to planning, shopping for, preparing, discussing, and finally eating one breathtaking meal after another at the end of which preliminary discussions and preparation for the next meal begin almost immediately" (Fergus 1988, 54). "Bird Hunting" in *Just before Dark* details not only one of their typical bird-hunting forays but some of the exotic, prodigious meals they prepare as well.

Behind the main house is the granary, Harrison's combination getaway/quasi-office/study. It, too, is unpretentious, comfortable, and rustic. On the walls are a picture of a younger Jim and Linda Harrison, with their daughter, taken in Linda's cornfield; Chief Joseph's picture with his words, "Today is a good day to die"; and animal skins. On a small table under the back window is an eclectic collection of keepsakes and artifacts: a Hopi rattle, some favorite stones, a prehistoric grizzly tooth, a brass body tag from the Wyoming Territory's Bureau of Indian Affairs. Above his desk and suspended from the low ceiling are Harrison's totems: a crow's wing, a pine cone from the forest where Lorca was murdered, a piece of dried grizzly dung, and a child's ragged tennis shoe he found in Florida after some Haitians had landed. Harrison recalls that the Haitians thought they were going to be shot when the police arrived, so they put their hands on the tops of their heads: "Another guy and I tried to convince them they weren't going to be killed. 'No pistola,' we kept saying. They left one little shoe in the boat. I took it along as a reminder" (Skwira, 14).

Although he has renovated the granary and the house and even added his famous Warner Brothers Memorial Wine Cellar (one of his splurges), lean times dogged the Harrisons for ten years as they struggled on his income of less than $10,000 a year. In *Letters to Yesenin*, he wrote:

What if I own more paper clips than I'll ever use in this lifetime.
My other possessions are shabby: the house half
painted, the car without a muffler, one dog with bad eyes
and the other dog a horny moron. Even the baby has a rash on
her neck but then we don't own humans. My good books were

stolen at parties long ago and two of the barn windows are
broken and the furnace is unreliable and field mice daily
feed on the wiring.[12]

With the publication of *Legends of the Fall* in 1979 came profuse wealth
and offers to write screenplays. However, Harrison says, "I lost my equilibrium": he squandered his money "with Leon Spinks' grace. . . . If
you're very poor for 20 years and then you get a lot of money, you're just
like any other fool who gets ahold of a bunch of money. . . . And after
you blow it you sort of look around like Alfred E. Neuman and say,
'*Huh!*'" (Skwira, 9–10). Noting that he made some bad investments in
English gambling stock, in Australian oil stock, in a Key West charter
boat, he observed, "If you get the idea I'm a financial moron you've
stuck the bandelero in the ass of the donkey."[13] Harrison worked even
harder to pay off his debts—they were into six figures—and managed to
do so within a year.

Despite the lean, hungry years and the now-affluent years, Harrison
emphasized that he had "what my wife and I wanted when I was thirty-
two—we had a small farm and a bunch of animals and a garden"
(Skwira, 13). Moreover, Harrison has described Lake Leelanau as "by far
the pleasantest place I've ever lived."[14] He warmly recalled that the
farm's previous occupant claimed that she could lie on the ground in the
pasture behind the house and "hear water running underneath. That's
quite something when you think about it."[15]

In "A Memoir of Horse Pulling," an essay in *Just before Dark*, Harrison
writes that his grandfather, John Severin Wahlgren, journeyed from
Sweden to Illinois in the 1890s and after a number of years had saved up
enough money to buy a farm "up in Michigan" (*JBD*, 103). Indeed, Jim
Harrison's roots have always been "up in Michigan": "I grew up in
northern Michigan. Both my mother's and father's families were farm
families from Osceola and Mecosta counties. I grew up within that
framework. It's whatever you get your juices from, your ideas from"
(Stocking 1977, 21). Harrison's "juices" and "ideas" are rooted in
Michigan, but they are also shaped by the metaphorical concentric circles that surround him.

The Family Circle

In "A Memoir of Horse Pulling," Harrison writes about his father: "I have
an old photo of my father, dead now as is my grandfather, leaning on the

plow handles looking very jaunty with the reins over his bare shoulder
and an old gangster-type fedora cocked on his head. He always helped
with the plowing during the Depression when he was unemployed"
(*JBD*, 103). Harrison's father was "physically, [an] enormously strong
person, and he was a wrestler on scholarship at Michigan State. . . . My
dad lived in a tent a couple of years—before he went to college—digging
pipelines. He was big across the chest, but he wasn't very tall" ("Lake").
After his father completed his undergraduate degree, he became an agricultural agent, work that required the family to move often; they lived in
Cheboygan, Boyne City, Reed City, and Lansing. Harrison's father "loved
his work, having come from a generation of many unprosperous farmers
. . . and considered farming an applied science and his job that of a missionary who spread the good news of effective farming methods" (*JBD*,
98). Harrison's father took him on his agricultural rounds "from farm to
farm, to farm, to farm"; "anything I had to write about was from that
experience" ("Lake").

Harrison's father started taking him fishing when he was five: "It was
a much more relaxed kind of thing in families then. There wasn't this distance that men unfortunately have now between themselves and their
sons where everything is programmed—Little League, Boy Scouts"
(Stocking 1977, 26). Both John and Jim Harrison recall that not only
were there books in their house—"We had *The Book House* when we were
growing up, and it's 12 volumes"—but their father began taking them to
Reed City's public library when they were very young ("Lake"). Their
father was also an avid reader who made his way through all of Erskine
Caldwell, John Steinbeck, and William Faulkner; Harrison would give his
father *The Bear*, which his father "just loved." For Harrison's 17th birthday, his father gave him a hardback edition of Faulkner's *The Mansion*.
Harrison attributes his "sense of language" to his father: "My father had
a delicious sense of language. He couldn't bear to say the same thing the
same way twice. I think that's more of the old oral tradition of people
telling stories around the supper table" (Stocking 1977, 21).

In 1962, tragedy invaded the Harrison house when their father and
younger sister Judith were killed in a head-on car crash with a drunk driver. Harrison has admitted that the accident "caused a lot of mental
problems for the next thirty years or so" (Sisyphus, 6). "When you start
out, you have a mother and a father. And for some reason, it takes forever to figure out those relationships. Then when a father dies, you're confronted with the first, big brutal fact in life—of your own mortality and
the utter transience of everything. The death of a loved one, especially a

father, can be an incredible thing in your life" (Stocking 1977, 25). According to Eric Siegal, the death of Harrison's father was the catalyst that started him writing seriously (Siegal, 20). "David" is a poem about his father's death, as told through his younger brother's eyes, and "A Sequence of Women" is a poem about the effects of his sister's death.

Even though she is in her seventies, Harrison's mother is very active and an avid bird-watcher. John Harrison says that she often drives from Michigan to Fayetteville, Arkansas, to visit his family. He says that she is "always astounded" by all the recognition Jim receives, then adds with a laugh: "She's very proud of him but doesn't know how she feels about what he writes. She has real reservations about some of the things he said—you know, about the morals of some of his characters and things like that. I don't know how she takes it now. She's always been upset over our broad language. . . . We'd always just shit her about it because we know she's a Swede, and you know how immoral they are as a people" ("John Harrison"). Jim Harrison recalled a quarrel between his father and mother: she objected to Jim's reading a Capote novel "simply because of the picture of Truman on the back"; his father responded, "Oh, for God's sake" ("Lake"). Harrison said, however, that he is not too concerned about his mother's approval of his characters and their morals; he laughingly recounted his mother once asking, "Don't your people ever have normal sex?" and he replied, "What the fuck is that? Give me a break. I don't allow it—normal sex" ("Lake"). He also recalled that "the first time I got my wife pregnant, my mother said, 'James, we've always catered to your aberrations.'"[16]

Because only 18 months separate their ages and they shared a bedroom growing up, a close bond exists between Jim and John Harrison. Jim lived with John and his wife, Rebecca Newth Harrison—to whom Jim dedicates *Selected and New Poems*—when they were first married and living in Boston. Rebecca was working at the Harvard Graduate School of Education, John was working at the Harvard library, and Jim was supposed to be interviewing for jobs. Both John and Rebecca recall that when they left for their jobs, Jim would "leap back into bed" ("John Harrison"). According to Rebecca, Jim stayed up late and wrote in their kitchen: "It was there he started writing that first book [*Plain Song*]. He had just six poems that were the basis for that book. . . . I always had this concept ever since Jim told me, 'I just had about six good poems that I knew were good, and then I interspersed other works into the core of that work.'" Early on Harrison had given Denise Levertov some of his poems, and when he got an envelope from her, he thought she was sending his poems back. Instead, she had written him a long letter informing him that she had just become poetry editor for W. W. Norton and wanted him to send her his manuscript. "Well," says Jim, "I didn't have but ten poems, so I got busy and got the rest of them written out. Then Norton published that book [*Plain Song*], and it received critical attention" ("Lake").

A significant aspect of the close tie between the two Harrison brothers is what John calls "vauntings." Jim will say that John is bigger in girth, and John will say that Jim is bigger. Rubbing his own stomach, Jim said, "This is all *good* food" and then vaunted, "John is an 'indiscriminate feeder' " ("Lake"). Naturally, their vauntings often relate humorous anecdotes about each other. John described Jim's territory when he worked as a book representative in Boston as "sort of this grand tour that took him from one oyster joint to the next" ("John Harrison"). Jim recalled that John started jogging, got down to 190 pounds, was sent to Crete as a consultant, gained back the lost weight, but defended himself with, "What are you supposed to do when they serve you a whole little lamb?" ("Lake"). Both Harrisons laugh about Jim's first visit to Fayetteville. At a Dickson Street restaurant, the waitress said, "Our lunch special today is venison stew." John says Jim ate three bowls, which forever fixed his admiration for Fayetteville and Arkansas; the restaurant had never had venison stew before, however, and according to John, "sure as hell has not had it since."

Jim Harrison's most significant and stable ties are to his wife Linda and his two daughters, Jamie Louise and Anna Severin. Harrison told Ric Bohy, "I've often thought that if I hadn't gotten married early, I'd be dead. I'm too self-destructive a human being" (Bohy, 21). Moreover, he told Jim Fergus, "I unabashedly owe my existence" to Linda (Fergus 1985, 118). He has attributed their long marriage to a "shared peasant tolerance" and to Linda's feminism: "Women that persist and insist on all their rights of every sort always get treated extremely well. And she's the least masochistic woman I've ever known" (Bohy, 14). Linda shares Jim's love for the outdoors, cooking, and reading, and like her husband, she is prepossessing and unpretentious. Although she drives Saabs, Harrison says they are her only extravagance.

Although Harrison has had several good editors—Leslie Wells, Pat Irving—his daughter Jamie now edits his work: "Starting with *Dalva*, Jamie did the best work on that, giving me little suggestions when I was shying away from certain things. She is just a profound reader and certainly has read more widely than anybody I know. And she is a good line editor. . . . She could remember, for example, that you used the same adjective 18 pages ago or that there's a slight incongruity in the plot" ("Lake"). After graduating from the University of Michigan, Jamie lived for about six years in New York, where she met Steve Potenberg, a law student; they married and moved to Livingston, Montana. As Jim jokingly remarked, being a lawyer does not "mean a lot in Montana, because nobody sues each other in Montana. It's slow going out there" ("Lake"). Even though it may be "slow going" for Steve, Jamie is busy working for Russell Chatham's Clark City Press, which published Harrison's *Just before Dark*. But as Harrison explains: "That cost me $125,000 to do it with Clark City Press. . . . I was so *pissed off* with the publishing world a year and a half ago—not with Sam Lawrence, I liked him. And I could have fulfilled my contract with that book, but then I said, 'I literally can't bear to have another book come out in New York. So here's this press run by friends and a daughter. I'll give them the book.' But that was a moral decision. And I like to reserve the right to make moral decisions like that" ("Lake").

The Potenbergs have a son named Will, and *Just before Dark* is dedicated to Steve, Jamie, and Will. John Harrison has said that, "if you read *Dalva* and *The Woman Lit by Fireflies*, you can see that" Jim's wife, daughters, and family are "central to his existence." Indeed, like Jim Harrison himself, the son, brother, husband, father, and now grandfather, Harrison's characters often find purpose, meaning, and stability within the circle of family love and solidarity.

The Circle of Friends

In addition to Harrison's family circle is his circle of very close friends, especially "the gang"—Tom McGuane, Russell Chatham, and Guy de la Valdene. McGuane says that he and Harrison were merely acquaintances at Michigan State—"Jim and I circled each other in those years, sort of suspicious of each other."[17] The Harrison-McGuane friendship was not forged until someone sent McGuane, who was living in Spain, a copy of *Plain Song*. When he returned to the United States, McGuane visited Harrison, they went fishing, and, said Harrison, "we've been friends ever since" (Stocking 1977, 22). When McGuane had problems with publishing *The Sporting Club*, Harrison helped: "I took it to Richard Locke . . . at Simon and Schuster, and he took only twenty-four hours to get it accepted there" (Ross, 228). When McGuane moved to Key West, he and Harrison called each other often until they realized how expensive long-distance calls were. They began writing letters instead and have been corresponding for over 20 years. Their correspondence is in Harrison's private papers at the University of Arkansas, but John Harrison has asserted, "The McGuane-Jim correspondence won't come out for a long, long time. I *can tell* you that. One reason why . . . it is just loaded with glosses, and things like that. It's an intensely personal correspondence. They've opinions about everybody" ("John Harrison"). Even Russell Chatham says that their letters are "unlike anything anybody would ever imagine existed. They really show off for each other."[18]

Russell Chatham met McGuane in 1967 in Bolinas, California; when McGuane invited Chatham in 1970 to fish in Key West, Chatham met Harrison. After following McGuane to Montana, Chatham started Clark City Press with the claim, "I'm only going to publish books that will be around a hundred years from now. . . . And, of course, my own" (Fergus 1989, 116). Not only have Chatham's paintings graced the covers of most of Harrison's books, but the seminal idea for Harrison's *Sunset Limited* arose from his attempt to imagine what the rest of the gang would do if one of them got into trouble, like Ted does in the novella.

According to Jim Fergus, Guy de la Valdene "had grown up in the privileged medieval world of stag coursing and driven bird shoots" (Fergus 1989, 43). In *Just before Dark*, Harrison's essay *"La Vénerie Française"* is about a stag hunt and sojourn at Valdene's French estate. Although neither an artist like Chatham nor a famous writer like McGuane and Harrison, Valdene does not begrudge his friends' artistic accomplishments: "I'm quite proud of their successes. It shows what good tastes I have in friends" (Fergus 1989, 115). Like Harrison, McGuane, and Chatham, Valdene is a hunter, a fisherman, a gourmand, and a gourmet chef—he has humorously referred to Harrison, Chatham, and himself as the "three fat guys." According to Jim Fergus, the gang has "shared a love of the arts, of the woods and the waters—and of each other"; in a "culture where both art and sport seem increasingly defined and circumscribed by voguishness and the dollar, they may be among the last of a generation to go about their business with original intention intact, on their own terms, without having kissed, as Russell Chatham once put it, 'one single undeserving ass'" (Fergus 1989, 40, 42).

Dan Gerber has been friends with Harrison since the two met at Michigan State in 1967, a friendship John Harrison thinks is "one of the major ones. I'd say Gerber and McGuane would be the big two." Harrison and Gerber often travel together on book tours or simply to collect new memories; in Harrison's "Don't Fence Me In," Gerber is the friend he calls the "Teacher." Gerber is also a Buddhist priest—his teachings as well as his friendship have helped Harrison. In "Everyday Life: The Question of Zen," Harrison writes about the works and people who have affected his own Zennist beliefs: "Through Dan Gerber, I met Kobun [Kobun Chino Sensei] himself, who has revived me a number of times. Through all of this I had the steadying companionship of Dan Gerber who is my teacher. Without this succession (or modest lineage!) I'd be dead as a doornail since I have been a man, at times, of intemperate habits" (*JBD*, 292). According to Gerber, his stability has a "calming effect" on Harrison, counteracting Harrison's occasional zaniness; indeed, their friends often refer to Gerber and Harrison as Bert and Ernie, Jim Henson's famous Muppets.

Harrison's other friends include the actor Jack Nicholson, who financially backed Harrison while he was writing *Legends of the Fall*; the musician and author Jimmy Buffet, whom Harrison and McGuane met in Key West (McGuane married Buffet's sister Laurie in 1977); Senator Bill Bradley, who arranged for Harrison to visit a dam site as part of the research for *Sundog*; the grizzly bear specialist Doug Peacock, who, during his television documentary special, was reading one of Harrison's novels (Patrick Swayze also reads a Harrison novel in *Roadhouse*); the writer Winston Groom and Jimbo Meador, the latter being one of the people to whom Groom dedicates *Forrest Gump*; the late Richard Brautigan, who gave Harrison the title of *Farmer*; Orson Welles, who cooked dinner for Harrison; the late editor Seymour "Sam" Lawrence. Another longtime friend is Bob Datilla, Harrison's agent for over 25 years. Harrison said that Datilla "always gets you the money faster than anybody can. He makes incoherent threats over the phone. He's the only person in the media to actually go to Columbo's [a reputed Mafia boss] funeral because he was invited" ("Lake"). Harrison also lists the late Loren Eiseley, Peter Matthiessen, Sean Connery, Roger Welsch, Barry Hannah, William Styron, and Rick Bass among his friends. Indeed, Bass has said, "A lot of little things added up to my becoming a writer, but the biggest thing was coming in touch with ['Legends of the Fall']." [19]

A Harrison Stew

Harrison notes that after he has worked tirelessly and constantly on his writing and must face the reentry into the normal flow and rhythms of life, he combats the usual adjustment problems by pursuing equal obsessions "for the natural world," which include cooking, hunting, and fishing (*JBD*, xii). Just as hunting and fishing are often therapeutic for his fictional characters, so they are for Harrison. He told Eric Siegal that fishing is "very therapeutic. . . . Most writers go batty because of the problem when they're not writing. It's very stabilizing to be able to stand in a river" (Siegal, 19). At the same time, not only are most of his characters connoisseurs of elegant food and expensive wine, but they are gourmet cooks. As is evident from his descriptions of food and wine in his fiction and in his essays about food and restaurants in *Just before Dark* and in his monthly *Esquire* column, appropriately titled "The Raw and the Cooked," Harrison himself is a connoisseur of wine and spirits, a gourmet cook, and a gourmand. In short, as he told Jim Fergus, "Fishing, hunting, cooking are all part of the same process. They restore the sense of playfulness and inventiveness an artist sometimes loses" (Fergus 1989, 114).

Harrison is an avid sportsman who respects game laws. He hunts only birds, especially grouse and woodcock, and he never kills more than the legal limit. Although he has often remarked that he is not above eating them, he avows that he does not kill mammals, especially bear and deer. He would not shoot a bear, primarily for "religious reasons";[20] John Harrison claims that Jim's aversion to killing bears stems from his respect for Native American customs and traditions ("John Harrison"). Harrison himself says he will not kill black bears because they have "always appealed to me as a huge, reasonably docile form of my daughter's teddy bear"; nevertheless, when backpacking he thinks of grizzly bears as "700-pound Dobermans that don't respond to voice commands" (*JBD*, 123, 144).

In "The Violators," an essay in *Just before Dark*, he explains why he cannot shoot a deer: "Part of the reason I would not have killed it is that I am no longer able to shoot at mammals. Grouse and woodcock, yes. But gutting and skinning a deer reminds me too much of the human carcass and a deer heart too closely resembles my own" (*JBD*, 64). In "A Sporting Life," Harrison describes a young buck that had been wounded in the spine, had one of its hind legs almost shot off, and had "much" of its rump torn off by a large collie. "Before the game warden dispatched it," writes Harrison, "the deer in deep shock stared at us, seemingly well past caring, some kind of runaway slave that had fallen victim to our fatal hobbies" (*JBD*, 151).

As an avid fisherman and hunter, Harrison deplores "The Violators" (in *Just before Dark*)—including "jacklighters," who spotlight deer at night, immobilize them, and then shoot them; and "snaggers," who foul-hook and snag coho, chinook, lake trout, and spawning steelhead. Writes Harrison, "I have seen sportsmen snag upwards of 200 pounds of lake trout—incredibly far over the limit—in the Leland River where the fish are in layers. . . . And these people have been led to think that they are fishing" (*JBD*, 66). Neither does Harrison think highly of those sportsmen who "harry and club to death both fox and coyote from snowmobiles" (*JBD*, 67). Harrison misses no opportunity to speak out against such violators. In "Don't Fence Me In," he recounts an incident at a bar in Jordan, Montana: when a man bragged about shooting "2,200 gophers that summer and was aiming for the 'record' of 4,700," the "lout" was not "amused when I asked him how he cooked the critters. . . . I get to ask such questions because I am not a shy, retiring shrimp of a fellow" (*JBD*, 191).

Harrison borrows Edward Abbey's phrase "cowboy consciousness" to describe the violators' belief that "the land is endless, unspoiled, mysterious, still remaining to be overcome and finally won. So shoot, kill, bang-bang-bang. WOW!" Although Harrison believes that city people who are hunters and fishermen possess more of a cowboy consciousness than rural sportsmen, many of whom sense a diminishing wilderness, he ominously concludes: "The true violator, though, will persist in all of his pathological glory. Even if there were no game left on earth, something would be devised. Maybe a new sport on this order: ganghooking Farmer Brown's pigs. A high-speed winch mounted on a vehicle hood is required, and a harpoon with large hooks. You shoot the harpoon over the pig's back and press the winch button. Zap! You've got yourself a squealer" (*JBD*, 71).

Harrison also deplores those man-made forces that despoil the land and the environment. In "Don't Fence Me In," an essay about his trip to the "Big Open" with Dan Gerber, Harrison admits that he refused to visit the Charles M. Russell Wildlife Refuge because a few years before about 2,000 antelope had starved to death when cattle consumed over half the forage. "The Bureau of Land Management administered a program by which land was rented to ranchers, so that the very name 'refuge' is a phony sop offered to environmentalists. . . . The Bureau of Land Management mess is scarcely unique in this area (read James Conway's *Kingdom in the Country*)" (*JBD*, 191). He is equally vehement when talking about realtors who want to make northern Michigan around Lake Leelanau "look like a damn suburb of Flint. They're going to cover every square inch with condominiums" (Stocking 1977, 21).[21] Harrison also rails about overpopulation, overgrazing, poaching, and

especially those Asians who believe that ground-up ivory is an aphrodisiac: "Think of the boggling sexual vanity involved in killing a seven-
ton beast for hard-ons" (*JBD*, 150). In another essay, however, he points
out that Americans themselves killed 80 million buffalo "out of greed"
(*JBD*, 186). As he told Jim Fergus, "Greed is killing the soul-life of the
nation. . . . It's destroying what's left of our physical beauty, it's pollut-
ing the country, it's making us more Germanic and warlike and stupid"
(Fergus 1988, 81).

In his essay "Going Places," Harrison writes:

> As a poet and novelist I have to get out of the study and collect some
> brand-new memories. . . . I'm planning a trip when I finish my current
> novel, for which I had to make an intense study of the years 1865 to
> 1900 in our history, also the history of Native Americans. I intend to
> check out locations where I sensed a particular magic in the past: certain
> culverts in western Minnesota, nondescript gullies in Kansas, invisible
> graveyards in New Mexico, moonbeam targets in Nebraska, buffalo
> jumps in Montana, melted ice palaces in the Dakotas. (*JBD*, 183)

Just as fishing, hunting, and cooking are therapeutic remedies for his
"reentry" problems, so, too, is traveling. Harrison records in "From the
Dalva Notebooks" the postscript that he "finished the novel in July and
have since driven 27,000 miles to get over it"; in "Going Places," he
remarks that his "spirit was lightened by the thirty-five days and 8,000
or so miles" (see "Log of the Earthtoy Drifthumper" for the account of
this journey); also in "Going Places," Harrison says that after an especially soul-draining tour in Hollywood that made him "ditzy," he logged
more than 5,000 miles in Michigan's Upper Peninsula, "lifting his sod-
den spirits and looking for good grouse and woodcock cover" (*JBD*, 289,
180, 182).

Although he has traveled to various foreign countries—England,
France, Russia, Africa, Mexico, Costa Rica, to name a few—Harrison is
particularly fond of traveling around the United States. While book
tours, business deals, and screenplay contracts often take him to New
York and Los Angeles—he satirically calls them "dream-coasts"—most
of the time he relishes driving on America's "blue highways" (he readily
praises William Least Heat Moon's *Blue Highways* and *Prairy Erth*). As
he travels the blue highways, he sets the cruise control, stands on the
seat with his head and shoulders out of the sunroof, and drives, a feat he
mentions in "Log of the Earthtoy Drifthumper" and "Going Places."

Jaunts on blue highways are restorative; in "Don't Fence Me In" he remarks about an "absolutely empty" 130-mile stretch of road, "I realize this is not everyone's cup of tea, but I draw enormous solace from this expanse" (*JBD*, 188). Harrison also has a special affinity for certain states—Iowa, Kansas, Nebraska, Montana, but especially Arizona and New Mexico.

While traveling provides him with "peace, solitude, inaccessibility, and the adventure," as well as the opportunity "to think up new novels and rest from the last one" (*JBD*, 185), Harrison believes that traveling should also be enlightening. In "Going Places," a delightful how-to-travel essay, he suggests that a traveler do research and reading about the region where he or she is headed: "For instance, if you're driving through Chadron, Nebraska, on Route 20, it doesn't hurt to know that Crazy Horse, He Dog, American Horse, Little Big Man, and Sitting Bull took the same route when it was still a buffalo path" (*JBD*, 181). One of his Arizona trips was entertaining and enlightening because he traveled with Douglas Peacock, the "grizzly bear expert . . . who knows every piece of flora, fauna, and Native American history in that state. In such company, the most unassertive mesa becomes verdant with possibility" (*JBD*, 181). Harrison lists the books he took along on his trip with Dan Gerber to the "Big Open": Thomas Mail's *The Mystic Warriors of the Plains*, Carl Waldman's *Atlas of the North American Indian*, Van Bruggen's *Wildflowers, Grasses, and Other Plants of the Northern Plains and Black Hills*, several bird books, and *Nebraskaland* magazine. An eclectic assortment, to be sure, but as he emphasizes, "Knowledge informs, gives shape to scenery" (*JBD*, 186). Harrison not only visits historical sites like the Little Big Horn or Wounded Knee but stops at museums like the Sturh Museum of the Prairie Pioneer in Grand Island, Nebraska, where he researched material for *Dalva*.

If "knowledge informs" and "gives shape to scenery," then Harrison's travels assuredly find shape and definition in his poetry and fiction. Whether he is describing Michigan's landscapes, an Iowa cornfield, the Nebraska plains, New Mexico's Anemas Mountains, or the singular actions of birds or animals, all are accurately and faithfully rendered because Harrison has been there, has experienced these things, and has seen them with the eyes of a poet and storyteller. At the same time, for Harrison a sense of place is essential to fiction: "Sometimes I think you tell the story that emerges from the locale. [In] my second book of poems, *Locations*, there seems to be a fable in the ground somehow. It's the place that determines the nature of the story" ("Lake").

Our House of Atreus Curse: Native Americans

Another essential feature of Harrison's life and writings is the Native American. "Native Americans are an obsession of mine, totally unshared by New York or Los Angeles for the average reason of moral vacuum" (*JBD*, xii, 22). And, of course, Native Americans and their plight are prominent in his novellas *Legends of the Fall*, *Brown Dog*, and *The Seven Ounce Man*; in his novels *A Good Day to Die*, *Farmer*, and especially *Dalva*; and in his *Esquire* articles and *Just before Dark* essays, especially "Poetry as Survival," an insightful discussion of Native American poets and poetry and the problems of Native Americans in the wider American culture.

As part of his study of Native American culture and history, Harrison visits Indian reservations; although he has "collected a large library" about Native Americans, he is "remarkably short on firsthand knowledge" of them (*JBD*, 297). However, he wanders around the reservations as a "quiet observer, quite shy in fact, because I [don't] want to be confused with the anthropologists and spiritual shoppers who drive these people crazy" (*JBD*, 298). In addition, he often attends Native American powwows, like the Crow Fair in Crow Agency, Montana, where he "watched the dancing for two days and nights, sleeping sporadically on the Custer Battlefield. It was a *spellbinding* experience, one of the few in my life, and there was a deep sense of melancholy that there was nothing in my life that owned this cultural validity except, in a minimal sense, my poetry" (*JBD*, 298). Another memorable experience occurred at a Chippewa powwow in Escanaba, Michigan:

> A very, *very* old man was doing his last Bear Dance. He was about ninety-three and dressed totally in the cape of a bear. He was shaking himself and dancing all around slowly, and it was just a beautiful thing. And next were prepubescent girls doing the Crow Dance. They had about eighty little girls under age ten out there and real fast music doing imitations of crows and ravens. They were uncanny. I thought, "Jesus Christ! What am I seeing here?" A complete transmogrification because some of them *were* ravens and crows. All the gestures were appropriate. It was unbelievable. ("Lake")

Harrison writes of the tragic injustices that result when the Native American culture collides with the white culture. He is, moreover, passionate, compassionate, and adamant about these injustices. He finds it "shocking" that very few people "know what happened to the hundred civilizations represented by the American Indians. . . . To me the Indians are our curse on the House of Atreus. They're our doom. The way we killed them is also what's killing us now. Greed" (Fergus 1988, 81). He is equally appalled with living conditions on reservations; after visiting "a half-dozen" reservations, he claims that if people "think these Indians are any better off than the blacks in Soweto you're full of shit. Some people think we got their land fair and square because of the Dawes Act. Well, sure, but none of the Indians had M.B.A.'s. Red Cloud had never been in a bank. . . . That area of our history is ugly, ugly" (Fergus 1988, 82). Harrison's grimmest denunciation of white injustice is the metaphor he conceived after visiting both the site where Crazy Horse was murdered and the church graveyard overlooking the Wounded Knee massacre. After asking the reader to imagine a U.S. map "covered with white linen as if it were a recently . . . murdered corpse," to note "where the blood is soaking through," and to ignore Civil War battle sites because "they constitute something we did to ourselves," Harrison continues:

> You will now notice that the rest of our linen map is riddled with the blood of over two hundred Native American civilizations we virtually destroyed, from Massachusetts to California. This is an unpleasant map and is not readily available for purchase or publication, especially not in history books or in what is blithely referred to as the "American conscience." Our nation has a soul history, not as immediately verifiable as the artifacts of the Smithsonian, whose presence we sense in public affairs right down to the former president's use of the word "preservation," or his cinema-tainted reference to oil-rich Indians. In any event, schoolchildren who we think need a comprehension of apartheid could be given the gist of this social disease by field trips to Indian reservations in big yellow buses. (*JBD*, 299–300)

Despite his compassion for Native Americans and his indignation over the social injustices plaguing them, Harrison has also been in some weirdly amusing situations because of his physical similarity to them. Ric Bohy reports that when young, the dark-haired, dark-eyed Harrison would lie sometimes, claiming "to be of Indian blood 'to get girls,' but when he quit lying, people believed it anyway" (Bohy, 14). Harrison recalled being in a northern Michigan bar with Guy de la Valdene and Russell Chatham and being refused a drink "because they didn't want to serve Indians": "Russell wanted to shoot them whereas I was charmed that I was mistaken for being from the Third World. Usually I have a temper, but this was wonderful. Then we went to the next bar and this very drunk woman came up and grabbed me by the collar and said, 'Are you Indian?' That

was two in a row" (Bohy, 14). John Harrison laughingly recalled the time
when Jim was standing outside a Chippewa gambling casino in Michigan
and a white man strolled up to him, playfully punched him on the shoulder, and asked, "Hey, Tonto, where's the action around here?" John says
that Jim first felt like punching the "son of a bitch" but then felt flattered
to be mistaken for a Native American ("John Harrison").

Not Machos, Just Nachos

In "The Macho Mystique," Peter S. Prescott reviewed James Salter's *Solo
Faces* and Harrison's *Legends of the Fall*. In defining macho fiction,
Prescott writes that women do not enjoy it because it celebrates a "fantasy of masculine self-sufficiency"; that while females are essential to the
plot, they never understand why a "man must blaze his solitary path in
a senseless world"; that men often leave their women behind, "preferably
pregnant," to wait a "year or two"; that women are especially useful in
macho fiction if they "can be killed in a baroque manner" (Prescott cites
Isabel Two's death in *Legends of the Fall* when the ricocheted bullet pierces
"her forehead like a red dime"); that the macho fiction writer prefers
plots that include fear, obsession, mutilation, and death; and that
although the "body counts tend to be inflationary," the plots end
"serenely with a certain rough justice achieved."[22] Prescott seems to conclude that Harrison was, and often still is, a macho fiction writer because
he hunts and fishes, and so do his male characters.

Harrison denies being a macho fiction writer. He adamantly responded
to Prescott's review: "What I don't like is the kind of review like the one
Peter Prescott wrote in *Newsweek* on *Legends* where I was a tool to explore
his interest in feminism" (Fergus 1985, 244). Regarding his love of hunting and fishing, Harrison retorts, "If you were born in Northern
Michigan, you hunt and fish. . . . Suddenly this is macho. It's just the way
you grew up, just the same as they play stickball in New York" (Skwira,
18). He defends his male protagonists: "All I have to say about that
macho thing goes back to the idea that my characters aren't from the
urban dream-coasts. A man is not a foreman on a dam project because he
wants to be macho. That's his job, a job he's evolved into. A man isn't a
pilot for that reason either—he's fascinated by airplanes. A farmer wants
to farm" (Fergus 1988, 71). Although John Harrison admitted that Jim
has had a reputation as a "sexist" and "relished it to a certain extent," he
added that the reputation hurt Jim's feelings because "it's obvious that
his wife and daughters are central to his existence."

Exactly what does "macho" mean to Harrison? He believes the word *macho* means a "particularly ugly peacockery, a conspicuous cruelty to women and animals and children, a gratuitous viciousness. . . . I am not all the men in my novels. How could I be? I'm little Jimmy back here on the farm with my wife and two daughters, and, at one time, three female horses, three female cats, and three female dogs. . . . So how can I be all these lunatics?" (Fergus 1988, 71–72). Harrison also believes that women should have the "same prerogatives in life" that men have, adding, "I've been sort of attacked for macho attitudes but I never felt that I misrepresented any woman. I'm writing fiction, not a tract. Politics can't enter into your artistic considerations" (Stocking 1977, 26). Or as he replies to his critics, "Tell them I don't believe in machos, just nachos" (Stocking 1980, 16).[23]

Writing and Reading

Harrison described for Ira Elliott and Marty Sommerness the way he writes:

> On a novel I crank up for a long time. I haven't written a novel that I haven't thought about writing for three years. When it gets ripe in my brain I just sit down and write it. I write the first draft in usually about six weeks. I work every day, all day. The kind of novel I've written, so far at least, you have to get it all down before you change your mind. The alternative is not bothering to write at all. That's something you're fighting all the time, what McGuane calls the loss of cabin pressure.[24]

Because he has mulled the material over for such a long time before putting pen to paper, Harrison does little editing, nor does he write numerous successive drafts: "I already have it all totally in my head before I start to write, or at least the general feeling. It's more of a feeling and images rather than the narrative. And then you turn yourself loose on it. It's sort of like winding out an old clock." According to Harrison, *Farmer* came from the smell of ivy in barnyards: "And it just took me back to those times when the farm used to be an old family farm. And then I started thinking that my grandparents had a son that would have been Joseph's age, but he died of flu in that epidemic of 1919 at the age of three. What would he have been like with these five sisters if he had stayed on the family farm?" Similarly, *Dalva* "started with a painting—I think Edward Hopper—of a girl sitting on a bed

looking out a window, and the wind's blowing the curtains of this room
in the house in the country." He admitted that since *Dalva* he has been
trying to become less intensive and to stretch the writing process out
because "the way I worked was totally ruining my health. . . . And I was
driving myself and everybody else totally insane" ("Lake").

While Harrison's fiction shares some settings, conflicts, and themes,
each of his works is singularly different. As he explained, "That's because
I would go crazy if I didn't bury everything, or try to do it in a new way.
I've always believed that anytime you hoped to create a work of art
without reinventing a form, it starts to expire" ("Lake"). He probably
inherited this tendency from his father, who Harrison says could not bear
to repeat a story the same way. Russell Chatham concurs that, "like all
great artists, Jim doesn't repeat himself" (Julia Reed, 506). At the same
time, as Harrison has complained, some book reviewers and fans do not
want him to change: "I have a certain bunch of followers who want me
to keep on writing *Farmer*, and then a certain bunch who want me to
keep on rewriting *Legends of the Fall* in that heroic mode which was a
one-time thing. . . . It's just odd where some of the people who loved
The Woman Lit by Fireflies are going to be discouraged by *Julip*. But that's
too bad. I'm the writer! Because it's finally, 'Who gives a fuck?'"
("Lake"). Harrison admits that he has "broken" himself of reading
reviews of his work unless he needs a "boost," and then he will read one
written by one of his avid supporters, like Bernard Levin, whose reviews
are usually interesting.[25] Usually, however, Harrison is too busy: "It's not
that I don't care. It's just that by the time the book comes out, I'm generally doing something else." Harrison also does not reread his works; he
cannot "all the time be backtracking and thinking about what I've
already done, or nothing new will arrive" ("Lake"). In his "The Raw and
the Cooked: The Morality of Food," he recounts the time he promised to
talk about himself at a gathering, but instead, he reports, "I actually
made a song out of my book, *Just before Dark*, and warbled it to the
assemblage, arms and feet akimbo, in the manner of Goulet, Tormé, and
Manilow. It was suggested that this indicated man in extremis. Not so:
Torpor makes one shameless, and I'm not interested in what I've written
after I've written it let alone chatting it up."[26] He does admit, though,
that he will probably have to reread *Dalva* when he begins the sequel,
tentatively titled *Earth Diver*.

Harrison may no longer read many reviews of his works or reread
them, but he does read, indeed widely. He prefaces his works with quo-
tations from other works and peppers his fiction, poetry, essays, and

Esquire columns with literary allusions and references. His knowledge of literature and certain authors is vast—see the section "Literary Matters" in *Just before Dark*. Moreover, his *Esquire* column reflects a deep familiarity with cookbooks and other food writers.

Harrison reads every night, especially in "down times" when he is not writing anything in particular. He reads very fast but slows down for works he appreciates, to savor the prose and the ideas. He claimed, for instance, that he read William Least Heat Moon's *Prairy Erth* at "exactly five pages a day, and that's how that book ought to be read. It's just a marvel. I loved that book" ("Lake"). Other authors he praises are, to name a few: William Faulkner, whose writings and life taught Harrison to endure as a writer; Ernest Hemingway, whose *A Farewell to Arms*, *Islands in the Stream*, and "Up in Michigan" are Harrison favorites; Saul Bellow, the "writer with the most mental equipment," or, "as Pooh would say, 'He is a bear with a very large mind'"; John Cheever, especially *The Wapshot Chronicle* because of its sense of place; some of E. L. Doctorow's works, especially *Loon Lake* because of the "eeriness of it all" ("Lake"); and John MacDonald—"I love to read MacDonald. I've read all fifty of them" (Elliott and Sommerness). Also in this company are Tom McGuane, Peter Matthiessen, William Styron, Larry Brown, Cormac McCarthy, and the many Native American authors Harrison discusses in "Poetry as Survival."

Full Circle

In "Bird Hunting," Harrison writes:

> We in the Midwest have to face up to the idea that no one on America's dream coasts will visit us except for very special occasions. True, we have the Great Lakes but they have the Atlantic and Pacific. They also have restaurants. Tom McGuane . . . said to me about the Midwest, "Mortimer Snerd must have bred five thousand times a day to build that heartland race." True, but the land as I find it, and daily walk it, is virtually peopleless, with vast undifferentiated swamps, ridges, old circular logging roads; a region of cold fogs, monstrous weather changes, third-growth forests devoid of charm, models, and actresses, or ballerinas, but somehow superbly likable. (*JBD*, 167)

Jim Harrison may have initially left Michigan to search for the right atmosphere in which to write, and he may leave to go on long driving sprees to collect new memories, but he always returns to Michigan, the "superbly likable" place where he feels the "best in the world." Moreover, he returns with new images and ideas about people he has met, things he has seen and experienced, and places he has visited—all of which become part of the man and the writer and, often enough, appear in his poetry, fiction, and essays.

Chapter Two

"Up on the Barn, Just Sort of Yelling": *Wolf: A False Memoir*

While the two were fishing in Key West, Tom McGuane suggested that since Harrison had a Guggenheim grant, he should write a "sort of auto-biographical novel."[1] "What had happened," says Harrison, "was I had a terrible hunting accident. I'd fallen down a cliff and it really screwed up my back and I had to be in traction at Munson [Medical Center in Traverse City]. I just sat there and said, gee why don't I write a novel" (Elliott and Sommerness).[2] The result was *Wolf: A False Memoir*. Because Harrison was so broke, he mailed the only copy of the manuscript to his brother John to photocopy, but it was lost in the mail for about a month because of a postal strike. John finally went to the New Haven post office and dug the package out of a mail bin. When *Wolf* was accepted for publication, Harrison says, "I was somewhat surprised. I thought, oh good, here's something else I can do because the dominant forces in my life had always been novelists, along with a few poets" (Fergus 1988, 61).

According to Harrison, *Wolf* did "quite well for a first novel" (Fergus 1988, 67). While noting its weaknesses, reviewers generally praised the novel. Jonathan Yardley, for example, noted that *Wolf* was a "raunchy, funny, swaggering, angry, cocksure book; it's also a poignant, handsomely written self-exploitation that deserves comparison, if it does not reach such heights, with Frederick Exley's *A Fan's Notes* and Frank Conroy's *Stop Time*—and . . . with the novels of Tom McGuane to whom it is in part dedicated."[3] Joyce Carol Oates believed that *Wolf* had very little "dramatic organization"; that it could have been "cut back neatly to one half its length"; and that it is a "novel of initiation that comes to no end, and it is, itself, an initiation, the kind of diary-like work many writers must publish before they can write their first significant book."[4] "Humor, irony, and above all, energy animate Harrison's prose," wrote H. L. van Brunt, adding that Swanson, the narrator-protagonist, is a "crybaby." "Ultimately," according to van Brunt, "his rages against life as it is and people as they are . . . sound like the howl of a mangy timber wolf unable to run with the pack—or perhaps merely unwilling to tolerate anyone's company except his own."[5] Jim Fergus believes that *Wolf* in its "sense of motion, its poetic language and imagery of the outdoors would become the earmarks of [Harrison's] work" (Fergus 1989, 112).

Because he could not think of "anything else to write about," Harrison admitted that *Wolf* is "probably eighty-five, ninety percent autobiographical" (Elliott and Sommerness). At one time he tried to reread *Wolf* but could not, simply because it was "basically true" and thus "too painful" and "too raw" (Skwira, 16). When Jim Fergus asked Harrison about *Wolf*'s angry tone, the author replied, "It reminds me of a heartbroken boy up on the barn roof, just sort of yelling," adding, "I've certainly become a nicer person over the years" (Fergus 1988, 61).

"Mainly Autobiographical"

While admitting the autobiographical nature of *Wolf*, Harrison emphasized that the novel is an "extremely direct, non-therapeutic attempt to come to terms with my life in the present."[6] The autobiographical elements are evident in the life and experiences of the protagonist-narrator, Carol Severin. In the Author's Note, for example, Swanson says that he was born in the "unusually nasty winter of 1937," and that he is 33, "a time when literary souls always turn around and look backward."[7] The birthdate and age approximate Harrison's. Similarly, within the narrative, Swanson reminisces about hitchhiking to California and working in "hot string-bean fields" in and around Stockton, Modesto, and San Jose. He recalls also his sojourn in New York—where he worked at a carwash, at a restaurant as a busboy, and at a bookstore—and his two trips to Boston, the second of which, he says, "came after an unsuccessful college career and two years of unemployment" and "when I was trying to make a new start, collect myself, get my head above water" (*WFM*, 63, 64).

Other autobiographical details either complement or augment known facts about Harrison's life. Swanson says that his father was the first on either side of the family to graduate from college, then worked as an agricultural agent. A young playmate blinded Swanson in his left eye, and he saved $1,000 for an eye operation: "Took three years to save the money and a kindly surgeon got it all in three hours for an incredibly unsuccessful hatchet job" (*WFM*, 152). The $20 typewriter and the five books Swanson packs into a cardboard box for his trip to New York are familiar details of Harrison's life. Because of his "dark complexion and vaguely Laplander or laplaper features," Swanson is often mistaken for a Native American: "Eastern college girls especially like the part Indian bit. . . . I vary with tribes from Cheyenne to Cherokee to Apache. Makes it harder to hitchhike though. Dirty minorities. I've been asked the question a thousand times: Are you part Indian or Mexican?" (*WFM*, 106). Swanson also recalls that he dug well pits by hand and laid blocks, "twelve-inch cement blocks, seventy pounds apiece, for a house that would have brick facing, perhaps a thousand of them in the walls. Unloaded in a day thirty-five tons by hand" (*WFM*, 40). He has also published "three extremely slender books of poems" and has had a "succession of not very interesting nervous breakdowns" (*WFM*, 137–38).

Other autobiographical references among the many in *Wolf* include: Swanson's conversion to religion and subsequent reconversion to the world and the flesh in Colorado; his stint as a waiter at a hotel out west; his vacations and the night walks he takes at the lake cabin built by his father and uncles; his experiences with peyote buttons; his injury during football practice, "a compound fracture across the bridge of my nose—bones sticking through and the blood a geyser" (*WFM*, 119). Swanson recalls that it has "been ten years since I shot at a mammal," and that when a deer is hung up and its hide stripped, "it looks a bit too human for my taste; in the hanging position the front feet appear to be atrophied human arms with the skin peeled back" (*WFM*, 117). Like Harrison, Swanson feels that "if you fish all day your continuous sanity is assured," and he would like to return to northern Michigan and have "dogs and cats and horses and children in a big dilapidated farmhouse" (*WFM*, 182). And, of course, Swanson remembers being 18 and leaving for New York "to live forever away from the vulgarities of the Midwest," but ironically he returns to northern Michigan to deal "mostly with the years 1956–1960" and to reestablish purpose and meaning in his life.

Harrison often comments about the traumatic effect the deaths of his father and younger sister had on him. He deals obliquely with their deaths in his poems "David" and "A Sequence of Women"; in *Wolf*, Harrison provides details that are not found in either the interviews or his poetry. For example, Swanson talks about how his younger sister was adept at killing and skinning frogs and loved eating frog legs; she also relished deer hunting with her father, even though "they tended to hunt in a desultory way with more interest in the walking than the kill" (*WFM*, 104). She and her father were, as a matter of fact, going deer hunting when the crash occurred. Swanson remembers:

> By mistake in the lawyer's office I saw the state police photos of the accident, the car tipped over with its engine driven into the trunk by

impact. Impossible to tell who had been driving. In one photo I caught
sight of her, in a split-second glimpse—I saw her forehead upside down
with a single thin trickle of blood on it, an irregular black line. A man
had hit them head-on going ninety, or they had hit the other car. . . .
For a year afterwards, I slept with my hands tightly clenched to my
chest so that in the morning my arms and shoulders would be sore from
exertion. (*WFM*, 104–5)

The autobiographical details in *Wolf* have a dual function. First, they are
the result of Harrison looking back over his life, like other "literary
souls" at age 33 (perhaps an allusion to Dante and the *Divine Comedy*); he
observes: "Most of the poisons have been injected, some self-inflicted;
how does one weigh mental scar tissue? At this point we must settle for
prose" (*WFM*, 11, 12). Metaphorically, the "injected" poisons could be
Harrison's personal traumas, like being blinded and the deaths of his
father and sister; the "self-inflicted" poisons could range from his exces-
sive drinking to his self-doubts and suicidal thoughts. Harrison told
Kathleen Stocking that he had a "mid-life crisis at 29. . . . That crisis
where you cease believing in anything in life. . . . I've certainly been
there and back a number of times" (Stocking 1977, 24).

In this sense, then, using "too raw" and "too painful" autobiographical details in his first novel "weigh[s] the mental scar tissue": writing
about them brings about Harrison's personal catharsis. At the same time
autobiography becomes the catalyst for future fiction, or as Harrison
explains: "I'm no longer interested at all in writing about myself, or versions of myself. . . . I don't think it's so much a process of outgrowing
something. You have to work with the strength of the autobiographical
juice, and then suddenly you start breaking out, writing about other
people" (Stocking 1977, 26).

The second function of the autobiographical details in *Wolf* is related
to Harrison's ambivalence toward writing fiction when he was recuper-
ating from his hunting accident. When he wrote *Wolf*, Harrison did
intend to write fiction; as Swanson says, "Here is the story, the fiction,
the romance" (*WFM*, 13). Harrison even emphasized the fictional nature
of the work in the subtitle, *A False Memoir*. In other words, the *memoirs*
will be Harrison's experiences, but they will be *false*, or fictional, as they
are transformed in Harrison's imagination into fiction and narrated by
the fictional protagonist Swanson. Is Swanson really Harrison, or is
Harrison really Swanson? In talking with Kay Bonetti about *Sundog's*
subtitle, *As Told to Jim Harrison*, Harrison admitted, "That was just to

have fun. Like Nabokov, I did that to throw people off the track. It is a little bit myself, but I had to have a contrast to Strang. . . . And I had to know both people. You could say they're almost extremities of the right and left lobes of the same head" (Bonetti, 70). Admittedly, thirteen years and five novels separate *Wolf* from *Sundog*, and these two novels mark Harrison's maturing skills as a writer. But when he wrote *Wolf*, Harrison was possibly having fun, "throwing people off the track," by using Swanson as a narrator who is "a little bit" like himself, especially in experience. Nevertheless, as Harrison often emphasizes, "I'm not all the men in my novels. . . . I'm little Jimmy back here on the farm" (Fergus 1988, 71–72). As Robert E. Burkholder notes: "Obviously *Wolf* is a 'false memoir' because it is a work of fiction, but Harrison also means to suggest by his subtitle that this memoir will paradoxically be truer than those usually called memoirs since, as the writer of an admittedly false memoir, he is free to invent characters and situations that better illustrate the truth as he perceives it" (268).

Soundings

Its autobiographical elements do not prevent *Wolf* from foreshadowing Harrison's fictional techniques, especially in terms of character, setting, and theme. Like Harrison's other male protagonists, Swanson experiences a midlife crisis precipitated by past events and experiences. Looming large, of course, are his being blinded, the deaths of his father and sister, his religious conversion and then reconversion, his *Wanderjahr* across the United States, and his "unsuccessful college career and two years of unemployment" (*WFM*, 63). In contrast, Swanson's older brother is settled and successful: "He is a librarian and has repressed his lowlife instincts for a good marriage, reading, fine food, and hard work. I admire him without reservation and never forget that back home he had been an Eagle Scout whereas I had been ousted from the troop as a chronic malcontent" (*WFM*, 81).

Although he yearns for purpose and stability in life, Swanson's odd jobs are as transient as he is. He picks beans in California; waits tables at a western resort hotel; buses tables at a Boston Italian restaurant; and in New York is a busboy, works at a carwash, and clerks at a bookstore. He either squanders his money on food and drink or saves enough to travel somewhere else. Swanson's desultory approach to work is evident in the ten job application blanks he carries around, on the backs of which he often makes notes. When the application blanks fray at their edges, he discards them, but first he spends "a great deal of time" transferring his notes, thus spending "more time making notes than filling out applications": "I could write my name with a great flourish at the top, but then begin to hedge at the address, home and local, and by the time I reached the social security line my energy would be sapped. All before reaching previous job experiences, spouse, mother-in-law's maiden name, references" (*WFM*, 65).

Swanson occasionally rides a Greyhound or Trailways bus, but mainly he hitchhikes; neither mode is conducive to lasting friendships. Similarly, the people he works with, especially the migrant workers, are just as transient as he is. Even more poignant is that Swanson is incapable of, and does not really desire, a sustained, serious relationship with a woman. He follows Marcia, one of his early loves, to Sacramento, but when he gets there, she has left for Santa Fe. By then, not only has he run out of money, but his interest in her has waned. "I didn't have a picture of her," he says, "and when I tried to envision her, the features would change vaguely and then I would have to start over as if dressing a bald mannequin, but then an eye would drop to the floor or the mouth would enlarge or the ear would disappear" (*WFM*, 27). That Swanson does not want a serious relationship is again evident when he candidly admits, "In the spring of 1960 I went back to New York for want of any place else to go. . . . I had found two girls to love back home and when I thought of them they seemed to resist each other's presence on earth with perfect balance. And the duplicity had settled in a sweet contradictory syrup in my brain so I chose the alternate of leaving them both" (*WFM*, 221). Even Swanson's marriage is faltering, and on one occasion he says that his wife is a "fine girl who doesn't want to be married to a drunk"; later he says that he "can't manage to stay married" because "monogamy usually involves retreat and cowardice" (*WFM*, 92, 212, 215).

At one time Swanson candidly says of himself, "I'm never cool enough but jerk around, a horse in double hobbles" (*WFM*, 192), a statement epitomizing the lack of connection between him and other people, his family included, and his jerking around between his northern Michigan family and roots and the places to which he goes. He always leaves Michigan, even though he admits, "Though I know this life I always leave it and where do I live when I leave home over and over on small and brutally stupid voyages" (*WFM*, 184). When he is in San Francisco, Boston, or New York, his thoughts about what he misses and wants are all earthy and homey images: "*sun bug dirt soil lilac leaf leaves . . . tree fish pine bluegill bass wood cock shore sand . . . horses . . . goldenrod sparrows rock deer chicken-hawk stump ravine . . . spinach bacon ham potatoes flesh death fence oriole corn"* (*WFM*, 25–26).

While Swanson enjoys the freedom and adventure of city life, he realizes he does not really belong to the city. In Boston, he writes, "I've lived there twice and both times quite miserably," and later he rationalizes, "It occurred to me that all of my miseries in Boston were invented and geographical—a simple move to New York City would change everything" (*WFM*, 48, 78). Once he makes the move, however, he discovers that "I couldn't handle the city; it seemed consistently malefic and I wanted to be elsewhere but I couldn't go home, having announced I had left forever" (*WFM*, 25). Swanson is thus doubly hobbled. He yearns for relationships, but he wants freedom from commitments. He knows he needs a job, but he detests filling out job applications. He wants to live away from his family and Michigan roots, but he yearns for and misses the life he knows. Metaphorically, he jerks around in his double hobbles from here to there because, as he himself says, "my mind is set convexly against the grain" (*WFM*, 212). This is the juncture that Swanson talks about in the Author's Note, a juncture at which, like Harrison's other protagonists, he must reestablish purpose and meaning in his life.

"Thirty Degrees or So in the Wrong Direction"

Like Lundgren in *Warlock* and Strang in *Sundog*, Swanson inevitably returns to northern Michigan after his travels. As the novel opens, Swanson is traveling across the Straits of Mackinac, through the Upper Peninsula, and into the Huron Mountains, where he will reassess his life between 1956 and 1960 and where he hopes to see a wolf: "There are only three or four hundred native wolves left in the United States. . . . I felt that if I could see one all my luck would change" (*WFM*, 83). However, just as Swanson could not cope fully with city life, neither can he adequately cope with life in the wilderness. On his first hike from his campsite, for instance, he carries a "worthless .30-30 rifle with bad sights" and a compass that is useless because of the "varying amounts of iron ore" in the ground. Two hours later he admits that he is "unfathomably lost." When he hikes to his car to "pack in" the rest of his food, his compass reading indicates that he is "thirty degrees or so in the wrong direction," and it takes him "ten hours to walk seven miles" (*WFM*, 77, 83). In other words, Swanson's life has metaphorically been 30 degrees in the wrong direction, a plight similar to that of Harrison's protagonists in *A Good Day to Die* and *Farmer*. Indeed, the lives of all

Harrison's protagonists are symbolically 10 to 30 degrees out of kilter, and their task is to restore direction in their lives.

Not only does Swanson become lost in the forest, but he often makes careless mistakes that underscore his inability to live in the wilderness. On the ten-mile hike to his car, for instance, after forgetting to apply "bug dope," a "small cloud of deer flies" trails him: "These little mistakes can cause great pain—a deer fly looks like a rather large house fly but their sting draws blood" (*WFM*, 77). On other occasions he does not gather enough wood for the night and he forgets to fill his canteen or to carry enough food when he hikes away from his camp. He frankly admits:

> True wilderness might destroy me within a month if I committed such fuckups. The only points in my favor were nonchalance and reasonably good health but I had none of the constant wariness owned by all good woodsmen. . . . I simply didn't have the functional intelligence of the explorer, the voyager and had only met a few people who were unilaterally stable in the wilderness. You have to know a great deal about food and shelter and the stalking of game and many of the aspects of this knowledge come only through astute, almost instinctive openness to your surroundings. (*WFM*, 173)

Then, underscoring his lack of openness to his surroundings, Swanson admits, "In Montana I nearly walked off a cliff dreaming of the peculiar flat shape of a whore's ass" (*WFM*, 173).

Swanson is also unsuited for wilderness life because he longs for civilization's amenities. Although his seven-day hiatus is an attempt to curb his addictions to cigarettes and alcohol, he yearns for them. "Oh for a cigarette," he groans. "When I get back to camp I intend to smoke ten in a row until I fall into a terminal fit of coughing and poisoning. Trade many dollars and shoes and shirt for tobacco" (*WFM*, 187). In a rare moment of fixed resolve, he buries his pack of cigarettes only to regret it, and later he must pretend to smoke an "imaginary cigarette." Similarly, he often wishes for a drink, a "large water glass filled with warm whiskey, or a succession of doubles with beer used as a chaser" (*WFM*, 20). He also wishes either that he had some aluminum foil so he "could eat finely steamed rather than scorched fish" or that a woodland nymph or starlet would appear for a sexual romp.

Unlike James Fenimore Cooper's Natty Bumppo, who finds solace and God's plenty in the forests and on the prairies and casts off the accoutrements of civilization to retreat to the wilderness, Swanson needs civilization and so casts off his wilderness accoutrements—specifically, his 20-pound pup tent—and escapes to civilization. He admits that he "wants tobacco. And a porterhouse and a bottle of Chateaux Margaux and a horse to ride back to camp where he would pack, and back to the car where the horse would be abandoned and the car driven straight through to New York City to the Algonquin or the Plaza where he would send an underling over to Bonwit's Bill Blass shop with his measurements and get outfitted for outrageous high-class low-down gluttony and fuckery" (*WFM*, 162). When Swanson returns to civilization, he does indeed pursue high-class, low-down temptations. He reserves a room at an Ishpeming hotel, buys new chinos and a Hawaiian shirt, and gorges on a "triple bourbon with water and no ice," "planked whitefish"—which he eats "in great gobbling chunks"—and a rare T-bone steak. After eating the steak, he even picks up and chews the bone, "to the disgust of Mr. and Mrs. America at the next table" (*WFM*, 206). When Swanson finishes eating and drinking, he "loosen[s] an uncontrollable, resounding belch" (*WFM*, 206). He further sates his hunger for civilization by buying all the available magazines and newspapers in town. Furthermore, on his drive home he buys pint bottles of whiskey, one of which he throws away even though it is still half full. Characteristically, he later wishes he had not been so impetuous.

"Bring It Back to Useless Life"

In interpreting the ending of *Wolf*, some reviewers and critics noted its less than optimistic tone. Joyce Carol Oates wrote that Swanson is "lost in the wilderness, and, we assume, he has always been lost; his life is as shapeless as nature itself" (462). Jonathan Yardley believed that in *Wolf* Harrison had "sharply portrayed the conflict between the urge to live— fully, meaningfully, exuberantly—and the circumstances we have created for life. [Harrison] has a keen eye for the problem, but his strategy for survival is a fantasy" (1971, 38). W. H. Roberson noted that Harrison's protagonists live in a society that provides "no stability or security" and thus must create their "own sense of meaning and belonging by finding something to personally place their faith in, an event or belief that will give [their] life form." According to Roberson, however, Swanson is a "failure" because he is "unable to make any lasting connections with life, nor with people, the family homestead he revisits, or even the wolf he seeks. He connects only with himself."[8] C. Lynn Munro correctly observed that Swanson is "alternately lost in the woods and lost in his own mental mires," that in both the woods and the city he is a "drifter searching, against the odds, to discover an ordering principle around which to unscramble his conflicting longings," and that his "Janus-headed nature" lures him to "both the land and the city." Munro concludes, however, that when the novel ends "one senses that Swanson has resolved very little. During his week in the woods, he has not only failed to see the wolf but has also failed to illuminate a route out of the riddle that only leads to another."[9]

Analyzing Swanson in light of Harrison's other heroes, John Rohrkemper wrote that at the end of the novel Swanson realizes "what many of Harrison's heroes will also learn: that while he is certainly not 'of the city,' and does not espouse the values of modern society, he is also not 'of the wilderness.' . . . Again like heroes to follow, Swanson accepts his fate with resigned good humor."[10] Burkholder also emphasizes the novel's affirmative conclusion:

> Unlike Thoreau in *Walden*, when Swanson leaves the woods it is not with a sense of optimism about the future but with an affirmation of the value of the past, including his own personal history. . . . To emphasize his commitment to the past, Harrison ends the novel with Swanson promising himself to saddle soap the harness his grandfather used for his team of Belgian horses to "bring it back to useless life." Of course, to Swanson the act of renewing the harness is anything but useless since it represents the commitment to his own past. (269)[11]

Other incidents in *Wolf* also suggest that its ending is not as hopeless as some reviewers and critics have argued. Swanson is somewhat healthier in that he had been 30 pounds overweight but lost "ten pounds of lard" and his muscles are tauter. Even his words and feelings are more hopeful as he leaves the woods. When he discards his 20-pound tent and throws it over the bulldozer seat as a "gift to the pulpers to keep their seats dry," he feels much happier for having lightened his pack (*WFM*, 197). As he sings songs ranging from the national anthem and Buck Owens's "It's Crying Time Again" to "The Old Rugged Cross," he feels "considerably more than ten feet tall" (*WFM*, 198). He plunges into a creek, and its cold waters become an "exhilarant" (*WFM*, 198). Worried that his car may not start, Swanson "totally" loses his "sense of panic" when the engine roars to life, and when he drives out of the woods, he feels a "new and curious calm" but doubts it will "last long" (*WFM*, 200, 201). As he reaches the main road, he feels "none" of his "usual fears," but he does admit to "a cautionary feeling" (*WFM*, 203). Swanson's words—"I doubted it would last long" and "cautionary feeling"—emphasize the tentativeness of his hope for the future. Furthermore, while he has retreated to the Huron Mountains to reevaluate and possibly to renew his life in true romantic fashion, he knows that there is "no romance in the woods in opposition to what fools insist. Our Indians were and still are great anti-romantics. Anyone who disagrees should be parachuted or landed by float plane in the Northwest Territory for a dose of romance" (*WFM*, 70). His comments ironically refute his prefatory statement that his narrative will be a "romance" (*WFM*, 13).

What does Swanson want? A simpler time: "I want twenty years ago and milking cows in the evening before dinner, pitch the silage in trough before the stanchions. Oats for horses with hay. Alfalfa too thick to walk through now" (*WFM*, 207). Just as he knows there is no romance in the wilderness, he also knows he cannot recapture the past, a fact underscored when he revisits scenes from his past. Though tempted to detour, he decides he does not want to see the cabin on the lake where his family vacationed. When he passes the house in Grayling where he was born, Swanson is "disgusted with the way the merchants had attempted to turn the town into an 'alpine village' by putting false-front shingled mansard roofs on their stores. Holy shit upon the birthplace but I felt nothing and continued south after buying another pint" (*WFM*, 208). As he drives by his childhood home in Reed City, he remarks, "Nothing is haunted and sentiment is a lid I don't need to manage the present" (*WFM*, 212). Even when he visits the house where his father was born, Swanson notes, "I wanted the impact of this to sink in but nothing happened" (*WFM*, 216). Though he feels a "terrible pull of homesickness" when he visits his grandmother's small, shabby farmhouse, he realizes that the "crazy gaiety about life" and the "three-day polka parties with tubs of herring and barrels of beer" are forever past. Yet, a vestige of the past exists here—the harness he "might bring back to useless life with saddle soap" (*WFM*, 225).

As do some of Harrison's later protagonists, Swanson may bumble along through life and occasionally rage against injustices and his own predicaments, but he is no fool. On the contrary, he correctly identifies his euphoria as temporary and cautionary; that is how the antiromantic world works in his life. Accordingly, he correctly assesses his life:

> I had changed my life so often that I finally decided there never would be
> anything to change—I could make all the moves I wished to on the sur-

face . . . but these moves were suspended on a thin layer that failed to stir anything below. A sort of mordant fatalism I lived within concerning geometrical matters—jobs, alcohol, marriage and the naturally concomitant joblessness, drunkenness, infidelity. Perhaps all true children of Protestantism are victims of such self-help—the notion of the law of life involving steps, paths, guideposts, ladders. (*WFM*, 201–2)

At the end of the novel, Swanson may connect only with himself, as W. H. Roberson pointed out, but that connection is essential because Swanson accepts certain truths about himself and his life. He admits that he can never fully live in the city or the wilderness, that his interests are anachronistic—"fishing, forests, alcohol, food, art, in that order"—that since 1958 his movements have been "lateral instead of forward," and that 1957 to 1960 were "unbearably convulsive" times (*WFM*, 215, 137, 217). Not only is he "exhausted from volatility"—those "unbearably convulsive" years—but he yearns for "something more final but doubt[s he will] get it barring dying" (*WFM*, 219).

Just as he still hopes to see a wolf, Swanson still searches for meaning and purpose in his life and is willing to "shed this old skin and add a new one" (*WFM*, 219). Since there are no steps or guideposts, if he changes, he must do it himself: "Fuck all the gurus on earth and advice and conclusions" (*WFM*, 202). What he wants, however, is the freedom to choose, to make his own decisions about his life. "If I want to be nothing," he rages, "it's my business," and later he says, "I'm talking about my own particular harmless sort of freedom" (*WFM*, 210, 215). Harrison underscored the idea of freedom when he told Elliott and Sommerness, "*Wolf* is basically about freedom, the compulsion to be free to work it out for one's self." The idea of working it out for one's self is also what motivates Harrison's later protagonists.

Despite the lateral movements, the "unbearably convulsive" times, the rages, and the wanderings, *Wolf* ends on a quiet but "cautionary" affirmative tone among the family's artifacts in his grandmother's calm house: his grandfather's brass spittoon, the Zane Grey novels, the Swedish Bible, and the worn harness. In addition, Swanson has ultimately returned to northern Michigan to renew himself and perhaps reshape even his own "useless life." When he leaves his grandmother's house, he will drive to his own home. All of Swanson's "brutally stupid voyages" eventually, inexorably, lead back home. As Swanson's father often reminded him, "Do as you will," but "you're always welcome at home" (*WFM*, 216, 211).

"Before I Wrote It"

"I diagrammed the form of *Wolf* before I wrote it," Harrison says, "just a picture of form, no words" (Fergus 1988, 77). He also admits that before he wrote *Wolf* he had not written "any fiction other than juvenalia, so naturally *Wolf* was a poet's book. I even have grave doubts whether it's a novel at all. That's why I called it a false memoir" (Fergus 1988, 61). Concomitantly, Harrison believes that the "artist must reinvent form," and reinventing form is what he does in *Wolf.*

Wolf combines two literary forms, the memoir and the autobiography. C. Hugh Holman writes that a memoir is a "form of autobiographical" writing that involves recollections of "prominent people" who have either witnessed or participated in "significant events," and that, while autobiography emphasizes the "inner and private life of the subject," a memoir stresses "personalities and actions other than those of the writer."[12] Following up on the book's subtitle, Swanson says in the Author's Note that the narrative is a "false memoir . . . and not even chronological" (*WFM*, 11). This false memoir, then, rather than being an organized, chronological narrative, has a more freewheeling chronology. For example, the novel's third chapter, "The West," includes Swanson's recollections about hitchhiking across the west to California and living in San Francisco, but it is also about his camping out in the Huron Mountains and specifically about his hike to the lake to watch an osprey nest. The chapter's narrative, however, alternates between these two experiences and thoughts about the deaths of his father and sister, his sexual experience at a drive-in movie, and his ideas about ecology, game violators, and the colon as a punctuation mark.

Not only does "false memoir" suggest a freewheeling chronology, but *false* also suggests that instead of recalling his relations with others, Swanson's memoirs focus on his own role in the significant events he relates. In this sense, *Wolf* is also an autobiography, because Swanson provides insights into his inner being and private life. In adopting both the memoir and autobiography forms, Harrison not only provides depth for Swanson's characterization and problems but, as Munro noted, "merges time and place in such a way as to convey a gestalt of experiences rather than a sequence of events" (Munro 1983, 1288).

Etcetera

In addition to improvising a literary form in *Wolf,* Harrison modifies certain literary traditions: the romance and rites of passage. As noted earlier, Harrison undercuts the romantic tradition when Swanson, like Natty Bumppo and Henry David Thoreau, retreats to the woods to reassess and renew his life. In *Wolf*, nature certainly does not minister to or soothe the protagonist. Rather than being the giant nanny that burps the world, true nature will destroy him if he commits too many "fuck-ups." Nor does nature assume romantic, pantheistic proportions. When he is wheezing from carrying his tent and other camping essentials back to his car, Swanson prays, "God send me a helicopter and I'll become a missionary to the heathen wherever you want me to go. Accept this little bribe and you won't be sorry" (*WFM*, 197). Instead of hearing answers from God to his prayers or hopeful clues from nature, Swanson says he heard "Silence except for the wind's wailing" (*WFM*, 197).

Harrison also modifies the rites of passage tradition. Although Swanson constantly separates himself from his familiar world, his Michigan home, his journeys do not reconcile him to the world and its ways. Even his ultimate separation, his retreat to the wilderness, does not end in an initiation. Burkholder pointed out that Swanson's week in the woods ends in an "uninitiation": he comes to the woods "to find himself" by "distancing himself from the civilization-gone-haywire that has corrupted him," but his thoughts continually revert to "his life in the West, Boston, and New York City, and to sex, alcohol, cigarettes, and all of the 'civilized' things and attitudes he has forsworn in an effort to find himself" (268–69).

Wolf may be an angry book, but it is also boisterously humorous; Swanson has a penchant for recognizing the absurdity in some of his predicaments, and he can also laugh at himself. He recalls, for example, a sexual debacle in a hammock: "I once went sixty-nine with a beautiful girl in a hammock and we became too preoccupied and violent and the hammock tipped us over onto the floor, at least a four-foot drop. She landed on top of me which made the etiquette of the accident proper but my shoulder was painfully wrenched. She thought it was very funny and was still juiced up but the pain in my bruised lips and nose and shoulder had unsexed me: full mast half mast no mast" (*WFM*, 51).

The novel's humor results also from Swanson's sexual fantasies, which, he claims, occur "without warning in everyone's technicolor memory—in the woods, the taiga, the arctic, to fighter pilots and per-haps senators and presidents" (*WFM*, 100). In one of his fantasies, he imagines living like a hermit rolling his own cigarettes and having star-lets parachuted into his "outpost to be reseeded—the poor girls will wander about aimlessly for a few hours. . . . I will follow them like a

Rima . . . sizing the cut of their haunches. Sex enters. To mate not once but a thousand times" (*WFM*, 139). In another fantasy, he imagines that a *Vogue* model walks out of a swamp, she thinks he is a "dark incredibly romantic savage," and they "play wood nymph." In another fantasy, a *Vogue* model pampers and financially supports him, but Swanson undercuts the fantasy when he admits that he is "too homely to be a kept man" (*WFM*, 78).

In his fantasies, Swanson is handsome and always sexually desirable, but when his fantasies are juxtaposed with reality, comedy results. His dreams about the starlets or the *Vogue* models, for example, could end in pratfalls in light of his experiences in the hammock and, later, in an alley: as he made love to a girl he met at a party, she only said "wow once or twice and hummed a little"; then after his climax, she looked at him "idly, straightened her skirt and went back to the party," while he stood there with a bottle cap stuck to his posterior (*WFM*, 85–86). Swanson's comic, absurd experiences complement life's general absurdities; more important, these experiences make him human and vulnerable as he searches for purpose and stability in his life, not the priggish bore that his rages would suggest.

Wolf also covers some of the subjects Harrison would deal with in his essays and succeeding novels. Swanson rages about game violators who "run fox to exhaustion with snowmobiles then club them to death"; about greed—"the merest smell of profit would lead us to gut any beau ty left. . . . We have been doing it since we got off the boat and nothing would stop us now"; and about pseudo-hunters, like the woman who "proudly told" of shooting a grizzly with a .375 magnum while it slept or about the archer who bought a buffalo "on the hoof" to kill as a trophy—"After shooting over thirty arrows into the beast from fairly close range the buffalo failed to die. . . . The state police were called and a trooper fanned his .38 into the slumping body. . . . The trooper trooped home after work and told his wife. . . . The archer told his friends that buffalo were tough, dangerous ole hombres and hard to bring down" (*WFM*, 45, 44, 94–95). Swanson comments about ethnic injustices: "It's a matter of contention now," he says, "who got fucked over the most, the blacks brought here as slaves or the Indians who were totally dispossessed. Sand Creek. Harper's Ferry. Like asking who in a war was murdered the 'deadest.' . . . Blankets purposely infected with smallpox, rapine, marches, slaughter, greed, and a hundred million pelts shipped back east" (*WFM*, 168). Swanson's reflections characterize him in that they arise from his own experiences in the world, and so, while he may often be the butt of his own predicaments, he is not a total fool but rather an intelligent, perceptive, compassionate person who perceives some truths about the culture in which he must live.

To "Practice It Pointillistically"

Harrison calls *Wolf* a "poet's book":

> Poets practice an overall scrutiny habitually, and what's good later for their novels is that they practice it pointillistically. You read some reasonably good novelists who tell a story well enough in terms of a flat narrative, but they never notice anything interesting, whereas a poet has folded and unfolded his soul somewhat like an old-fashioned laundry girl with the linen. His self is his vocation. As W. C. Williams said, "no ideas but in things." (Fergus 1988, 61)

Just as in pointillism, a postimpressionist school of painting, small dots and brush strokes blend into a whole picture, in *Wolf* the small segments of Swanson's life add up to the novel's narrative. The interest Harrison shows here in the "things" of life foretells the techniques he would use in his succeeding poetry, novellas, and novels.

Chapter Three

"Out of the Feeling of the Late Sixties": *A Good Day to Die*

Like *Wolf*, *A Good Day to Die* has its detractors and its acclaimers. Sara Blackburn claimed that Harrison wasted his "excellent narrative talent" on a "kind of super-machismo a-man's-a-man stuff," and she noted that despite the protagonist's "constant assertions that he's variously weak, guilty, self-serving, jealous, small-minded, greedy and self-hating . . . both he and his author clearly want us to see him as somehow tragic, a heroic if lost figure upon the vast American landscape." Concluding that the narrator is not "grandly tragic or heroic," Blackburn deemed Harrison's novel an "adolescent book by a talented writer who, on the basis of it, is experienced enough to know better than to preach its me-burned-out Tarzan dogma."[1] W. H. Roberson believed that, while it is a "darker, more unsettling, and less successful work," *A Good Day* continued to develop one of Harrison's major themes, "being out of sync with the twentieth century" (30).

Although noting that *A Good Day* is "more sketchpad than novel," and that if "read as fiction it must be found wanting" since there is "very little evidence" that Harrison "knows how to find a story and then find his way through it," William Crawford Woods still praised *A Good Day* as a "poet's book" with metaphors as "sharp as jagged bone," "bright, dizzying language," and adroitly characterized "rural and urban types."[2] The anonymous *Choice* reviewer praised Harrison as a "fine writer" and the novel as "noteworthy": "Its characters are real, its language is genuine and poetic, and its themes are aesthetically embodied in, rather than painted onto, its 'Westward' plot."[3]

"Such Disinherited Children"

Harrison admitted that, after the autobiographical *Wolf*, he wanted to "write a straight short novel"; *A Good Day* comes "out of the feeling of the late sixties" and is the "first Vietnam book" (Fergus 1988, 63). Raymond Chandler and John D. MacDonald were major influences on this novel's more traditional narrative form: "I wanted to tell one of those simple tales that has a great deal of narrative urgency, propelled by characters who, once you've met them, you know it's going to be a godawful mess" (Fergus 1988, 63).

Harrison confessed that the novel's three central characters—the unnamed narrator, Tim, and Sylvia—are "people that nobody wants in their living room . . . except maybe Sylvia, in her white cotton underpants" (Fergus 1988, 63). He conceded that a great many readers hate *A Good Day* because of its three characters. Alfred Kazin complained, for example, that they are "simply the nastiest people" and "they don't exist," but Harrison countered that such people are "all over. It's just that people don't write about them" (Bonetti, 76).

A Rainer Maria Rilke quotation prefaces *A Good Day*: "Each torpid turn of this world bears such disinherited children to whom neither what's been, nor what is coming, belongs." The narrator, Sylvia, and Tim are all disinherited, for different reasons. Tim's Vietnam experiences have not only alienated him but ravaged him physically and mentally. He has been "through too much shit, too many drugs and Saigon whores for it ever to be quite the same again."[4] Tim is badly wounded in Vietnam, and the right side of his face is so "distorted with a bleached twist of scar tissue" that his eye is a "few degrees off center" (*AGD*, 42). After his discharge, he does not want to return to Georgia Tech, nor does he want to be a garage mechanic like his older brother or a gas station attendant like his younger brother. More important, Tim realizes that he no longer loves Sylvia, his high school sweetheart, with whom he has had an "on-again, off-again relationship ever since" (*AGD*, 42). When he thinks she is pregnant, he volunteers for another tour in Vietnam "to avoid marriage" (*AGD*, 29). At the same time, the more she loves him and the more she talks of marriage, the more he abuses her. Not only does he go off with whores when he is with her, but he even suggests that she and the narrator have an affair. Also symptomatic of Tim's alienation are his self-destructive actions: his Seconal-alcohol–induced dazes, his reckless driving, his frequent brawls, his romantic illusions about working on the Alaskan pipeline or becoming a mercenary in Africa; even his favorite song, Janis Joplin's "Get It While You Can," says the narrator, is "unequaled in modern music for sheer relentless desperation" (*AGD*, 111).

Sylvia is likewise disinherited and out of sync with the twentieth century. She barely tolerates her job filing insurance claims and willingly leaves it to travel west with Tim, who is a major factor in her alienation:

"She merely waited. And was punished. And there was no real majority of the sane to be a member of. She had gradually by the act of waiting for Tim cut herself off from all but a few like Rosie and Frank and her mother whom she exchanged letters with" (*AGD*, 131). Ironically, like Harrison's later heroines, Sylvia possesses innate virtues and values that could stabilize her in a world of flux. The narrator describes her as an "antique," as "helplessly feminine"; she reminds him of those "comparatively simple country girls" of a decade before. Sadly and inevitably, Sylvia's greatest virtue is her "naive altruism which, although battered, daily centered in her wanting to wholly love someone and to be loved as totally and faithfully in return" (*AGD*, 131). The narrator sheepishly confesses: "Sylvia was right and Tim and myself were wrong . . . she was that purportedly normal group that formed such a stunning majority. I saw us as goats who stood for alcohol, dope, dynamite, errant promiscuity, while she was some hearth goddess who was sweet, virtuous, gentle, kind and faithful" (*AGD*, 130–31). Spurned by Tim, lusted after by the narrator, and doomed to marry someone she does not love, Sylvia is adrift in an impersonal modern world that batters her altruistic values and her very being—or as the narrator says, she does not "seem to belong to the twentieth century," although she bears "so many of its characteristic scars" (*AGD*, 69).

The narrator is disinherited because he is unemployed—he has never found "anything suitable"—has been separated from his wife and daughter for six months, and will probably not reconcile. He attempts to return once, only to park three blocks from his house and watch through binoculars as his wife and daughter go to and return from the grocery store. He feels that he is becoming less interested in and adept at fishing, a therapeutic sport for many of Harrison's heroes. Even his romantic illusions about himself become ludicrous. In one of his reveries, for example, he heroically climbs a mountain and mistakes a lightning bolt for a "power vision"; his body is blasted into a charcoaled "crescent smile." In turn, the local people name the mountain Big Smiley and create an anti-legend: "At fourteen his heifer took last place at the fair; at twenty-two he had difficulty staying awake; at twenty-six his wife asked him to leave but to please not take the car; at twenty-eight he climbed a mountain and made a smile" (*AGD*, 141). His idiotic Big Smiley grin—perhaps an allusion to the vacuous Alfred E. Neuman grin of *Mad* magazine fame—symbolizes his alienation and only tentative interest in life, or as he admits: "I did not qualify even as an observer let alone a pilgrim. Or to make it tiresome, I was not in the stands watching or on the field playing, I was down in some sub-basement regarding the whole base structure indifferently. My friends no longer existed, neither did my wife; I had no state or country, no governor or president. We used to call such people nihilists but that is much too strong a word for a vacuum" (*AGD*, 55–56).

Tim's life is "conceived and lived only in terms of the act," and his idea of a "proper life" as "swashbuckling" springs from an "old Errol Flynn movie." The narrator, by contrast, cannot act decisively (*AGD*, 45, 69). Indeed, he even says, "I've always been psychologically geared to retreat"; he has "never committed an act without a consequent fuck-up" (*AGD*, 90, 45). Whereas Tim refuses to pay his car notes, the narrator is terrified that someone will "get" him if he fails to pay the telephone or the gas credit card bills. "Once I was a week late on a two-hundred-dollar note," he confesses, "and a banker . . . lectured me at his desk about financial responsibility and how the economic health of the nation depended on the individual citizen. I blushed but stayed and took my 'medicine'" (*AGD*, 41). While women are strongly attracted to Tim's "velocity . . . waitresses, whores, bar girls or ranchers' daughters in Jackson Hole" (*AGD*, 152), the narrator candidly admits: "How often I had wanted to be Bob Bold and swagger around our great land having at every attractive girl, throwing in a homely waitress or two, even a grandmother out of kindness. It was never to be. Sadly, I never had trouble with whores but I knew that was because the act was so totally devoid of any response except the sexual. Like dogs. A very rare girl, Sylvia for instance, would throw me into a frenzy of trepidation: hollow stomach, trembling hands, dry mouth and all of that" (*AGD*, 82). Accordingly, the narrator's assessment of his personality faults, his judgment of his Big Smiley adventure as an "anti-legend," and his realization that their plans are wacky and not heroic clearly mark him as an absurd, comic figure, not an attempt at a tragic figure, as Sara Blackburn claims in her *New York Times* review: "Both he and his author clearly want us to see him as somehow tragic, a heroic if lost figure upon the vast American landscape" (4). The narrator constantly admits he is lost, but he never claims to be a tragic figure capable of heroic or tragic actions.

Epitomizing the characters' alienation is their journey from Key West to Arizona, where they intend to blow up a purported dam in the Grand Canyon, a scheme the narrator and Tim concoct when both are in an alcohol-speed–induced haze. In a journey somewhat reminiscent of Jack Kerouac's *On the Road*, Harrison's protagonists speed westward, whoring and ingesting prodigious quantities of beer, whiskey, marijuana, and other drugs. No dam exists, however, so they decide to dynamite a rancher's earthen dam near Orofino, Idaho, that "prevented steelhead from moving upstream to spawn" and was "built out of greed and in contempt of the natural world" (*AGD*, 83). The sheer folly of their adventure becomes apparent as the narrator ominously realizes that theirs is a "mindless, disorganized plot" that is "ten degrees off in the direction of wacky," and that there is "no sense of balance left in anything we are doing" (*AGD*, 55, 77).

The closing scenes of *A Good Day to Die* focus on the final preparations to blow up the Idaho dam. As Tim and the narrator wait for dusk—ironically disguised as Indians with pigtailed hair and lipstick-painted faces—sinister omens plague the narrator. The weather turns cold and stormy; Tim kills a Doberman pinscher guard dog; Sylvia mires the trailer in the soft earth; oblivious cattle amble down the slopes; Tim loses control in a Seconal-speed daze; and the narrator feels "terminally disconnected with the way things were going wrong" (*AGD*, 168). In the explosion, Tim is killed when he rushes back to frighten away some cattle ambling toward the dam. Tim's absurd death underscores the folly of their plan. In addition, the narrator's and Sylvia's immediate plans are jumbled as he wonders what to do with Tim's car and frets that the trailer, hastily abandoned at a roadside park, may have fingerprints on it. While the narrator worries about whether he will be arrested and Sylvia worries about what to tell Tim's family, the less than heroic nature of their act comes home to the narrator when he realizes: "An act that I had conceived as heroic would probably go unnoticed except by a rancher who might wonder why his dam had never washed away before, or why his Doberman was dead, or why he was missing two cattle. Two dead and two missing" (*AGD*, 175). With Tim's death, a stable relationship is possible between Sylvia and the narrator, but he knows he cannot commit himself to it. Because of his tentative hold on life, he finally admits: "Someone should take care of her but if I had any qualities of kindness and mercy left, any perceptions of what I was on earth however dim and stupid, I knew it couldn't be me" (*AGD*, 176).

A Good Day, like *Wolf*, ends indeterminately in that both Swanson and the narrator are not sure what the future of their families and their own lives will be. Yet despite the "godawful mess" their alienated lives and crazy plans have caused, the narrator affirms, "I felt oddly alive. Suicide wasn't the question." Both those assertions contrast with his earlier comment: "Suicide was a thought that consistently held vitality" (*AGD*, 175, 112). In contrast, he definitely knows he cannot make a mess out of Sylvia's life, a fact that he has learned from his own marriage and what he terms "that long pull of boredom in marriage" (*AGD*, 135). When he decides to let her go, however, he does so out of kindness and mercy—one of the few times he truly considers the feelings of others.

Our House of Atreus Curse: The Nez Perce Theme

In *Wolf*, Swanson's diatribes about social injustices, especially against Native Americans, arise from his observations and experiences; while they are part of his characterization, they are not wholly integrated into the plot. In *A Good Day*, however, the allusions to the Nez Perce Indians complement the plot, characterizations, and themes. First of all, the novel's prefatory quotation from Rilke about "disinherited children" suggests the Nez Perce's heroic action and tragic surrender. According to Francis Hanes, the Nez Perce were "friends of Lewis and Clark, seekers after the 'Book of Heaven'. . . renowned fighters, yet eager for peace; kind, intelligent, gentle, proud of their blood and culture."[5] The Nez Perce loved their land for its abundant game, natural resources, and breathtaking beauty, but that love would clash with the settlers who encroached on their land. As more and more settlers pushed westward, the Nez Perce were doomed by the inevitable scenario: "A council was held and a treaty made, Indians ceded lands in return for presents and promised annuities; boundary lines were marked and declared inviolable. Peace lasted a few years but was destroyed by the encroachment of settlers who crossed the line to hunt, prospect, graze stock, and farm. These invasions brought protests, massacres, battles, and ultimately victory to the troops."[6]

The Upper Nez Perce sold their lands, moved to the Lapwai Reservation, and were treated shabbily and humiliated. However, Chief Tuekakis, Chief Joseph's father, counseled his son, "No man owns any part of the earth. No man can sell what he does not own. My son, never forget my dying words. The country holds your father's body. Never sell the bones of your father and mother."[7] After his father's death, Chief Joseph diplomatically refused every request to move his people onto the reservation. In 1877, when General Oliver O. Howard threatened to "drive" Joseph and his people onto the Lapwai Reservation, Joseph gave in, but only because he was thinking of his people's lives first. When cowboys deliberately provoked some of Joseph's younger, more volatile warriors, killings followed, war became inevitable, and Joseph, again thinking of his people, decided to lead them peacefully to Canada. The U.S. government sent Howard's command in pursuit, and thus began the Nez Perce's epic 11-week, 1,600-mile trek during which they engaged "ten separate U.S. commands in thirteen battles and skirmishes and in nearly every instance either defeated or fought them to a standstill" (Chalmers, 265). Because they were finally trapped and many of the old and young succumbed to the rigors of their winter journey, Chief Joseph surrendered to General Howard at Bear's Paw in Montana. With his characteristic pride and dignity, he promised, "From where the sun now stands, I will fight no more, forever." Although they lost their lands and eventually surrendered, the Nez Perce never lost either courage or dignity, and if anything, in defeat they had their greatest victory. Their heroic, tragic journey and struggle contrast with the narrator's and Tim's wacky plans and less-than-heroic lives.

Their "lack of balance" and disorganization are especially evident when the narrator fishes Idaho's Big Hole River, site of the first battle between the U.S. Army and the Nez Perce. Because the narrator's courage waxes but mostly wanes, he marvels that the Nez Perce could say, "Take courage, this is a good day to die," and "mean it" (*AGD*, 139). He wishes that he could receive some instructions from Chief Joseph, but when he recalls Chief Joseph's abiding love for his two wives and nine children, the narrator admits that Joseph "clearly wouldn't like me and I didn't very much either" (*AGD*, 143). While Chief Joseph and his Nez Perce were dedicated to preserving a way of life that was unjustly being taken from them, the narrator and Tim have not been as unjustly treated as they think they have, and their plan to dynamite the dam is indeed "ten degrees in the direction of wacky." And if the narrator's courage always wavers, Tim's courage is "out of control" and dangerous, in contrast to the Nez Perce's dedicated, selfless courage. Similarly, Chief Joseph's unstinting devotion to his wives and children and to his people contrasts with the narrator's desertion of his wife and daughter and with Tim's inability to love Sylvia. In defeat, the Nez Perce never lost their dignity, but all that is left for Harrison's protagonists once they blow up the dam is an act that "would probably go unnoticed except by a rancher" (*AGD*, 175). It was not, after all, a "good day to die," nor was it a good day to live.

Perspectives

Like Swanson, the narrator in *A Good Day to Die* is from Michigan, but he does not return there to renew himself and to reestablish purpose and meaning in his life. Furthermore, he, too, experiences a midlife crisis (though at 28) that results from a number of causes. He not only realizes that the pristine fishing streams and rivers are vanishing—he drives "around the country in a veritable frenzy to cream the good fishing before it totally disappeared"—but gradually loses interest in fishing: he takes "several good fish," he says, but "with no pleasure" (*AGD*, 92, 114). In addition, the narrator cannot hold a job: he has lost three jobs in one year. When he decides he wants to own a "fishing tackle and sporting store," his parents and his wife's parents object and then arrange for him to work in the sporting section of a large department store, a job he detests because "the people who came in to buy the junk we carried . . . were collectively less charming than a drunken bowling team" (*AGD*, 136). He organizes a "beautiful fly display case" that no one notices, orders expensive fly rods that no one buys, insults customers, and even alters licenses by reducing heights and vastly increasing weights. The job, according to him, "precipitated the breakdown" (*AGD*, 135). Another major cause of his crisis is his boredom with his marriage and realization that "love" as he knows it will not "hold enough energy or velocity to hold interest after three or four years" (*AGD*, 135). In fact, when his wife drives him to the airport, he admits it is "an emotionless process that followed months of talk where no one was really wrong because no one had ever been right" (*AGD*, 57).

While he enjoys hunting and fishing, the narrator possesses no macho characteristics like "macho self-sufficiency," courage, or a desire to "blaze" his solitary way through a "senseless world" (Prescott, 72). Again, his Big Smiley anti-legendary adventure, his not being a "Bob Bold," and his lack of courage emphasize his absurd, rather than macho stance. Although Tim is more macho than the narrator, Harrison undercuts Tim's machismo. For example, as he watches Tim play pool, the narrator says, "This sort of player can be very accurate but he plays with his balls, his manhood, and never leaves himself well for the next shot, except by accident: a pointless arrogance, a kind of dumbbell 'macho'" (*AGD*, 19–20). Not only do Tim's reckless driving, fistfights, alcohol-drug binges, and living only in terms of the act symbolize his dumbbell machismo, but his machismo is especially evident when he is pointlessly killed in the dam explosion as he tries to run in "those gaudy blue cowboy boots," which symbolize his arrogant macho stance (*AGD*). Like his pool playing, Tim's actions are fatalistic and never leave him "well for the next shot."

In discussing with Jean W. Ross the accusation that he presents shallow women characters, Harrison replied: "I think in *Warlock* that's definitely not true. Someone told me . . . that [Diana] was my first major woman. It's just that I don't suspect I ever knew them well enough. . . . When I've presented a shallow woman, it was because she *was* a shallow woman; she was no more shallow than the man—as in *A Good Day to Die.* Also, I certainly don't want to pretend to more knowledge about women than I have, just to curry favor" (Ross, 228). While she may not be as strongly feminine and as well understood and finely drawn as Harrison's later heroines, Sylvia is Harrison's first hearth-goddess figure whose virtues—her desire to love and be loved totally, her "gentle, kind, and faithful" nature—could provide purpose and stability for Tim or the narrator in a world of flux. The autobiographical details in *A Good Day* contribute to the characterizations and themes. Noticing on Tim's face the "whorl of scar tissue" resembling a "knot in a white oak board," for example, the narrator recalls when he and his brother built a Slocum boat out of a white oak they "skidded out of the woods with a Belgian mare in the winter" (*AGD*, 43). He also recalls the Model A automobile that his father taught him to start with a crank, a car that contrasts with Tim's new Dodge muscle car with "four on the floor" and an engine that growls and is "too aggressive"—further symbols of Tim's dumbbell, arrogant machismo. Other autobiographical details are evident as the narrator fishes for tarpon in Key West and reminisces about his affair with a New York woman, whom he would "break from that evening," and about being "so generally strung out by urban life that I felt I must return to the 'land' which proves even now to be a rather literary urging" (*AGD*, 55, 92). In other words, after Harrison begins working with the "strength of the autobiographical juice," he then breaks out and writes "about other people" (Stocking 1977, 26).

Harrison uses very little symbolism in *Wolf*, but in *A Good Day* symbols augment characterization and theme. As previously noted, the novel's three main characters and the Nez Perce symbolize Rilke's "disinherited children" and the fate of the late 1960s generation, who would be alienated and dislocated by the Vietnam War. In addition, the rancher's dam that despoils a steelhead-spawning stream and the Nez Perce's tragic fate suggest the greed that is "killing the life-soul of the country," a subject of Swanson's diatribes and Harrison's own essays. The plan that is "ten degrees off in the direction of wacky" is also symbolized in the narrator's feeling "terminally disconnected" and in Tim's scarred face that draws his right eye a "few degrees off center." Even the songs Harrison alludes to in the narrative suggest the world in flux. In addition to Joplin's "Get It While You Can," Tammy Wynette's "Divorce" is a "mournful song" in which a husband and wife spell the word so their child will not know what will disconnect him from one of his parents; Merle Haggard's "I Can't Hold Myself in Line" suggests the narrator's vacillation and Tim's dumbbell macho actions, or as the narrator says, "The singer was mournfully going 'off the deep end' because of love and whiskey. It was painfully accurate and I wanted to turn it off" (*AGD*, 158).

Compared with *Wolf*, *A Good Day* reflects Harrison's maturing literary technique. Far from demonstrating that Harrison cannot "find a story and then find his way through it" (Woods, 4), *A Good Day* is a unified narrative that unfolds logically and chronologically. Not only does Harrison show how the three characters create a "godawful mess," he also captures the chaotic dislocation of the late sixties and the aftereffects of the Vietnam War, on Tim in particular but also on Sylvia and the narrator. If, as Joyce Carol Oates believes, *Wolf* is the "diary-like work" that must come before the "first significant book," then *A Good Day to Die* is a necessary step toward *Farmer*, as well as toward each of Harrison's succeeding novels.

Chapter Four
"The Heartbreaker for Me": *Farmer*

Harrison told Jim Fergus:

> *Wolf* actually did quite well for a first novel, and *A Good Day to Die* did all right, but the heartbreaker for me was the absolute failure of *Farmer*. That was something I couldn't handle because it just slipped beneath the waters. I think Viking took out one one-inch ad for it. That was a difficult period and I couldn't maintain my sanity. I had a series of crack-ups. I was at a point where I couldn't pay my taxes. . . . That was the period out of which I wrote *Letters to Yesenin*. (Fergus 1988, 67)

Ironically, while it may have been a heartbreaker for Harrison, *Farmer* generally received good reviews, even though some reviewers faulted its minor weaknesses. The anonymous *New Yorker* critic praised the novel for its "graceful descriptions of rural northern-Michigan life and robust, emphatic portraits of country people" but said that the story is "vapid and stale" and that Harrison is "at his worst when he is describing relations between the sexes and since the school teacher's problem is resolved rather vaguely, one ends up feeling cheated of a real story to attach to all the beautiful descriptions of geese, deer, woodcocks, and streams."[1] Similarly, Parkman Howe praised as the novel's "true touches" its "descriptive passages," which "flare up appealingly behind the ghost figures, such as the almost indiscernible, relentless coming on of the seasons in upstate Michigan." But Howe criticized Harrison for not managing enough "ironic distance," so that "Joseph's tribulations are treated with teenage seriousness."[2] While asserting that *Farmer* "stumbles into a patch of moralizing banality at its end" as Joseph goes to Chicago to "think himself out of his dilemma," the anonymous *Newsweek* reviewer noted the novel's strengths: "Harrison cannily fractures his story and reveals each treasured facet only gradually. Flashbacks and flashforwards slowly fill in the details of the author's disjointed meditation on a complicated person. His features build up in an apparently uncalculated order that is itself carefully designed to raise a dozen questions at each meander and to put the reader inside Joseph's head."[3]

Webster Schott, on the other hand, wrote: "Harrison's earlier novels, *Wolf* and *A Good Day to Die*, suggested the intensity of his talent. *Farmer* shows it maturing. He writes beautifully. . . . He moves us rather than overwhelms us. He creates an art small except in its grace."[4] William H. Roberson believed that *Farmer* is "arguably" Harrison's "finest novel," and that it "strengthens Harrison's theme of the individual's realization of the certainty of death and his subsequent search for identity" (31). C. Lynn Munro argued that *Farmer* does not suffer from an "ironic distance" and that it is a "parody of the Romantic novel; throughout the book, Harrison burlesques Joseph's inability to attain 'a place that refused to arrive' and with mock seriousness describes self-pity as 'an emotion [Joseph] had never allowed himself.' That Harrison is intent upon effecting a parody is also made clear by his inclusion of several stock characters and a segment in which Joseph's brother-in-law, Frank, stages a grade-B robbery attempt" (Munro 1983, 1291).

"Titles Are a Quarter This Week"

Even though *Farmer* may have "slipped beneath the waters," it eventually resurfaced. Harrison explained to Wendy Smith how *Farmer* was "utterly and totally rejected," how what he "valued most, no one in the literary community valued," and how he slid into a "long clinical depression" from which he gradually recovered. At the same time, he told Smith, although *Farmer* initially sold only a "couple of thousand copies," it sold ten times as many in 1989.[5] In explaining the genesis of *Farmer*, Harrison recalled that the idea originated from the smell of "ground ivy in barnyards," the image that opens the novel proper: "Ground ivy, *glecoma hederacae*, or called gill-over-the-ground. . . . The weed smelled vaguely of dishwater or the slop pail for pigs. . . . It was a fact of life."[6] The ground ivy's smell, according to Harrison, reminded him in turn of the times when the farm "used to be an old family farm" and of the fact that his grandparents' son, had he not died in the 1919 flu epidemic, would have been Joseph Lundgren's age. Accordingly, Harrison began to wonder what the son's life would have been like if he had stayed on the family farm with his five sisters ("Lake"). Richard Brautigan, Harrison's fishing and drinking friend, gave *Farmer* its title when Harrison complained to Brautigan that he had written a novel but did not know what to call it:

"Give me a quarter," Brautigan said.
"OK, but what for?"

> "Titles are a quarter this week," he said.
> After I gave him the quarter, he said, "What's it about?"
> "It's about a farmer that . . ."
> He says, "Call it *Farmer.*"
> And that's how I got it. Then it sort of struck me—just *Farmer*
> ("Lake")

When asked why Joseph Lundgren in *Farmer* has the same last name as John Lundgren in *Warlock*, Harrison explained, "I liked that name. . . . I also like the trick of why can't people have the same last name and be different people." *Farmer* opens with its ending, a device Harrison adapted from the Greek tragedians. "Everybody knows how the story's going to end," Harrison says, "but that doesn't change it. So I told them the end of the story in *Farmer*, and then I make them forget it. Then you get, 'Well, yes, that's where they are'" ("Lake").

"Who's Least Like Myself": *Farmer*'s Protagonist

Kathleen Stocking remarked that Rosealee resembles Linda and Joseph Lundgren resembles Harrison, but Harrison said that Joseph is "really the person I've created who's least like myself." Harrison then explained that, while he and Linda are always going somewhere or doing something, Joseph and Rosealee are "trapped in their situation. Whether socially or financially. . . . There were so many people in that generation who never went anywhere or did anything. Joseph's 43 years old and still dreaming of seeing the ocean. There's that notion that not only do you own the farm, but the farm owns you. You had to be there. Cows, pigs, horses needed to be fed" (Stocking 1977, 24). After alluding to his own midlife crisis at 29, Harrison elaborated:

> That crisis where you cease believing in anything in your life and for some reason, almost biological, that tends to happen to men between the ages of 36 and 50, somewhere in there, and that's when they get into the most trouble. A man will have a year or two within that period when he can't handle anything. When he has, almost in the clinical sense, a nervous breakdown. . . . And then, too, there's a certain sexual crisis for men in their 40s. Where they know they are no longer young and life is no longer full of infinite possibilities of any sort. They are largely already what they are, and it's facing up to that back wall that is your own personality, that creates this sort of tremendous crisis. (Stocking 1977, 24)

Harrison's comments apply not only to his other protagonists and their crises but also to Joseph Lundgren, who, in fact, explains his mood shifts and erratic behavior to Rosealee as "a change of life. . . . Men my age go through a change of life. They know they're going to die without doing what they wanted." Later he tells Dr. Evans, "Maybe I'm having a nervous breakdown" (F, 49, 99).

Most of Joseph's life has been circumscribed and routine—"he remembered his passions: he had loved Rosealee for thirty years, he had hunted and fished for thirty-five years and worked hard on the farm nearly that long . . . and he had taught twenty-three years though that was more menial habit than passion" (F, 17). When changes affect these "simple things" he knows "so intimately," an "edge of panic entered him on considering that they might simply blow away like clouds" (F, 17). In turn, these changes knock his life off center—perhaps the "ten degrees out of kilter" that affects northern Michigan's people as spring approaches (F, 57). Joseph must resolve his midlife changes—metaphorically the "back wall"—and then transcend them to realign his life. Like Harrison's other protagonists, he finds external forces bearing down on him, and while he knows change is inevitable, he resists those forces. Like Swanson, he wants the freedom and the time to make his own decisions about his life.

Although Joseph no longer hunts deer (this "prey was too easy") or shoots ducks (they are easy targets and "simply too fascinating to watch"), one change is that he also loses all desire to hunt or fish, those therapeutic pastimes for Harrison's heroes. Doc Evans even says to Joseph, "You show all the signs of cracking up. You didn't bird hunt with any interest last fall and you've hardly fished this spring" (F, 136). Another significant change is that the small rural school where Joseph has taught will close, and since Joseph does not have a college degree, he will lose his job. At the same time, Joseph's mother is dying, another change that will force his life out of its circumscribed rut: he stayed on the farm to nurse her and thus "relieved his sisters of their burden of guilt over their mother" (F, 5). Once his mother dies, Joseph must decide if he will marry Rosealee, lease his farm, and move three miles up the road to her house.

The most unsettling change, however, and the one that exacerbates the other changes, is his eight-month affair with Catherine, his 17-year-old student, whose mother is an alcoholic and whose father is a retired army major. Compared with Joseph's former and present students, Catherine is more "vivacious and sophisticated," but more important,

"she is from the outside world and this clearly interested him no matter
how dangerous the situation was" (*F*, 10). She represents the unknown
world that Joseph often thinks about, even the ocean that he dreams
about visiting. What also interests Joseph is Catherine's blatant sexuality, which also suggests the changing sexual mores of the outside world.
She unabashedly takes her clothes off, readily performs fellatio, sprawls
obscenely on Joseph's couch, and walks around bare-breasted in front of
Joseph and Dr. Evans.

That Catherine will jar Joseph's circumscribed life a few degrees off
center is evident in several of his blunders. After their first assignation,
for instance, Joseph is hunting, stops to rest, and absentmindedly walks
off and leaves his rifle resting against a tree stump. During the same
hunt, not only does he miss several shots at grouse—"After each missed
shot he would yell shit"—but as he walks down to drink from the creek,
he flushes three grouse and can only watch them fly away because he left
his rifle on the hill—"He watched their graceful curving flight . . . and
yelled shit again . . . with all the power of his lungs" (*F*, 21). On one
occasion he forgets to feed the chickens and the geese, and another time
he almost trips in a river "while wading and thinking about Catherine's
ass" (*F*, 89), a blunder that recalls the incident in *Wolf* when Swanson
almost walks off a cliff while thinking about a whore.

Even though Joseph admits that he is "addicted to Catherine as the
dope addicts are addicted to their drugs," when the newness of his attraction wanes, he sees Catherine's flaws (*F*, 60–61). He admits, for example,
that she is a "classic neurotic," a "secret conniver and ultimately no
good," that she is "by turns, possessive, bitchy, conspiratorial" (*F*, 61, 77,
150). Moreover, Catherine is very unstable, and her "instabilities" would
become even more obvious once the "novelty of country life wore thin"
(*F*, 78). Even her father tells Joseph, "I can't say what's going on in her
mind. . . . She's flighty like her mother and gets bored easily. . . . She's so
scatterbrained I don't think she belongs in this world" (*F*, 107, 108).
These qualities are evident when, after hearing that Joseph has lost his
teaching position, she says, "Let's get married in June and just take off,"
and then adds, "I hope the Jeep isn't stuck" (*F*, 41). When Joseph is ill,
his thoughts about Rosealee become more appealing, while his thoughts
about Catherine "sour"; he "wondered how he could have been so stupid
as to get involved with her" (*F*, 77). Nor do he and Catherine share common interests: "He could not imagine her camping by the ocean with
him. She had no interest in his fishing or hunting; no interest in lakes and
rivers" (*F*, 78).

Torn between his lust for Catherine and his love for Rosealee, Joseph's life has certainly been wrenched out of its rut: "All the strictures, habits, the rules of order for both work and pleasure seemed to be rending at even the strong points" (*F*, 15). At the same time, Joseph wants his life to return to normalcy and stability; he knows he must reconcile with Rosealee. On the class trip to Chicago, he not only loses his sexual desire for Catherine but rekindles his love for Rosealee as he looks out the hotel window: "The warm still evening outside . . . made him want to be home or trout fishing or sitting on the porch swing with Rosealee with their laps perhaps covered with the glossy equipment catalogs that had been such an integral part of their lives. Any talk about the future was always full of catalogs and maps. Should it be a Massey-Ferguson, John Deere, or Farmall and was it to be Oregon or Florida or Georgia on their first trip to the coast" (*F*, 157–58). The words and images in this passage suggest purpose and stability. The word *home* suggests Joseph's strong ties to his northern Michigan farm; trout fishing suggests that Joseph has regained his love for fishing, and fishing will be therapeutic; the equipment catalogs and the questions about the different tractors imply that Joseph will continue to farm; finally, the maps and the questions about the various destinations foreshadow Joseph and Rosealee's honeymoon. Joseph strengthens, in other words, the strong points in his life— the "strictures, habits, the rules of order for both work and pleasure."

Hearth Goddesses

Generally, Harrison's hearth goddesses are women who, because of their family background, experience, and perhaps profession, represent stability and purpose in the heroes' lives. They usually assert their individuality and independence without losing any of their feminine qualities. Although Sylvia in *A Good Day to Die* is described as a hearth goddess who is kind, gentle, faithful, and loving, she may not be a fully realized female character simply because Harrison did not yet understand the female psyche. In *Farmer*, however, Joseph's mother and Rosealee mark the development of Harrison's understanding of the same.

In her midseventies, Joseph's mother is a vestige of old world values and beliefs. She has given birth to seven children but lost two of them, Carl Jr. and Dorothea, "dead before the First World War of something mysterious called diphtheria" (*F*, 6). Because her husband Carl desperately wanted a son and was disappointed when his daughters were born, Joseph's mother, to quote Dr. Evans, is "heartbroken because she

couldn't come up with the son he wanted" (*F*, 96). She always reads her
Swedish Bible, and her somewhat antique virtues and beliefs are evident
when she tells Joseph, "I heard you and Dr. Evans talking. I shouldn't
say anything because I wasn't meant to hear it but you should marry
Rosealee and stop messing with that girl" (*F*, 68). When Joseph spends
the night with Rosealee, his mother mildly chides him, "You have to
marry Rosealee if you are going to sleep all night with her," adding,
"You weren't brought up to act that way" (*F*, 54). Joseph's mother thus
echoes communal traditions and mores, or as the narrator says, "A serious flirtation could only end in marriage in these parts" (*F*, 10).

Joseph's mother is dying from stomach cancer. Harrison says, "I
picked stomach cancer [because it is] the most brutal pain conceivable.
You're never free from it. There's no pain like that. The body is literally
rotting from the inside" (Elliott and Sommerness). Although she suffers
terribly from the cancer, she suffers stoically. Joseph mentions, for example, that he wakes up sometimes and hears her weeping. When the pain
becomes too great and she feels she is imposing on Joseph, she admits,
"I'm tired of this. . . . I'm not alive for months now. Your father never
taught me to shoot a gun" (*F*, 79). In other words, she wishes to die, a
wish both Joseph and Dr. Evans fulfill when Evans administers a lethal
drug dose. Dr. Evans emphasizes her hearth goddess virtues and stoicism
when he tells Joseph: "Your mother died in a great way. She had more
guts than you and Carl and me and ten more like us" (*F*, 97).

Rosealee's hearth goddess virtues are evident when Joseph first meets
her. At 13, she knows how to cook and make jams and jellies. She reads
all the books and magazines at Joseph's house, and she sews well. When
Joseph has the flu, Rosealee not only cooks for him and his mother but
nurses him and even does some of his farm chores. Such care and work
scatterbrained Catherine could not and would not do. And, of course,
Rosealee shares common interests with Joseph. She relishes venison and
wild game and enjoys camping, rivers, lakes, and oceans; she even sympathizes with Joseph's love of hunting and fishing.

As does Joseph's mother, Rosealee endures many heartbreaks during
her life. Her husband Orin, who survived World War II as a pilot, vol-
unteered during the Korean War and died when his plane crashed into
the China Sea. When she finds a love letter to Orin from an Italian
woman, Rosealee almost has a nervous breakdown. She also accepts the
fact that her only son, Robert, is a homosexual. More important, however, she must cope with Joseph's midlife crisis. Deeply hurt when she
learns of his affair with Catherine, she lambasts him: "Why are you

doing it? Aren't I enough? I've given my life for you. . . . Oh god. You sat here thinking and messed up your life and now I pay for it. . . . I'm not going to get another chance. . . . Oh goddamn you. I hope you die" (*F*, 85). After her angry outburst—something Sylvia in *A Good Day* never indulges in—Rosealee tips the kitchen table over in his lap, scattering his fishing flies, and she almost runs over him when he follows her outside. Her anger is part of her individuality and independence—she has her own house and farm and a secure teaching position. Although she loves Joseph and has invested six years in their relationship, she can survive on her own, a fact Joseph soon realizes.

When Joseph invariably compares Catherine with Rosealee, Rosealee's hearth goddess virtues and her stability far outweigh Catherine's mood swings and flightiness. Although Catherine kindles his lust, when he thinks about making love to Rosealee Joseph realizes, "With Rosealee it was sweet and pleasant, precisely what he imagined it would be like to be married to someone you deeply cared for" (*F*, 12). In the novel's closing pages are two images of Rosealee—on the porch swing with equipment catalogs in her lap, and riding a horse around the barnyard. Each image suggests her hearth goddess role and the stabilizing influence that Joseph needs to realign his life, which has gone ten degrees off center. Furthermore, although Joseph hunts, fishes, and enjoys sex, he is not a macho hero, primarily because he needs Rosealee to stabilize his life and also because he is, at heart, sentimental, compassionate, and loving.

"Some Happy Endings": The Structure of *Farmer*

Harrison reminded Kathleen Stocking that "there actually are some happy endings. There really are in life some tremendously lovely things. And just as you can't neglect the grotesqueries, you can't neglect the beautiful" (Stocking 1977, 24). As previously noted, *Farmer* begins with its happy ending, the italicized material detailing Joseph and Rosealee's honeymoon: "*Imagine a late June evening in 1956 in a seacoast town—say Eureka, California, or Coos Bay, Oregon. Or a warm humid evening in Key Largo or the Sea Islands that are pine-green jewels in the Atlantic south along the coast from Savannah*" (*F*, 1). From this fairy-tale opening, the plot unfolds the realistic events in both Joseph's and Rosealee's lives that will culminate in the novel's last sentence without its end punctuation, and that, in turn, will recall the novel's beginning.

The novel's second section, which opens with the ground ivy image, is set in early June, the time preceding the "late June evening" of the honeymoon. Not only has Joseph's mother died, but his sisters, with the exception of Arlice, have returned to "pick over what they wanted from the house" (*F*, 4). Joseph has been "laying the farm to rest since last autumn," and the things his sisters take, as well as the old family trunks Joseph has shipped to Arlice, his twin and favorite sister, all mark the final stages of that process. He will then move "three miles up the road past the schoolhouse to Rosealee's" after they are married (*F*, 5). The early June time frame suggests spring and a new beginning for Joseph, Rosealee, and the farming cycle. It is after the time when Joseph "almost destroyed" his relationship with Rosealee, "like some madman burning a barn or shooting his animals" (*F*, 8). The novel will flash back to "that pivotal year that had begun so easily with the grace of last October" and his almost disastrous affair with Catherine (*F*, 8). Furthermore, the second section's last sentence about the "pivotal year" of "last October" merges into the next section's opening sentence: "Joseph liked the long cool sunny autumn days when even the shadows on earth were clean and specific" (*F*, 9). On one of these sunny October days, the day on which their affair would begin, Catherine brings her horse to Joseph's farm to be stabled. The rest of the narrative relates the unsettling effects of their eight-month affair.

Interspersed within the narrative are italicized passages that flashback to significant events in Joseph's past. One of the first flashbacks occurs when Joseph is on the "verge of sleep" and he remembers when he first met Rosealee when they were both 13. Joseph then remembers when Rosealee came to school, how she and Arlice became friends, and how he, Rosealee, and Arlice swam nude in the beaver pond. When he is suffering from chills and fever, he dreams about the time when he and Rosealee were 14, sneaked glasses of beer from a party, and became drunk. In another flashback, Joseph recalls the accident that mangled his leg. As he sits on the porch swing, his conscious thoughts are about being dragged around the barnyard by the team of plow horses and about his and Orin's attempt to ride a cow. In the flashback of the novel's last sentence, the sentence with no end punctuation, Joseph watches Rosealee ride a horse around the barnyard: "*She slows the horse by the grape arbor and he takes the halter and she smiles at him, the miniature violets on her cotton dress*" (*F*). Technically, not only do these italicized flashbacks underscore Joseph's links with the more stable, meaningful past before Catherine unsettles him and his life, but they occur as he attempts to realign his life. Moreover, most of these flashbacks, especially the last one in the novel, are about Rosealee, who provides stability and purpose for Joseph's life.

Potpourri: Autobiography, Setting, Themes, Symbols

While Harrison uses some autobiographical details in *Farmer*, the novel
reflects his further move away from his "autobiographical juices." There
are no references to experiences in San Francisco, Boston, and New York,
and though Joseph's father dies, it is from drowning in a river when his
car overturns down by the bridge pilings. Instead of being blinded in
one eye, the fate of Joseph's favorite nephew, Joseph himself suffers a
mangled leg while "buzzing" logs. Even the more direct autobiographical references arise logically from Joseph's characterization and so complement the plot, setting, and conflicts. Joseph's ancestors, for example,
are hearty, jovial Swedish farmers. His father owns Tom and Butch, a
"well-matched pair of Shire-Belgian horses weighing a ton apiece," and
they win the "pulling contest at the fair two years in a row" (*F*, 39).
Joseph also spends some of his spare time restoring a harness that is
"cracked from neglect" (*F*, 39). Joseph detests "jacklighters" and other
game violators like the "hunters who shoot crows for what they call
'sport,'" and he also yearns for a pristine time when "Michigan wasn't a
game farm for hunters, when natural predators, the puma, wolf, coyote,
and lynx lived there. And the Indian. Not man hunting for sport and
house pets gone wild and utterly destructive" (*F*, 18, 46).

Farmer is firmly grounded in northern Michigan and thus establishes
the fictional world that figures prominently in Harrison's later works. In
"Northern Michigan," one of his poems, Harrison describes the land as
having the "juice taken out of it,"[7] a description equally appropriate for
Farmer's setting. Joseph's northern Michigan is a land of empty or marginal farms, or farms that the "managerial class" has bought. Most of the timber stands were overforested when the "first wave of lumbering . . . scalped
the land of its giant white pine" (*F*, 93). Despite its bad points, Joseph
loves the land for its beauty, and so do Doc Evans and Catherine's father,
to whom Joseph says: "You probably saw enough that this place looks real
good. I think it's a fine place, though I don't know any other" (*F*, 108).

Harrison suggested one of the themes in *Farmer* when he told Elliott
and Sommerness that in this novel he wanted to "somehow pay some
debt to a way of life that was almost totally vanished. That is, a small
farm as a way of life." The encroachment of civilization, a secondary
theme in *Wolf* and *A Good Day to Die*, is especially strong in *Farmer*. The
vulnerability of the small farm as a way of life is evident in Joseph's decision to continue farming when he moves to Rosealee's much larger
acreage but to lay his own farm to rest. While he admires the "frayed,

energetic" look of active farms, he despises those farms the managerial classes buy and modernize with false shutters, white board fences, and bright red outbuildings like those in Kentucky or New England. Because farming as a way of life is vanishing, families move away; as Joseph notes, "The loss of students was easily explained by the number of empty, marginal farms in the township" (*F*, 59). The closing of Joseph's school and the subsequent loss of his teaching position reveal the influx of the modern world.

Another indication of civilization's influx are the dogs that become "feral with neglect" and the "neighbor dogs" that join them, returning to "more ancient instincts" and decimating deer herds. Joseph "was not so much disgusted with the dogs," the narrator says, "as he was with people who didn't take care of them" (*F*, 43). Like Swanson's desire to see a wolf, Joseph wants to see a coyote, a vestige of the time when Michigan was not a "game farm for hunters." That the outside world encroaches upon northern Michigan is also evident in his sisters' husbands: "They all lived in the city and to them wrenches and garden tools took favor over such valuables as a scythe, harness, corn picker, manure spreader, hay rake" (*F*, 4). Frank, Charlotte's husband, returns to steal the coins that belonged to Joseph's father. Joseph even refers to his nieces and nephews as "awful city children and potential pyromaniacs intent on burning down the barn," and he calls Frank's children "thuggish" (*F*, 29–30, 4). And, of course, Robert's homosexuality and Catherine's blatant sexuality are further evidence of the influx of the outside world and its changing sexual mores.

Another theme becomes evident when Joseph realizes that life is a "death dance and that he had passed through the spring and summer of his life and was halfway through the fall" (*F*, 14). Complementing the aging theme are the autumnal scenes and images when the narrative begins. The novel is filled with endings and beginnings. Joseph's rural school will close, but it will be consolidated with the city schools. Joseph begins his affair with Catherine, a metaphorical dead end, only to end it and marry Rosealee. Joseph lays his farm to rest, only to farm again at Rosealee's. Even Joseph's insistence that he and Rosealee make love with the lights on is a beginning: sexually reawakened, Rosealee says, "This is fun" (*F*, 52). Joseph's midlife anxieties result in part from his realization that his life is slipping away and he may not be able to do or see the things he dreams about.

The major symbol in *Farmer* is the ocean about which Joseph reads, thinks, and dreams. His main wish is to live by the ocean, to study it and its sea life. When he goes to a restaurant with Rosealee, he always orders "shrimp and salt water fish even though he knew both had been frozen for months. But they were from the sea, and had a salt smell to them, however vague" (*F*, 30). He also drinks rum at the restaurant because rum is "exotic, coming from the Caribbean, a place he thought of in travel poster terms: white beach, deep blue water, fish, lovely women in scanty bathing suits" (*F*, 30). Harrison has said, "It's like Hemingway said, the ocean is the last wilderness" (Stocking 1977, 27). The ocean symbolizes, as does Catherine, the outside world, but it also suggests the wilderness that Joseph wishes still existed in northern Michigan. The wilderness of the ocean also echoes the freedom that Joseph longs for but is afraid to seek until he is forced out of his ruts. And finally, as the last sentence of the first section suggests, the ocean has a cleansing, calming effect: "*He pokes at the ocean with his cane, staring at it with the raptness he felt for the northern lights as a child*" (*F*, 2).

Even though *Farmer* may have been a heartbreaker for Harrison when it was first published, it does indeed mark a maturing of his literary techniques. Its characters are more fully realized, its setting more poetically described, and its ending more definite. Time should prove that *Farmer* is one of Harrison's finest works.

Chapter Five

"No One's Going to Publish These": *Legends of the Fall*

In 1990 Harrison explained the origins of *Legends of the Fall*: "I had written three novellas and my agent at the time said, 'No one's going to publish these.' I thought Sam Lawrence had a good record for taking literary writers and giving them a shot so I sent them to him. Then Clay Felker did the whole of 'Legends of the Fall' and three quarters of 'Revenge' in *Esquire*" (Smith, 60). *Legends of the Fall* was Harrison's first commercially successful work; indeed, according to Harrison, he earned more money the year of its publication than his father made in his entire life (Stocking 1977, 21). He further admits that *Legends of the Fall* is the "one [that] started the problem,"[1] perhaps a reference to his meteoric financial rise and subsequent plummet when he squandered his new-found wealth.

Despite its commercial success, some reviewers and critics faulted *Legends*. While praising Harrison as a "stylist" who, like Hemingway, uses "simple declarative sentences, cast out like fishing lures in pursuit of an elusive cast," the anonymous *Atlantic Monthly* reviewer concluded: "But there is something facile here; the taut lines of prose eventually reel in only small, bland, truths. These stories skim dangerously near the category of thrillers and while they are exciting to read, they leave a disappointing aftertaste."[2] W. H. Roberson judged *Revenge* and *Legends of the Fall* to be "impressive stylistic achievements and exemplary pieces of storytelling," but they "lack substance. The characterizations are shallow and underdeveloped" because Harrison moves "away from the minds of his characters, the mental and emotional lives that his other works are centered around," and focuses "more upon action and physical activity" (33–34).

Other critics were divided about which of the three novellas is the best. Vance Bourjaily, for instance, ranked them as "good, better, and best"—the "best" being *Legends of the Fall*, "better" *The Man Who Gave up His Name*, and "good" *Revenge*.[3] Although *The Man Who Gave up His Name* suggested that Harrison had "better fiction in him," Keith Opdahl

thought that *Legends of the Fall* was the "crudest fantasy of the three"; he
then rhetorically, and somewhat erroneously, asked: "Has Harrison seen
too many gangster movies, too many Westerns, too much TV? He seems
to *believe* all this, though I would guess that he is either doing movie sce-
narios, attempting to tap into the great American Dream Machine . . .
or has trained himself as a poet to be too honest, too direct to soften
these American fantasies?"[4] Terming *Legends of the Fall* a "trilogy of tough
masculine stories reminiscent of Hemingway in terseness of style, sar-
donic philosophy, and even heroes who are not too far removed from the
much over-used and abused 'grace under pressure' code," Anne V. Kish
concluded that *Revenge* is the "most nearly perfect" because its action is
compressed into a few months and thus focuses on a "single thread of
revenge"; that *The Man Who Gave up His Name* "spreads itself a little
thinly over 20 years"; and that *Legends of the Fall* "suffers the most"
because it should have been a novel: "There is too much time covered,
there are too many actions, too many involvements to be squeezed into
81 pages. It should be a trilogy in itself."[5] The collection is a "triumph,"
claimed the anonymous reviewer for the *New Yorker*: "The subject here is
obsession. . . . The last, the title story, is perhaps the best, but all are
strong stories, rich to almost the point of melodrama yet alive and shat-
teringly visceral."[6] Robert E. Burkholder noted that *Legends of the Fall* is a
"dramatic departure" for Harrison, presenting yet another "opportunity
for structural experimentation," and that the three stories are "closely
related through the recurring themes of obsession, revenge, and violence" (271).

"Implausible Anguish between Two Friends": *Revenge*

Revenge is about the friendship between J. Cochran, a 41-year-old retired
fighter pilot, tennis player, and outdoorsman, and Baldassaro Mendez, an
extremely wealthy and socially prominent gang lord whose nickname is
Tibey, from the Spanish *tiburón* (shark). Cochran's affair with Miryea,
Tibey's 27-year-old wife, goads Tibey into a frenzy of revenge. Cochran is
savagely beaten and left to die in the Mexican desert. Tibey slices Miryea
across the lips—"the pimp's ancient revenge for a wayward girl"—doses
her on heroin, terrorizes her with rattlesnakes, and puts her in a seedy
Durango brothel.[7] Out of greed, the brothel madam cuts Miryea's heroin
dosage, and Miryea is aware enough to stab one of her customers while he
is making love to her. Because the customer is a foreman for a big ranch
and a scandal occurs, Tibey sends Miryea to an asylum operated by nuns,

whom he bribes with exorbitant donations as long as Miryea is there. The novella's plot revolves around Cochran's obsessive need to take revenge against Tibey and his attempts to find Miryea. Typically, however, in Harrison's hands, the plot is not a traditional revenge story. As Harrison explains in "Revenge," an essay in *Just before Dark*:

> Years ago, I wrote a novella, *Revenge*. . . . The story concerns the nearly implausible anguish between two friends . . . caused by an act of betrayal. The relatively innocent woman over whom they are fighting dies. I don't think good novels are written for dogmatic reasons, to offer principles of right conduct, and I certainly didn't figure out the soul of revenge other than that, like many other forms of human behavior, it destroys innocent and guilty alike. As Gandhi said after Hiroshima, 'The Japanese have lost their bodies, now we will see if the Americans have lost their souls.' (*JBD*, 277)

Not only does the novella's title declare its plot and theme, but so does the prefatory quotation: *"Revenge is a dish better served cold,"* a Sicilian adage Bob Dattila gave Harrison (Bonetti, 65).[8] The plot involves other instances of revenge as well. When a boatmate seduces Miryea's 13-year-old sister, their father has the seducer "conveniently drowned" during a long boat trip. The Texan, the expert horseman who gives Cochran a ride, boasts of his vengeance: "I blew the foot off a man years ago who screwed my wife. Did a year for it but I smiled thinking of the bastard's empty boot" (*R*, 55). When Cochran is healing from his near-fatal beating, other characters sense and even sanction his vengeful ire. The old ex-*Maderista* and then pro-Zapata Mexican believes that it is "a just and proper pleasure to shoot his enemies" and that life is indeed better "if you were no one's victim" (*R*, 41). Mauro gives Cochran a lucky, pearl-handled knife that is "razor sharp, and perfect for cutting off the balls of those who had beaten [Cochran] and left him for dead," and even Cochran's loyal friend, the Aereomexico pilot, understands and accepts his "matter of unavoidable vengeance" (*R*, 43, 42). Not only does Amador help Cochran find Miryea and track Tibey, but he owns a "Latin patience not possessed in any degree by Cochran," letting "grudges pass for years until the appropriate time came to relieve himself of their burdens" (*R*, 81). And, of course, one of Tibey's henchmen believes that Tibey should have slit Miryea's throat when he caught the lovers in the cabin. Regarding this propensity for revenge, the narrator says, "There is an impulse for vengeance among men south of the border that leaves the sturdiest Sicilian gasping for air" (*R*, 44), an idea Harrison explains further in his essay "Revenge": "Classical revenge demands a purity of hatred against a backdrop of a specific code of honor usually only found in cultures that have not lost their traditional underpinnings—Sicilians, Corsicans, Mexicans come to mind" (*JBD*, 270). This specific code of honor dictates the machismo beliefs and actions of the old Mexican Mauro, the Texan Amador, and especially Tibey and Cochran. Once their pride and manhood are sullied—Cochran's by his beating, Tibey's by the betrayals— each seeks revenge; as far as Cochran was concerned, "somebody had stolen his soul and he meant to have it back" (*R*, 58).

Although Tibey subtly warns Cochran with the white rose, money, champagne, and one-way ticket to Paris and Madrid and even forgives the illicit lovers their first "clandestine meetings" because he understands the "vagaries of a woman's emotional life," when he hears the taped conversation in which Miryea admits to her sister that Cochran is her "final great love" and that she may run away with him, Tibey becomes "desperate" and avenging (*R*, 45). While Cochran's vengeance is more instinctual and perhaps indirectly influenced by his knowledge about and love for the Spanish culture, Tibey's vengeance typifies not only his heritage—his mother was "half Mescalero Apache, a tribe not noted for its humility and gentleness" (*R*, 44)—but the machismo code of the underworld, which demands terrible retribution in order to redeem both pride and manhood. Otherwise, he would be a cuckold: "He would teach her a lesson that would accompany and mitigate any gossip about the cuckoldry. . . . Tibey could easily call the infamous . . . assassin, El Cociloco, but it was necessary in the crime of cuckoldry to do your own revenging. He drank incessantly to work up his rage because he, in fact, was so tired of it all that he wished to go to Paris, say to the Plaza Athénée, eat and drink and forget. But that would mean an end of his pride and he would have nothing left except money" (*R*, 46).[9]

Cochran's initial impulse, like Tibey's, is revenge—to kill Tibey and find Miryea, even if he dies trying, or as the Aereomexico pilot's brother tells him, "I know it's probably better to die than to live with it" (*R*, 63). In a cantina restroom, Cochran's first revenge occurs when he encounters "the Elephant," the huge man who savagely beat him: Cochran guts him from testicles to sternum and then slices open his neck with Mauro's knife. He later confides to Amador, "Killed a man I hated today. I want to lay in bed and think how good it felt" (*R*, 55). Learning that Tibey has put Miryea in a whorehouse, Cochran's rage becomes "far past weeping," and he feels "murderous" (*R*, 69). When he and Amador raid the whorehouse where Miryea is supposedly held, Cochran's rage becomes "uncontainable" as he kicks in doors in a "state of whirling whiteness so that the gun he held on its occupants held a terror beyond a simple gun: its owner had become red-eyed, utterly berserk" (*R*, 80). When he fails to find Miryea, he "howl[s]" and runs from room to room, beating up pimps, until Amador restrains him. Consumed with vengeance, Cochran later suggests to Amador that they go to Tepehuanes to kill Tibey: "It would be fun . . . to watch the mother-fucker buck and somersault through the air with half his head disintegrating into separate pieces of meat" (*R*, 79).

The revenge sought by both Tibey and Cochran provides the gripping suspense, but the plot is neither a typical revenge story in which evil is punished and good triumphs nor a classic western, which traditionally ends with a man-against-man, hero-against-villain shootout. The novella's gripping opening sentence certainly leads the reader to expect one of these types of stories: "You could not tell if you were a bird descending (and there was a bird descending, a vulture) if the naked man was dead or alive" (*R*, 3). Structurally, with this sentence, the plot opens in medias res, after Tibey's malefic revenge, so that Harrison can focus on and examine the effect that revenge will have on Miryea, Cochran, and especially Tibey, the one who initiated the cycle of vengeance. Just as Gandhi wondered about the Americans after Hiroshima, Harrison is interested in whether these three characters will lose their souls. As Tibey realizes, "The die was cast so deeply in blood that none of them would be forgiven by their memories" (*R*, 77).

The Die So Deeply Cast in Blood: Aftereffects Miryea's disfigured face may be the direct consequence of Tibey's vengeance, but the aftereffects of all she has borne begin to destroy her spirit as well. She is described, for example, as "traumatized to a degree that her thoughts return mostly to her childhood summers in Cozumel" (*R*, 60). When she dreams of being with Cochran again, she often loses "contact totally in her dreaming," and when she becomes "conscious again," she is "surprised" that she is alive (*R*, 61). When her "dread" becomes too great and she thinks of escaping but realizes escape is not possible, she hides and weeps until she regains her composure. Inevitably, her condition worsens, and no one, especially the mother superior, understands that Miryea is "what a previous century had called 'pining away,' drawing inward on her own peculiar autism caused by love and the aching vacuum of love, so that her nights had become insomniac and barren of hope; nights of extreme consciousness shared by those on the edge of severe breakdown, terminal patients in the cancer ward whom drugs have assuaged into a state of nonlocalized dread" (*R*, 75). Besides being the extreme aftereffect of the cycle of revenge, Miryea's death personifies Harrison's belief that revenge "destroys innocent and guilty alike."

Because he begins the violent cycle of revenge, Tibey suffers the most terrible consequences as he is racked between his underworld machismo code and his love for Miryea. Even during the brutal night of the revenge, once his anger cools, he tries to "expunge his near regret and near horror," and so "partly for histrionics," he "screamed and ranted" so the "men in the car would spread the story of his vengeance" (*R*, 46). When Miryea is in the brothel and then the nunnery, Tibey is "in mourning in his soul," and he "deflowered a number of *peóne* girls in manic fits which alternated with periods of despondency so severe he wished to go to the whorehouse, and after that, the nunnery and try to claim back the happiness that had been so briefly his" (*R*, 47–48). Furthermore, when Tibey's mastiff tears the hand off a *peóne* who tries to steal a mallard from Tibey's private flock, instead of punishing him, Tibey pays him $100 a month and even moves the peasant and his family to "better quarters" because, says the narrator, Tibey has "begun to do oblique penance for what he had done to his wife, no matter what her sins" (*R*, 76).

Furthermore, once he knows Cochran is alive and that he should kill Cochran and poison Miryea—"to wipe the slate clean and have something that resembled a fresh start"—Tibey realizes the idea is absurd, and so he decides to let Cochran "eat his heart away in the fruitless search for his beloved" (*R*, 77). Later Tibey is described as "sickened with his revenge"; he has "given up the notion . . . of going into Durango and shooting Cochran. He was tired of love and death. . . . Now he wanted Miryea to live or he would surely go to hell, or at the very least, continue to live in hell" (*R*, 87–88). Ironically, in his attempt to adhere to his macho code to "get his soul back," Tibey loses both his manhood and his soul; as one of his bodyguards realizes, "His boss had become so distracted and drunkenly sentimental that he had begun to lose his manhood. Tiburón had become so suddenly older. . . . It was all this nonsense over his faithless wife whose throat should have been cut the night in the cabin" (*R*, 86).

Similarly, Cochran's rage alternately boils and cools as he wavers between wanting to kill Tibey and loving Miryea. For example, after he suggests killing Tibey, Cochran admits that he is "only exercising" his "fantasy life": "I don't even want to shoot him. I want to take her away.

That's it. Plain and simple" (*R*, 79–80). Later, when Amador remarks that it is too bad they could not just shoot Tibey, Cochran says, "I figure it's far past killing him unless it's necessary. I'd like to think he knows when he's beat" (*R*, 90). Amador's reply is significant: "Neither of us know when we are beat. How can we expect it of him? Losing a woman isn't being beat, it's losing a woman. It happens to everyone" (*R*, 90). Ironically, Amador and Cochran have lost their wives—Cochran's married his brother—yet neither man killed their wives or the other men involved. As Cochran says, "The business of killing doesn't make good husbands" (*R*, 90).

Amador's comment that "losing a woman" is not being beat is similar to the remark of Tibey's bodyguard about "all this nonsense over [a] faithless wife." This nonsense is Tibey's and Cochran's machismo code, which dictates that they get their souls back, that one "beat" the other, but in so doing, they sacrifice what is meaningful to both of them, Miryea. During one of his reveries about himself and Miryea, Cochran recalls a minor quarrel they had "over a silly literary matter about who killed whom in *Pascual Duarte*," and during the reverie Cochran realizes that he was arguing "on hormones, stirring his brain with his dick" (*R*, 64). Metaphorically, in their initial rages, their subsequent posturings, and their attempts to "beat" each other, both Tibey and Cochran react to their male hormones and stir their brains with their "dicks."

During the inevitable final confrontation, the plot twists unexpectedly when Tibey, after saying, "Perhaps we should both die now," throws his gun into the brush and says, "I ask you as a gentleman and a former friend to ask my forgiveness for taking my wife away from me," and Cochran does indeed ask Tibey's forgiveness (*R*, 94). While each moves beyond senselessly killing the other because of some inane code, each admits his own sin—Cochran for having betrayed the bonds of friendship, and Tibey for his irrational vengeance. Tibey also realizes that his love for Miryea has deepened and moved far beyond the macho reason he married her: "Miryea was an implausible showpiece, a woman striven for over a period of years, and finally an access to Mexican social life that had been totally denied him" (*R*, 45). Because of his tormented sense of guilt and his love for Miryea, Tibey lies to the mother superior and tells her that Miryea is Cochran's wife. Once Cochran, Tibey, and Amador reach the convent, another plot twist details the aftermath of revenge. Miryea is so close to death that neither Tibey's doctor nor Cochran's words and presence can save her. The novel ends as Cochran finishes digging her grave, kisses the bouquet of wildflowers on her casket, and throws in "some earth with a thump that he would hear on his own deathbed" (*R*, 99).

With that thump, *Revenge* ends with a sense of emotional exhaustion, loss, and emptiness. Betrayal, infidelity, and especially revenge are self-defeating and life-negating; nevertheless, there are no facile answers or explanations, Harrison seems to say, for what happens in revenge except that the guilty as well as the innocent suffer.

Mainly about Machismo and Crisis   In his *Newsweek* review, "The Macho Mystique," Peter S. Prescott used the novellas in *Legends of the Fall* to discuss Harrison as a macho writer. *Revenge* is certainly about violence and bloodshed, cruelty to women, masculine codes, and what Harrison himself calls "ugly peacockery." If anything, in the novella's denouement, Harrison underscores the unconscionable evil of machismo. To paraphrase the old ex-*Maderista*, life is indeed better if one is not a victim, but as Tibey and Cochran try to avoid being victims, they victimize each other. More important, they not only victimize Miryea but doom her. This is "ugly peacockery" at its worst, as well as Harrison's criticism of machismo.

Like Harrison's other protagonists, Cochran endures a midlife crisis: "He had been at the end of his tether for two years in a time when the meaning of tether had long since been forgotten" (*R*, 15). The "end of his tether" metaphor echoes the realization of other Harrison protagonists that their lives are ten degrees out of kilter. Cochran's crisis partly results when he divorces his wife, a nurse he met on Guam and married "by the force of nostalgia alone": she was also from an Indiana farm family. His marriage, however, was only "an affectionate companionship" (*R*, 29). Somewhat similar to the effects of Tim's experiences in *A Good Day to Die*, Cochran's Vietnam experience erodes the marital bond: "His tour in Laos among other things (alcohol, womanizing, an incapacity for sitting still) had broken his marriage" (*R*, 16). Moreover, his retirement from the navy compounds his crisis; he spends "two years trying to get the handle on civilian life" (*R*, 18). During these two years, he irresolutely travels around in the battered Lincoln Mark IV he bought on a drinking spree, and he has a "half-dozen solid infatuations," one of which is with a "far too young and daffy" girl from Corpus Christi, an affair he has "willed" himself into "out of unrecognized boredom" (*R*, 18). Ironically, Cochran believes his stasis is over when he becomes "unbearably in love" with Miryea, a love he holds "onto as the first totally grand thing in his life in years," but instead of providing stability and purpose to his life, his love for Miryea provides only violence and chaos (*R*, 28). Because it does not end with a vague hope for the future, as do *Wolf* and *A Good Day to Die*, and certainly not as positively as *Farmer*, *Revenge* is the bleakest of the four works.

"Getting out of the Life He Had Created": *The Man Who Gave up His Name*

Harrison told Kay Bonetti: "I always loved the work of Isak Dinesen, and Knut Hammsun, who wrote three or four short novels, so I thought I would have a try at it. I called the first one *Revenge*. . . . The second of the novellas is called *The Man Who Gave up His Name*. I wrote it in a time of extreme duress. I envisioned a man getting out of the life he had created for himself with the same intricate carefulness that he'd got into it in the first place. I suppose I was pointing out that if you're ethical you can't disappear" (65–66).

The Man Who Gave up His Name is about Nordstrom, a midwesterner from Rhinelander, Wisconsin, and a magna cum laude graduate of the University of Wisconsin, where he met his wife Laura in a modern dance class. A week after graduation, they marry, move to California, and within a year Sonia, their only child, is born. Nordstrom becomes vice president of finance at Standard Oil, and Laura works for a flourishing documentary film company. Although they are both financially successful, their marriage gradually erodes and, in fact, was "unhappy for years before it ended amicably" (*TMW*, 112).

As with *Revenge*, and in keeping with the compact form of the novella, *The Man Who Gave up His Name* begins in medias res: "Nordstrom had taken to dancing alone" (*TMW*, 103), Harrison believes this to be a "durable" image, one that "totally concentrates on character" (Smith, 59) and enables him to focus on his protagonist's efforts to extricate himself from the life he has created. Nordstrom's midlife crisis at 43 years of age occurs with his divorce and subsequent efforts to change his life and "escape into the world rather than from it" (*TMW*, 114).

Flashbacks explain not only how Nordstrom and Laura met and married but how they inextricably drifted apart once they were married. The narrator, for example, describes Nordstrom and Laura as "successful but never together"; their "sole meeting point" and "only mutual concern" has been Sonia, but when she gains "health and vitality," they fade even further into "their careers" (*TMW*, 112). When she is 16, Sonia underscores the stasis in their marriage by calling them "cold fish," a remark that stings Nordstrom, who thought he was being a "model father" (*TMW*, 113). He then tries to talk more intimately with Sonia, and also with Laura, about taking a less demanding or even a different job, but neither Sonia nor Laura really understands.

Nordstrom's realization that he should change his life occurs when he wants to make love to Laura before she leaves on a two-day business trip to New York. Because it would rumple her clothes, she declines, but she does offer fellatio. Even that fails, ending with "half a blow job" when the driver rings the doorbell. After Laura leaves, Nordstrom suddenly feels completely alone and on the "edge of panic" when he wonders, "What if what I've been doing all my life has been totally wrong?" (*TMW*, 114). After brooding all night, Nordstrom decides "to escape into the world rather than from it: there was nothing particularly undesirable or repellent in his life, only a certain lack of volume and intensity" (*TMW*, 114). Since he has never really learned how to play, he begins to add intensity and play to his life. He reads biographies and novels, shoots skeet and hunts quail, skis and plays tennis, buys a sailboat and a sports car, changes his hairstyle, smokes marijuana with Sonia, and learns how to cook after resigning from Standard Oil to become vice president for a wholesale book dealer. None of these middle-age-crazy attempts makes him entirely happy, however, and he broods even more, especially about his "boredom with money," Sonia's departure for Sarah Lawrence, the number of affairs Laura may have had, and his own potency, the latter having failed him when he visited a San Francisco whorehouse to fulfill his fantasy about being in bed with two women: "It cost him three hundred dollars not to get a hard-on, his first experience at unsuccessful love" (*TMW*, 116).

The "final grace note" of his marriage occurs the night Laura performs a "mock dance" to the same Debussy music she used 19 years before in the modern dance class. He realizes that "their marriage was over and she knew it and was perhaps unwittingly dancing a swan song. Her body had changed very little but the grace had somehow been tainted with an almost undetectable hint of vulgarity" (*TMW*, 117). After he weeps alone in the bathroom, he and Laura make love "nearly as passionately" as the first time in college, but as the narrator says, this time it is the "terrible energy of permanent loss that wound them together and made them repeat every sexual gesture of their lives together" (*TMW*, 117).

The phrases "mock dance," "tainted," a "hint of vulgarity," "nearly as passionately," and "permanent loss" not only underscore the widening gulf between them but also contrast with their first years together. When she first danced to the Debussy music, Laura danced with "inconsolable grace," and afterwards Nordstrom felt like a "moon walker with feet of tingling fluff" (*TMW*, 107). When they first made love in the winter wheat, the narrator says, "such simple events last lovers a long time" (*TMW*, 111). Moreover, the "half blow job" contrasts with Nordstrom and Laura's lovemaking odyssey early on: before their senior year at Wisconsin, he brought her back from California and they made love in the car, in gas station restrooms, and "on a picnic table in North Dakota, on motel room floors, in a sleeping bag in a cold fog near Brainerd, Minnesota, in a movie theater (*East of Eden*) in La Crosse, Wisconsin" (*TMW*, 111). According to the narrator, it was the "sexual mystery that made their marriage last eighteen years" (*TMW*, 111). However, the mystery becomes tainted with Laura's infidelities—"she saw life as too exasperatingly short to know only one man"—and with Nordstrom's "intoxicat[ion] with his business success." As Sonia realizes, he is "lovable" but also an "introverted ignoramus, lacking even a touch of ease and spontaneity" (*TMW*, 118, 119).

Though painfully depressing, Nordstrom's divorce eventually enables him to make his life simpler and more fulfilling as he begins to shed certain aspects of his former life. Once he moves to Boston to work for the book dealer, several events reshape his perspectives. In Boston he is still "so dead to himself," but he begins to dance alone in order to "keep moving, to work up a dense sweat and to feel the reluctant body become fluid and graceful" (*TMW*, 103). In addition, having learned to cook in California, Nordstrom reads cookbooks and cooks gourmet dinners for himself. When a short-order cook fails to report for work at a delicatessen Nordstrom frequents, he cooks during the breakfast rush. At the seaside house in Marblehead, he cooks for Sonia and her friends, some of whom even mistake him for the cook. When Sonia chides him about this, he tells her, "There's nothing wrong with being a cook" (*TMW*, 131).

Besides foreshadowing his eventual job as a cook at a Florida seaside restaurant, cooking forces a major change in Nordstrom's life. At the Marblehead vacation house, as he prepares a leg of lamb on the antique cast-iron grill "from an earlier time when people prepared feasts rather than meals," he experiences a strange feeling just above his heart, after which he sighs, "Oh, fuck it": "He was rather suddenly not much interested in past or future, or even his breaking heart that perhaps now felt the first itch of healing. But he didn't know that and cared less. The sigh seized his backbone, rippling his vertebrae to his brain which felt delicately peeled, cold and clean. The feeling was so abruptly powerful that he decided not to examine it for fear it would go away: (*TMW*, 131). As suggested in his lack of concern about the past, the future, or even his breaking heart and by the image of his brain being peeled clean and cold, Nordstrom begins to transcend the "deadness" of his past. As he writes in his diary later: "All those years with Laura and the gradual deadness and then three years of true deadness" (*TMW*, 162). That Nordstrom is shedding his past and is more concerned about living in and appreciating the present becomes evident when the frayed tomcat eats the lamb scraps and returns Nordstrom's stare: "It seemed to him it was the first cat he had ever truly looked at in his life. They gazed at each other unblinking until tears formed to moisten his unblinking eyes" (*TMW*, 132). Even Sonia detects a subtle change in her father's personality. When she wonders what he is celebrating by insisting that she and Philip invite some houseguests, Nordstrom replies: "I have no idea really. Why not? Maybe I know it's unlikely there'll be another month like this. Also I want the excuse to cook for a lot of people, to be honest" (*TMW*, 133).

According to Aleksandra Gruzinska, this strange feeling and Nordstrom's refusal to examine it make him "feel alive at a time when various relationships, including his family, seemed doomed to disintegrate." Gruzinska also explains that Nordstrom's culinary preoccupations—reading cookbooks, choosing recipes and wines, mixing and preparing ingredients—are "very absorbing" and thus "keep the body and the mind occupied and decrease the chance of succumbing to the call of the void without obliterating it."[10] Similarly, just as his middle-age-crazy binges are attempts to feel more alive as his marriage fails, so, too, is dancing alone: "The point was to keep moving . . . to feel the reluctant body become fluid and graceful." Even Nordstrom's diary is an attempt not only to channel his "rage for order" but to realign and assess his life, which seems to have crumbled so quickly.

In spite of his impotency in the San Francisco brothel and the fact that his "sexuality had been wonderful for eighteen years and then vanished" (*TMW*, 122), Nordstrom makes love to one of Sonia's friends, the "plain girl" with "pear breasts," an act further indicating that he is reawakening and reshaping his life. When he takes the girl to the airport the next morning, he meets a business associate who consoles him about his divorce and who thinks the plain girl is more than just one of Sonia's friends. Afterwards, Nordstrom is buoyantly happy, because "not only had he made love rather wonderfully, the word and idea of divorce no longer knotted his stomach or threw him into a fretful melancholy state" (*TMW*, 139). Later he writes in his diary that, although he often longs for "that girl at the kitchen sink in Marblehead, it is the nature of such things not to return" (*TMW*, 151). Just as he realizes he will probably not have that moment again, he also probably realizes his marriage is over.

Finally, Nordstrom realigns his life after his father's death. Like Harrison's other protagonists who return to the land and their roots to restore order and purpose in their lives, Nordstrom returns home and sees "death itself. . . . He was convulsed with loss and the unthinkable fact of death" (*TMW*, 141). He weeps until he has no tears left, walks out of town into the woods, and sits on a stump. He thinks about how his father preferred "looking things over" and how his father thought everything "was fine . . . beyond a subsistence level." Suddenly Nordstrom realizes that his own life seems "repellently formal," and he begins to transcend the pain of divorce and the formalities of his corporate life when he understands that life is "only what one did every day":

> He seemed to see time shimmering and moving up above him and through the leaves and down around his feet and through his middle. Nothing was like anything else, including himself, and everything was changing all the time. He knew he couldn't perceive the change because he was changing too, along with everything else. There was no still point. For an instant he floated above himself and smiled at the immaculately tailored man sitting on the stump and in a sunny glade back in the forest. He got up and pressed against a poplar sapling swinging back and forth to a harmony he didn't understand. He looked around the clearing in recognition that he was lost but didn't mind because he knew he had never been found. (*TMW*, 142)

In this passage, certain images suggest transcendence: the way time itself moves above, around, and through him, the way he swings on the poplar like a child, and the way he floats above and smiles at himself sitting on the stump. In conjunction with this transcendence are the clues that nature furnishes him: everything is changing, including himself, and he is literally and figuratively lost. His literally being lost is remedied when he climbs a white pine tree (another type of transcendence) to see where he is and "to look things over," as his father had often done.

Other plot details suggest Nordstrom's transcendence. For instance, during his trek in the forest, he not only sheds his trench coat, because of the heat, but ruins his $400 suit and Florsheim shoes. As he walks out of the forest, he thinks about suits and the government and decides that he does not believe in either anymore and that he is "as guilty as anyone for wearing [suits] for twenty years" (*TMW*, 144). More important, after he returns to Boston, he resigns from the book company and gives his money to Sonia and his mother. Nordstrom explains to his psychiatrist that he became bored with money after his divorce, that perhaps both his and Laura's ambition ruined their marriage: "I didn't so much lose faith in it all as I totally lost interest. . . . My dad who died last October always said he liked to look things over. Maybe that's what I want to do. . . . I sort of came to life again last July and it's been pleasant. Most days I'm quite excited about living for no particular reason" (*TMW*, 159).

In contrast to *Revenge*, *The Man Who Gave up His Name* has a positive ending in that Nordstrom moves to Islamorada, Florida, lives in a one-room tourist cabin, and cooks in a small seafood restaurant "at an abysmal wage." His life is indeed simpler and more fulfilling: he continues "to look things over" and has become a "water, wind and cloud watcher" (*TMW*, 191). The story ends as it begins, with Nordstrom dancing, but this time he dances in public for the first time, with the restaurant's two waitresses and "anyone else willing until four in the morning when the band stopped. Then he danced alone to the jukebox until four thirty in the morning when everyone had to leave" (*TMW*, 192). Dancing in public with the waitresses and then alone symbolizes the spontaneity and play that his life lacked before.

More about Machismo   As he does in *Revenge* and *A Good Day to Die*, Harrison obliquely undercuts the absurdity of macho thinking and posturings in characterizing Slats, Sarah, and Berto. Slats is a "nickel ante dope pusher," Berto is a "cutout from the movies of a gangster psychopath," and Sarah is a "bad actress," not a "human being"—"There was the quality of a photograph or mirror image about her" (*TMW*, 172, 170, 177). Because of Slats's clothes and actions, Berto's affinity with movie gangsters, and Sarah's attempts to be a macho woman—she talks tough and often parrots Slats's words—Nordstrom thinks of them as waltzing around New York "like violent peacocks," the word *peacocks* suggesting Harrison's idea that machismo is "ugly peacockery." They mimic, in other words, what they think is macho, a mimicry inspired no doubt by the media's romanticization of "this nonsense." They have been successful before with their shams. For example, Sarah explains that it is a "way of making money, a gig": "rich men sympathized with the mistreatment and advanced her money to get out of Slats' clutches" (*TMW*, 187). Because they mistakenly assume that Nordstrom is "simple-minded," he outwits them. He knows that the people who "tripped most often and fatally did so out of greed, not understanding that it was a limited though convoluted game" (*TMW*, 187, 174).

Symbol and Theme   The ocean is a major symbol in *The Man Who Gave up His Name*; as in *Farmer*, it stands for the freedom that Nordstrom unconsciously and then consciously seeks. Indeed, his eventual fascination with the ocean may result from having discovered as a youth in Wisconsin a certain sense of freedom swimming in ponds, streams, rivers, small and big lakes. He becomes aware of his attraction to the ocean at Marblehead during the month that fuels his "departure from what he thought of as normal life" (*TMW*, 132): "The sea took over then and Nordstrom was incredibly pleased that he had had the sense to take this huge stone house on the water. . . . Best of all Nordstrom liked to take his morning coffee on the veranda and stare at the sea, leaving newspapers, magazines and business correspondence unopened in favor of the sea, watching the surface with the same intensity whether stormy or becalmed" (*TMW*, 131). At Marblehead, Nordstrom not only has the sharp pain in his chest, looks at a cat for the first time, and rekindles his sexuality but watches the sea and forgets the outside world with its newspapers, magazines, and business letters. Finally, in Islamorada, Florida, he boats on the ocean, swims in it and under it, and studies its sea life. That the ocean has had a positive effect on his life is evident when his psychiatrist thinks of Nordstrom as having a "stolidity" like the fishermen near the psychiatrist's summer home in Maine.

Nordstrom copes with his midlife crisis by learning to play, dancing alone, writing in his diary, and cooking, but these pastimes also allow him to accept his own mortality and a fuller, simpler life, as his words to the psychiatrist indicate: "I sort of came to life last July." He gives his money away—after which he writes that he feels like he has "levitated"—and becomes more aware of people around him. Whereas he was known as a "hatchet man" in the corporate world for firing people and increasing profits, he does not fire the two stockboys who fight over a girl: "I hadn't the heart for it. In high school I thought it grand to fight over a girl and these emotions swept over me" (*TMW*, 123). An old man from the shipping department is dying of cancer, and Nordstrom arranges a bonus so the man can die in Galway, Ireland, his birthplace. Nordstrom helps an old man and his wife who are stuck during a Boston snowstorm, and he feels compassion for an old black man "lying in a pool of vomit" in a Roxbury neighborhood. And, of course, he regrets hurling Berto from the window and rather likes Slats despite the latter's pseudo-machismo.

Finally, Nordstrom's renewed sense of being alive is evident in his deeper interest in the world around him. He studies a flounder fillet

closely to get a better sense of what he is eating; he pauses to look at the
Charles River; he watches a woman in a loose green skirt as she plays
with her son; he is humbly awed at a Celtics–Denver Nuggets basketball
game when David Thompson "floated through the air in a three-sixty,
and dunked the ball backward over his head and didn't even smile"
(*TMW*, 147–48). Nordstrom becomes a lover of the wind, the clouds,
and the sea. With its humor and optimistic ending, *The Man Who Gave
up His Name* is a respite from and a bridge between *Revenge* and *Legends of
the Fall*.

"The Heart of That Story": *Legends of the Fall*

Harrison has said that his wife's great-grandfather, Colonel William
Ludlow, is the basis for the character Ludlow in *Legends of the Fall*.
According to Harrison, Linda returned from her ancestral home in
Michigan's Copper Country over 20 years ago and said, "You might like
my grandfather's notebooks" ("Lake"). Harrison read the notebooks and
Ludlow's original report on the Black Hills expedition, a report his
brother John had also been able to send him. Harrison uses some of the
journals in *Legends* because Ludlow "was such an elegant writer," had a
great deal of "probity and grace," and thought that Custer was a "low-
bred turd" ("Lake"). The idea for *Legends* began, however, when Harrison
wondered what would have happened if Ludlow had ended up in
Montana instead of Michigan's Copper Country.

Although Ludlow inspired the story, Tristan, his son, is the central
focus. According to Harrison, it "was interesting to find the heart of that
story. I think I got so much out of reading the Bible so much when I was
a kid. . . . Like that story of Cain—his hand was raised against all hands,
and all hands were raised against him. That idea of Tristan, of his incredible hubris—so I liked him for that reason even though I made him up.
That powerful image of someone who can accept nothing" ("Lake"). To
create the powerful image of Tristan, who can accept nothing, Harrison
innovatively combines two literary traditions, the epic and the saga.

Somewhere between the Epic and the Saga   Reviewers and critics have been divided about whether *Legends of the Fall* is an epic or a saga.
John Wilson noted, for example, that it is "less a novella than a densely
compressed and transmogrified family saga which defies summary."[11]
William Roberson wrote that *Legends* is a "novella of epic proportions"
(33). On the other hand, while remarking that *Legends* is a "complete

two-generation family saga," Vance Bourjaily said that not only does the "opening line establish both the voice and the epic storyteller, who deals in great vistas and vast distances," but the "steady, singing epic voice assures and reassures us that we are hearing—as the title claims—legend, not reality. In compression, unexpectedly, lies credibility" (14). After mentioning an editor who thought *Legends* would have made more money if it had been 450 pages, Harrison himself declared, "The whole reason it works is that it's only a hundred pages. Tristan isn't Tristan if he's babbling. And the grandeur is in the people's minds" (Fergus 1988, 80). Actually, somewhere between the epic and the saga lies the grandeur of *Legends of the Fall* in that Harrison combines the two traditions to establish the narrative's historical and legendary sweep.

War is the ominous background for epics, and World War I looms portentously as *Legends* begins: "Late in October in 1914 three brothers rode from Choteau, Montana, to Calgary in Alberta to enlist in the Great War" (*LOF*, 195). Another war coloring the plot's background is the one between the United States and the Indians, experienced by Ludlow alongside Custer in Dakota's Black Hills. As with wars in epics, these two wars affect both the nation and the Ludlow family. Epics often encompass sweeping vistas, and the settings for *Legends* include North and South America, the Caribbean, Europe, Africa, and the Far East. Like his epic counterparts, Tristan acquires a larger-than-life stature as well as international, national, and local fame. Some old Canadian veterans still remember Tristan's vengeance for Samuel's death and his receipt of Britain's Victoria Cross for his gun-smuggling mission. His national fame is for horse breeding, and his local fame is assured in the ongoing speculation of the old men in and around Choteau about "whether it was alcohol, jail or grief, or simply greed that made Tristan an outlaw." In the 40 years since Isabel Two's tragic death, Tristan is "still an object of fascination, somehow the last of the outlaws, rather than a gangster" (*LOF*, 255).

Sagas combine history and legend in chronicling the exploits of a prominent family. Beginning with Tristan's grandfather, who sails to far-flung corners of the globe, *Legends* chronicles almost 100 years of Ludlow family history. As a mining engineer, William Ludlow, Tristan's father, ranges from Maine to Mexico and from California and Arizona to the Copper Country of Michigan's Upper Peninsula. He is also famous for traveling, along with George Bird Grinnell, into the Black Hills with Custer in 1874. In 1875 the Government Printing Office published Ludlow's account of this expedition, *"Report of a Reconnaissance of the Black Hills of Dakota*, made in the Summer of 1874 by William Ludlow, Captain of Engineers . . . Chief Engineer Department of Dakota" (*LOF*, 206). Not only does Ludlow detest Custer—who when angry mimics Ludlow's English accent ("an inexcusable frivolity in a fellow officer")—but he celebrates "privately" when he hears of Custer's defeat and death at the Greasy Grass (*LOF*, 206). Moreover, when the government scorns his recommendations about the Sioux and their lands, he resigns his commission and goes to Vera Cruz. At 35, Ludlow marries Isabel, a Boston socialite, but their marriage, initially described as "mutually unlikely," gradually burns itself out. Nevertheless, they remain friends. While Isabel prefers the civilities of Boston in winter, where she indulges in various discreet love affairs, Ludlow prefers his semireclusive life on his Montana ranch.

Besides the Indian wars and World War I, the Ludlow saga spans other cataclysmic events that shaped the family's and the nation's destiny, including Prohibition, the stock market crash, the Depression, and the coming of the automobile. Alfred deals shrewdly in wheat futures and Standard Oil stock and with the help of Susannah's father becomes an influential state senator. The Ludlow family becomes more prominent when Tristan breeds thoroughbred mares to one of his father's blooded stallions named Arthur Dog Meat, a name Tristan gave the horse when Susannah's father sniped, "The horse would serve a better purpose as dog meat" (*LOF*, 209). Although the foals are not as sturdy as quarter horses, they are "exquisite cutting and class pleasure mounts, pretty faced and spirited," and "powerfully fast at the quarter mile" (*LOF*, 251–52). Arthur Dog Meat's stud fees provide the ranch's sole income during the Depression, although Tristan and Decker also earn money racing the offsprings at fairs and Texas cattlemen and horsemen come to Ludlow's ranch to buy horses.

Finally, both epic and saga plots hinge on ominous and tragic actions. With its emphasis on the Great War, on Ludlow's "farewell breath" rising in a "small white cloud" toward the stable roof, on the cold, hard wind blowing against the "yellowed aspens" and skittering leaves across the high pasture, and on the doleful howl of a wolf at midday, *Legends* opens ominously enough. Tragedy and doom stalk the Ludlows: Samuel is killed in the war; Tristan goes temporarily insane and scalps German soldiers; Ludlow's marriage erodes; Tristan marries, abandons, and then divorces Susannah, who in turn marries Alfred, Tristan's older brother; federal agents accidentally kill Isabel Two; Susannah retreats into her melancholy and dies in a private asylum. The plot's epic proportions, however, only heighten the powerful image of Tristan, who defies everything and accepts nothing.

Tristan Ludlow: An Atypical Harrison Hero   "If you wrote a novella called *Legends of the Fall*," remarks Harrison, "somebody's going to know that things aren't going to go well in there. Like [Isabel] Two with that little red dime in the middle of her forehead because life is terrifying. It was even more so back then" ("Lake"). While speaking generally of the tragedies that plague the Ludlow family, Harrison was also referring particularly to Tristan, the central focus and Harrison's atypical hero.

Tristan's life, for example, brims with more adventure and violent action than that of any other Harrison hero, including Cochran in *Revenge*. Tristan fights in World War I, goes temporarily berserk, scalps German soldiers, is straitjacketed and sent to a military hospital near Paris, and escapes within a week. He smuggles guns for the British, who honor him with the Victoria Cross. He captains his grandfather's schooner all over the world and is involved in the ivory, opium, and bootleg liquor trades. He and his Mexican crewman are set upon by four thugs in Manila, one of whom the Mexican beheads with a machete. Tristan also crushes the skull of a federal agent and avenges himself against Irish mobsters, two of whom he stalks at the racetrack in Saratoga Springs. He kills one by jabbing him in the head with a manure fork and the other by breaking his neck and stuffing him into a garbage barrel.

Tristan also leads a more tragic life than do any other Harrison protagonists. Samuel, his beloved younger brother, is killed on a reconnaissance mission near Calais; after cutting out Samuel's heart and encasing it in a paraffin-filled ammunition canister for burial in Montana, Tristan howls, "Goddamn God," scalps German soldiers, and makes a necklace of the scalps. Because he wants a son to replace Samuel, Tristan marries Susannah—"in essence a cruel impulse he knew, but could not help himself" (*LOF*, 226). When he sails away on the schooner—"a matter he knew to be unmistakably perverse but he could not help himself"—he dooms Susannah to melancholy, madness, and eventual death, especially after he writes her that he is "forever dead" and to "please marry another" (*LOF*, 226, 245). These tragic circumstances are compounded when Susannah marries Alfred, Tristan's older brother, who has been secretly in love with her, and when Alfred finds Susannah and Tristan in a compromising situation. Like Miryea in *Revenge*, Susannah's melancholy and death are the result of unrequited love. "Susannah's character," says the narrator, "owed more to the early nineteenth than the early twentieth century and as an abandoned lover she was unwilling to commiserate with anyone" (*LOF*, 232).

As the opening of chapter 3 forebodes—"What doomed him again (for there is little to tell of happiness—happiness is only itself, placid, emotionally dormant, a state adopted with a light heart but nagging brain)"—Tristan's most tragic loss is the absurd, tragic death of Isabel Two (*LOF*, 253). As Tristan, Two, One Stab, and others are returning to the ranch with ten cases of illegal liquor, two federal officers fire warning shots into the air and accidentally kill Two sitting in the Packard's backseat "with a ricocheted bullet from the canyon wall piercing her forehead like a red dime" (*LOF*, 253). As he did when Samuel was killed, Tristan goes "berserk then, reached for a nonexisting gun, then slugged each startled officer, putting one of them near death for months"; similarly, he also howls in a "language not known on earth" as he carries Two's body through the rain (*LOF*, 254). In both cases, Tristan's madness and howling underscore the depth of his tragic pain and its consequences, especially from Two's death.

Unlike Harrison's other protagonists, Tristan endures no midlife crisis, nor does he wish to find purpose and meaning by escaping into life. On the contrary, he is always outside social conventions as he isolates himself from the world, much like a legendary western outlaw hero. When he is 14, for instance, he quits school to trap lynx, and later he borrows his father's Purdey shotgun, disappears for three months, and wins enough money at sporting club shooting matches to buy gifts for One Stab and Samuel and to send Alfred on a trip to San Francisco. Tristan often separates himself from the world. After his engagement dinner, for example, he and One Stab "inexcusably" disappear to track a marauding grizzly, and when Arthur, Susannah's father, denigrates Arthur Dog Meat, Tristan refuses to join any of them for a later supper. Epitomizing Tristan's rebellious alienation are his sea voyages, which "never really ended, except as it does for everyone: in this man's life, on a snowy hillside in Alberta late in December in 1977 at the age of eighty-four," where his grandson finds him dead "beside the carcass of a deer he had been gutting" (*LOF*, 229, 230).

Other plot details signal Tristan's self-imposed isolation. Compared with Alfred's bedroom, with its "sentimental bric-a-brac, dumbbells, self-help books," and Samuel's "littered with microscopes, stuffed animals . . . [and] botanical specimens," Tristan's room is "stark and bare," with its "mule deer skin on the floor, a badger skin covering the pillow on the bed, and a small trunk in the corner" that contains a "pair of Spanish spurs Ludlow had given Tristan on his twelfth birthday . . . some cartridges for a Sharps buffalo rifle, a rusty handgun of unknown origin,

a jar of flint arrowheads, and a bear claw necklace, no doubt a gift from
One Stab whom Ludlow often felt was more of the boy's father than he
himself" (*LOF*, 205). While his trunk's memorabilia may represent
Tristan's eventual status as the "last of the outlaws," it also suggests a
past when men were fiercely independent, self-reliant, and responsible
for their own ill-fated or fortune-graced destinies. In their formative
years, Samuel was babied, Alfred was "stodgy and methodical," and
Tristan was "uncontrollable"—personality traits that also surface in their
military experiences:

> In the month of training before shipping by train to the troopships in
> Quebec, Alfred quickly became an officer, Samuel an aide-de-camp due
> to his scholarly German and ability to read topographical maps. Tristan,
> however, brawled and drank and was demoted to wrangling horses,
> where he felt quite comfortable. Uniforms embarrassed him and the drills
> bored him to tears. Were it not for his fealty to his father and his notion
> that Samuel needed looking after he would have escaped the barracks and
> headed back south on a stolen horse on the track of One Stab. (*LOF*, 199)

That Tristan chafes "under army discipline" is apparent when he visits
Alfred, who has shattered his knee and broken his back in a fall from a
horse near Ypres; Tristan is "sloppily dressed with manure on his boots"
and fails to salute one of Alfred's fellow officers, much to Alfred's cha-
grin. As Ludlow knows, Tristan "would like Cain never take an order
from anyone but would build his own fate with gestures so personal that
no one in the family knew what was on his seemingly thankless mind"
(*LOF*, 215, 209).

Tristan's disdain is not only for the military but for anyone who would
attempt to demean or intimidate him. He tolerates neither his father-in-
law's haughtiness when he snipes about Arthur Dog Meat nor his mother's huffiness when she denies him permission to marry Susannah
because it is "improper to marry even before [Samuel's] funeral." He
becomes "curt and manic telling her she might attend if she wished"
(*LOF*, 224). He retaliates against the Irish Gang who beat him savagely
and the four thugs in Manila who attempt to rob him. He is equally
repelled by Alfred's "ostensibly important friends" and refuses to take
them hunting after a "rich haberdasher shot a grizzly sleeping on a hillside" (*LOF*, 262). Tristan damns himself most when he twice curses God.
When he is 12 years old and his mother leaves to winter in Boston
despite his protests, Tristan prays that she will return by Christmas;
when she does not, he curses God, becomes a "steadfast nonbeliever,"

and later tells his mother that he "could not believe in God because he had already cursed Him" (*LOF*, 214). He again curses God when Samuel is killed.

Like Harrison has said, Tristan's hand is raised against all hands, and all hands are raised against him. Harrison's other protagonists experience crises that knock their lives out of kilter, but then they all attempt to realign their lives, even though some of them long for the very freedom that being out of the mainstream may have brought. Not so with Tristan. He finds meaning and purpose outside of conventions, as symbolized in his smuggling, his disdain for military rank and life, his refusal to take orders from anyone, and his defiance toward both the world and God. He is the "last of the outlaws"—self-reliant, fiercely independent, and the creator of his own destiny through his own personal gestures.

More about Setting, Theme, and Machismo   Despite its many international settings, the primary setting in *Legends* is Montana. Like Harrison's protagonists who return to Michigan to renew themselves, Tristan periodically returns to Montana to renew himself. His most significant and restorative return occurs after seven tumultuous years at sea: back in Montana, he falls in love with and marries Isabel Two, the daughter of Roscoe Decker, the ranch foreman, and Pet, his Cree wife: "Tristan's life seemed to be moving through time in increments of seven and now he was to have seven years of grace, a period so relatively peerless and golden in his life that far into the future he would turn back to that time. . . . No grace is isolate, and it was to a greater part the people he loved, but could scarcely comprehend as people when he left, who led him into light and warmth" (*LOF*, 250). The words *grace*, *golden*, *light*, and *warmth* contrast with his dark, violent wanderings over the earth after Samuel's death and after his abortive marriage to Susannah. Significantly, when he makes love to Isabel Two, "all the loneliness faded at last from the earth" (*LOF*, 249). Moreover, not only is the idea of leaving again "remote from his thoughts," but he builds a lodge house for Isabel Two and himself, breeds and races horses, makes the ranch self-supporting, and fathers two children, Samuel Decker and Isabel Three. However, in keeping with the implications of the words *legends* and *fall* in the novella's title, Tristan's happiness is short-lived: tragedy dooms him again when Two is killed. The "reader, if he or she were a naive believer, might threaten God saying leave him alone or some such frivolity. No one has figured out how accidental is the marriage of the blasphemy and fate" (*LOF*, 272).

As in *Farmer*, one of the themes in *Legends* is the encroachment of civilization and its effects on Montana. Ludlow settles in Choteau, Montana, to escape the unconscionable horrors and chicanery of the U.S. government, especially its treatment of the Indians. Other settlers, like Arthur, Susannah's father, purchase land solely for "prudent business practices"; some of the "grandest ranches in north central Montana were actually owned by absentee Scottish and English noblemen" (*LOF*, 227, 199). As suggested by his buffalo robe, Ludlow is one with the land, and he preserves its natural resources: he limits the number of cattle "out of a lack of greed" and to keep the game birds from leaving. In contrast are people like Sir George Gore, "of suspicious noble birth," who enrages the Indians by "killing a thousand elk and an equal number of buffalo on a 'sporting trip,'"[12] or Alfred's "ostensibly important friends" who, instead of hunting, merely come to the ranch to play cards, drink all night, and have the Cree fill their "elk and deer licenses" (*LOF*, 212, 206, 262). Besides the automobile, other signs of civilization's encroachment are Prohibition, the Depression, the federal officers, and the two Irish mobsters who come to kill Tristan. All of these changes ultimately doom Tristan, the last of the legendary heroes.

As an adjunct theme to the encroachment of civilization, *Legends* also deals with the plight of the Native Americans, whom civilization dooms. Ludlow, for example, champions the Sioux cause in his report and recommends that their lands remain inviolate: "The region is cherished by the owners as hunting grounds and asylum. The more farsighted, anticipating the time when hunting the buffalo, which is now the main subsistence of the wild tribes, will no longer suffice to that end, have looked forward to settling in and about the Black Hills, as their future permanent home, and there awaiting the gradual extinction which is their fate. . . . The Indians have no country farther west to which they can migrate" (*LOF*, 207). Furthermore, he vehemently condemns the whites' wanton slaughter of wildlife, especially the buffalo: "A man who shoots a buffalo and not eat the entire body and make a tent or bed of the skin should himself be shot, including the bone marrow which Stab says restores all health to the human body" (*LOF*, 208). In a larger sense, the greedy, wanton slaughter of buffalo and other wildlife is similar to the wantonness behind Custer's Black Hills expedition, or the murder of the Nez Perce women and children in their tents—"Nothing is quite so grotesque as the meeting of a child and a bullet" (*LOF*, 231).

Harrison suggests, moreover, the harmony that could, but sadly will not, exist between the red and white worlds in the relationship between

Ludlow, Tristan, and One Stab, the aging Cheyenne warrior who is Ludlow's friend and Tristan's surrogate father. Unlike Alfred and Samuel, who tend to ignore and even laugh at One Stab, Ludlow and Tristan respect and even honor his heritage and traditions. On one occasion, Ludlow permits One Stab to perform a "private ceremony" when Isabel Two is ill, and another time he knows and privately approves of One Stab's "coup bag full of scalps, not a few Caucasian" (*LOF*, 204). Tristan severely thrashes a tavern keeper who refuses to serve One Stab, goes outside to drink with the Indian, and does not laugh when One Stab, vowing not to get drunk until he returns to Lame Deer, only rinses his mouth and spits out his drink, even though he likes its taste. The potential harmony between the red and white cultures is also evident in Decker's marriage to Pet and Tristan's marriage to Isabel Two.

Of Harrison's heroes, Tristan may come closest to personifying the macho hero about whom reviewers cavil. For example, he hunts, traps, breaks and trains horses, is insubordinate, refuses to become a victim, and during his sea voyages drinks excessively, whores, fights, and even kills. Although he knows it is cruel, he marries Susannah just to father a son to replace Samuel, and then he compounds the cruelty by sailing about, hoping that "time and distance would reveal to him why Samuel died" (*LOF*, 237). His actions do indeed coincide with Peter S. Prescott's contention that in macho fiction a woman never understands why her man must leave to "blaze his own path in a senseless world," that a woman must be left behind, "preferably pregnant," to wait, that a woman must be killed in a "baroque manner," and that her death ennobles her man. A closer reading of *Legends*, however, suggests that it is not macho fiction, and that Tristan is not a macho hero.

Rather than not understanding why he must leave, Susannah tells Tristan that "she could tell that he needed to go and she would wait for him forever" (*LOF*, 229); moreover, she is not pregnant, nor will she ever be. For his part, as soon as Tristan realizes his hypocrisy in their marriage, he writes Susannah to say that he is "forever dead" and to urge her to marry another, surely a cruel but honest confession. Tristan is unaware, however, that his absence and then his curt letter will doom Susannah to madness. When he learns of her condition, he is remorseful but tries to avoid her, even though fate curses him twice—once in the pantry when at her insistence he makes love to her to calm her torment, and the second time when Alfred sees them embracing. Had Tristan been a macho hero, he would certainly feel no compunction for his acts, yet he broods "about his betrayal of his brother, no matter the circumstances. He placed not a shred of blame on Susannah recognizing that she was periodically less responsible for what she did than the youngest of children. His heart ached over the confusion and pain he had caused on earth" (*LOF*, 264). Furthermore, in refuting allegations of machismo in *Legends*, Paul H. Lorenz argues that if the story is macho fiction, Harrison "would have followed Tristan's career exclusively, but Harrison takes the time to describe the effects of this behavior on Susannah."[13] Indeed, as he waits at the train station for her—he does not know she is dead—his thoughts are anything but macho: he imagines that "he would spend the rest of his life caring for Susannah though he envisioned that she might finally get well at the ranch" (*LOF*, 272). Finally, Tristan loves the people close to him, especially during his seven years of grace.

While both *Revenge* and *Legends* are bloodily violent, *Legends* does not end with the emotional exhaustion and emptiness of its companion work. As suggested in Harrison's remark about Tristan's "incredible hubris" and in the plot's central tragedies, *Legends* ends in a classic catharsis: not only is there a final suspense before Ludlow kills the two avenging Irish gangsters—who, uniformed as police, have come for Tristan—but there is also an assuaging of tragic pain as Tristan, still nobly irresolute, goes into exile with his children. The novella's concluding scene of the Ludlow graves suggests a melding of chaos and pain into a universal harmony.

The novellas in *Legends of the Fall* mark Harrison's further development as a writer. He innovatively adapted the novella form—each story's opening sentence declares the heart of the plot—and, as Bourjaily observed, discovered that "in compression" lies "credibility." Moreover, Harrison's increasing skill at landscaping his settings, poignantly capturing human emotions and psyches, and, above all, telling a good story is evident. *Legends of the Fall* is a logical bridge to Harrison's next novel, *Warlock*.

Chapter Six

"To Tilt My World": *Warlock*

Like Harrison's previous works, *Warlock* has been damned and praised. Among its detractors is Paul Stuewe, who wrote in *Quill and Quire*: "The book attempts to bring comedy, tragedy and irony into a simple moral tale of good versus evil but succeeds only in making a pretentious mess out of some not terribly promising material. Most likely a case of success inspiring an overly hasty follow-up, and, in any event, a surprisingly inept piece of fiction."[1] Less harsh is John Buckley's comment that *Warlock* would have been an "excellent novella" rather than a novel; though it has "some exciting scenes, some well drawn characters and . . . a good story," it is "flawed in its timing, taking forever to start and then no time to end. There is rich irony in that ending, but it is less conclusion than punch line."[2] Similarly, John D. Casey faulted the story's pacing: "Mr. Harrison takes the first lap too slowly and the last lap too fast. But that's better than starting out too fast and winding up too slow." While commenting that *Warlock*'s opening section is reminiscent of Thomas Berger's Reinhart series, especially *Reinhart in Love*, Casey also noted that there arc "pleasures of all sorts to be had—farcical, reflective, luscious, gritty—in this stylish entertainment"[3] Although he felt that *Warlock* "casts doubts on Harrison's art," especially in light of his previous achievements, George Held concluded that "Harrison's ribald and playful imagination makes *Warlock* a good read, if not a work of 'serious consequence.'"[4]

J. D. Reed, on the other hand, provided some interesting insights into *Warlock*, particularly in terms of its spoof of detective fiction. "If Henry Miller, S. J. Perelman and Walt Whitman had holed up in a Michigan roadhouse to concoct a mystery yarn," Reed writes, "the resulting melange of cosmic erotica, snappish humor and hisuite lyricism might resemble this send-up of the 'tecs.'" Reed concluded that Harrison "scores well on the firing range: his humor usually strikes in the killing zone. Dashiell Hammett's low-rent realism made the mystery novel fun to read. *Warlock* demonstrates that it is equally enjoyable to spoof."[5] While also noting *Warlock*'s flawed pacing, William H. Roberson linked its plot and protagonist to Harrison's other works: *Warlock* is about the "testing of the individual in his search for identity outside of the restrictions of society, the beauty and support of the natural environment, and the perception and reality in one's life" (39). According to C. Lynn Munro, *Warlock*'s uneven pacing results from the "unconventional wedding" of two genres, the "false memoir" and "detective fiction"; Munro also noted *Warlock*'s relation to Harrison's other works: "Warlock [the protagonist], like Swanson in *Wolf* and Joseph in *Farmer*, is a romantic dreamer; he is also a man ruled by elemental desires, who repeatedly becomes embroiled in ill-conceived liaisons and who 'belongs' in northern Michigan despite the fact that he has a habit of getting lost in the woods" (Munro 1983, 1291, 1294).

When Ira Elliott and Marty Sommerness asked him why he decided to write a comic novel, Harrison responded, "I don't mean comic in the term of slapstick. I mean comic in the classical sense that everything is not tragic. In good comic novels people do die. I just wanted to tilt my world. I never can bear to do the same thing in two books in a row." In fact, in the prefatory quotation, Harrison declares his intention: *Warlock* "is an attempt at a comic novel not ruled by Irony" and "aims to draw its energies from more primary colors, say from the dance that is *A Midsummer Night's Dream* to those two archfools Don Quixote and Walter Mitty, with the definite modification of a venal Quixote and a gluttonous, horny Mitty."[6] While Harrison metaphorically tilts his fictional worlds in *Wolf*, *A Good Day to Die*, *Farmer*, and *The Man Who Gave up His Name*, nowhere had he tilted it so completely toward pure comedy as he does in *Warlock*.

The Comic Tilt

C. Hugh Holman writes that comedy is about people in their "human state" who are "restrained and often made ridiculous by their limitations, faults, bodily functions, and animal nature," that comic laughter or satire results from the "spectacle of human weakness or failure," and that comedy juxtaposes appearance and reality "to deflate pretense" and "to mock excess" (89). The comic tilt in *Warlock* results primarily from Lundgren's human limitations and weaknesses and from his attempts to distinguish appearance from reality.

The novel's spectacle of human weakness and failure occurs when Lundgren decides to change his life: he writes on his legal pad four self-help maxims—*EAT SPARINGLY, AVOID ADULTERY, DO YOUR BEST IN EVERYTHING*, and *GET IN FIRST RATE SHAPE*. Because

these maxims represent the norm and the ideal, any deviations from
them not only emphasize Lundgren's human limitations and weaknesses
but provide the comedy. Of the four, the two he violates the most are the
proscriptions against overeating and adultery.

While waiting to reshape his life, Lundgren watches too much television and eats too much, especially his own exotic, highly seasoned dishes
ranging from fried squid and hasenpfeffer to rutabaga filled with turkey
leg gravy. In fact, next to making love to his wife Diana, Lundgren's
greatest pleasure is eating. He decides to lose weight when he dreams of
his own death and then realizes that "at 42 his interest in mortality rates
has increased," that "Milestones in *Time* magazine had become more
poignant," and that "gluttony was creeping up from all flanks" (*W*, 10,
52). His firm resolve to diet is short-lived: on his first undercover assignment to Michigan's Upper Peninsula, he drives along munching on
Diana's health-food mix, complimenting himself on his willpower, but as
his hunger becomes acute, his willpower wanes. Unable to resist his
craving for food, he stops at the Rathskeller and consumes a heaped
"platter of sauerbraten, spatzle and red cabbage" (*W*, 121). As he continues his trip, his eyelids grow heavy, his spirits droop, and he readily
blames not his lack of resolve but the food: "The food was good, but not
good driving food, much less secret mission food. . . . Many of the problems the world has had with Germany in the past century, he felt, could
be traced to this leaden, fascistic diet. It sucked out the aerial spirit and
made one fart and feel unkind" (*W*, 121–22). Lundgren remorsefully
thinks about dieting again but then justifies not devising a "new diet on
a full stomach, having done so a hundred times, a number far in excess
of what it takes to teach wisdom to a Pavlovian dog" (*W*, 122).

Other eating bacchanalias follow. After a late afternoon pickled herring gorge, he lies to Diana about his pickle-fouled breath. "It must be
ketosis," he says. "The breath of starving people becomes foul. I read
about it. India is chock full of bad breath" (*W*, 158). After Diana leaves
for work the next morning, a guilty but determined Lundgren throws
away the "last, somehow symbolic, piece of herring," but as he eats the
remaining pickled onions, he rationalizes that they do not "seem central
to the issue" (*W*, 159). After his sexual interlude with Laura Fardel, he
goes to a black barbecue shack, orders "beer, beef and pork ribs,
hamhocks and greens, baked beans and a side order of raw sliced onion,"
and tells the astonished waiter, "Love has stolen my energy. I haven't
eaten in recent memory" (*W*, 204). He also consumes quantities of wine,
beer, or bourbon with his meals and, to help settle his ample fare, finish-

es up with brandies, mixed drinks, or peppermint schnapps. The next morning he suffers for his overindulgence with either terrible hangovers or sessions over the toilet bowl, "ridding himself of the rainbow colors of the evening" (*W*, 220).

Lundgren's determination to avoid adultery provides opportunities for more comedy; as Elmer M. Blistein observed, the "behavior of people in love or heat has long been considered comic by objective observers."[7] One of Lundgren's typically comic infidelities involves Patty, a "smallish cheerleader type" who works at the unemployment office and bowls at Timberlanes on Thursday nights. His vacillation between avoiding adultery and lusting after Patty occurs ironically after he pens the precept about avoiding adultery. He fantasizes about her butt, which "bobbed" like "pistons," but then decides: "No . . . I got more than I can handle at home, a saw not less true for being so often repeated. Adultery was messy, both in the inevitably sneaky structure of carrying it off and in the emotional messiness that followed. He'd best keep his nose to the grindstone of the future. What about the grindstone of Patty, the Unemployment Office cheerleader and champ bowler? Probably a pretty grindstone. It was a bold man that ate the first oyster, his dad used to quote Swift" (*W*, 53). In this typically comic struggle between the spirit and the flesh, he thinks about how easy it would be to leave Diana a note saying he was having a drink with Clete, a friend who would alibi for him, and then take Patty to a "tourist cabin where he would roger her loose little joints" (*W*, 53). Although his "dick rose with despair," he finally decides to remain faithful, or as he says, "It seemed that the act of making a coda defiled the spirit of the coda" (*W*, 53).

Like his resolve to avoid overeating, his resolve to avoid Patty is short-lived. After Diana throws a bowl of oxtail soup in his face during an argument, Lundgren hastens to the bowling alley and Patty. When she hears about the soup incident, Patty sympathizes: "Poor Johnny. I hope you kicked her in the cunt. . . . Let me give you a quick B.J. to get the pressure off. . . . I got one more game and then we can go to a motel and go all the way" (*W*, 58). As Patty begins to relieve the pressure, Lundgren is appalled about "woman's inhumanity to woman": he has "never struck a woman and couldn't imagine kicking the fair Diana in the cunt" (*W*, 58). Somewhat contrite, he even tries to imagine Patty is Diana, but he fails since Patty is "far more experienced, having perfected the rare technique of deep throat" (*W*, 58).

The full comic effect of his tryst with Patty culminates when he is in West Palm Beach and scans a *Reader's Digest* article excerpted from

Psychology Today entitled "Is What Is Good for Peter, Good for Petra?"
The piece, he learns, is not about a Greek couple but rather about cou-
ples with an unlikely combination of names, like Paul and Paula, Gene
and Janine, George and Georgette. Realizing that "some wives paid husbands back tit for tat, and some new wave types frittered through life as
Don Juanettes," Lundgren tearfully wonders about Diana's fidelity and
just as tearfully attempts to assuage his own conscience:

> The angle of tit for tat was bothersome, but Patty's blowjob in the bowl-
> ing alley parking lot couldn't be held against him. It was obviously up in
> the air whether a blow job constituted adultery in the first place, the
> Bible making no mention of the act. Rules had to be laid down in some
> form. The distant night in Corona, and the more recent three day session
> with Aurora in Sault Ste. Marie presented more difficulties to his waffling
> spirit. Diana in a weak moment had once said she could forgive him for a
> one night stand with a lady of the night if he were drunk. He tried
> mightily to remember being drunk throughout the three days with
> Aurora. (*W*, 192–93)

Conscience-stricken, he wants to pray, but since he can only remember
the words to "Now I Lay Me down to Sleep," and since "they kept
changing the translation of the Lord's Prayer," Lundgren gives up "after
an hour of this self-defeating nonsense," smokes a huge marijuana cigarette that Diana had hidden in his luggage, and returns to Gloria
Rabun's art gallery, where earlier, as he was leaving, he had stared at her
with a "slight suggestion of savage lust, of a possible undreamed afternoon that would be the spiritual equivalent of a mud wallow" (*W*, 193,
188). When he sees her this time, she looks so appealing that he hornily
forgets "in a trice the recent horror of adultery." Similarly, after his sexual escapade with Laura Fardel, Lundgren postulates, "If this be adultery,
so be it!—not comprehending that a man in a questionable moral situation is given to pompous stands" (*W*, 203).

The novel's comedy also results from Harrison's juxtaposition of
appearance and reality, exemplified in Lundgren's Mittyesque sexual
flights of fancy fueled by his avid reading of *Penthouse*, *Playboy*, and *Oui*—
he "eschewed hardcore" (*W*, 30). One of his earliest fantasies occurs
when he is 14 and grows five inches. According to one of his graphs, by
the time he is 21, he should be over nine feet tall and a professional basketball player living in Chicago with Janet Pilgrim, a former *Playboy*
centerfold model, to whom he is faithful "except on extended road trips
when his huge body would no longer be able to control its dark gorilla

lust and cheerleaders would line up at his hotel door crooning their cheers for attention" (*W*, 66).

Another sexual fantasy occurs after he shops at the local IGA supermarket and sees the stockbroker's attractive wife in a yellow tennis outfit. Flustered, he blurts out, "You're pretty," grabs a package of turkey legs, which he had not intended to buy, and hurries away. Sitting at home and realizing that he bought the turkey when he looked at her "brown, damp legs," he fantasizes: "What would she look like in the back of his Subaru in that yellow outfit without undies? Please, Johnny, I need you, she said pointing a Converse skyward" (*W*, 47). In another Mittyesque reverie, he imagines a Girl Scout, a "hundred and thirteen pound waif," who is lost in the forest; he would rescue her and then lead her to a "woodland stream where she (the usual hygiene) bathed" (*W*, 122). He would make love to her well into the afternoon so that the "poor thing was crazy for him" and she "couldn't be stopped" (*W*, 122). Actually, no lost Girl Scout appears when Lundgren is lost in the forest and cowers by his campfire all night amid strangely terrifying woodland sounds.

Parodying the diction and content of the letters printed in *Penthouse* and *Playboy*, one of Lundgren's most explicit but comic fantasies is about the three young girls he has seen earlier on a Lake Michigan beach. While he sits at his kitchen table, they swim out of the surf and into his brain. He imagines them

> in a bathhouse, or in a loft of a cottage, or in a large California-style bathroom. They are beginning to peel off their wet suits when Warlock enters by mistake. No, stay, they say in unison. Dry our backs! They gently strip him and they all hop into the shower. (All his fantasies included a shower to avoid the natural but gamy exudate of bodies)
> . . . They said one potato or eenie-meenie-mynie-moe to see who would go first. Warlock lay down and hoisted one onto his chops while the other slammed down on his rude rouser. There was a knock. No there wasn't. These gratuitous interruptions the mind throws up. He dandled the third with a spare hand. A chorus of moans. He humped all three until they couldn't walk, talk, crawl. Each had exactly seventy-seven orgasms, his lucky number. (*W*, 36)

The purportedly confessional letters in *Penthouse* and *Playboy* always claim that sex readily and often occurs in department store dressing rooms, ascending or descending elevators, airplane lavatories, swimming pools, and university libraries, classrooms, and offices. Similarly, not only do Lundgren's imagined sexual escapades occur in odd places, but he is

always a sexually desirable hero who is capable of prodigious sexual per-
formances, and willing but attractive women—most with cheerleader
bodies and some, no doubt, sans undies—croon and moan for his sexual
favors. In reality, however, when he does meet a woman like Aurora,
who has a thigh that "rumbled his weiner" but also a "nervous disposition" that makes her "orgasm resistant, or hard to bring off, as the magazines say," Lundgren is exhausted and completely "fucked out" (*W*,
140, 147).

As part of the juxtaposition of appearance and reality, Lundgren's sexual interludes with the women he meets on his detective missions are
shattered by reality. When he meets Aurora, for example, she says she is
a Chippewa Indian; as he waits for her in the motel room, Lundgren
imagines her on the reservation scrubbing "her buckskin clothes by the
river while being watched by deer and raccoon," but Aurora is actually
of Armenian descent and a Detroit third-grade teacher. After his sexual
romp with the supposedly crippled Laura Fardel in Florida, Lundgren
fantasizes about taking her to Michigan for successful surgery, after
which Diana would nurse her in an old farmhouse where all three of
them would live. In reality, Lundgren is a victim of the Fardels' "living
drama" series in which, pretending to be crippled, Laura lures men off
the beach and into sexual encounters while her voyeuristic husband,
using binoculars and hand signals, videotapes the action.

The major comic thrust of the juxtaposition of appearance and reality
is Lundgren's job with Dr. Gerald Rabun, whose appearance impresses
both Lundgren and Diana. Rabun's reputation rests on his brilliance as
an inventor of medical devices, such as valves and filters for dialysis
machines, computerized blood testing systems, and storage facilities for
organs awaiting transplants. In addition to being an excellent gourmet
cook and wine connoisseur—talents that impress Lundgren—Rabun is a
successful businessman who owns vast timber preserves, assorted stocks
and bonds, a Kansas Chrysler dealership, and a Florida health spa.
Rabun complains that people swindle him, especially his wife Gloria and
his son Ted, whom Rabun claims is a homosexual.

In reality, Rabun's nefarious past includes a socially embarrassing incident in which he was found in bed with teenage girls to whom he had
given drugs. There was also an expensive coverup when he injured an
underage girl with one of his weird sexual inventions. Rabun also married his wife for her money and then through financial chicanery gained
control of her money and his son's estate. According to Rabun, his most
prized invention is a heat-controlled, "utterly lifelike" dildo. "I've imitat-

ed here the shimmying of a porpoise's skin as it moves through the water," he says. "I deserve the Nobel but it's never given to a pragmatic genius" (*W*, 110). In fact, while Lundgren is in Florida, Rabun semidrugs Diana and persuades her to perform some final tests with the dildos while he films the tests. Not only is Rabun the villain alluded to in the novel's epigraph (the "foe who embodies perverted sex, drugs, greed, and the destruction of the social contract"), but according to Lundgren's father, a streetwise former cop, "Rabun is the biggest pervert in the country. I wouldn't trust a Holstein in his vicinity. He should be destroyed like a rabid dog" (*W*, 242).

In comic fashion, the novel ends happily without any violence or tragedy. Rabun is not killed like a rabid dog, nor is he sent to prison, but at a staged and choreographed meeting he is forced to return the bulk of the money he swindled from his wife and son. Although Lundgren's jealousy about Diana and the dildo test is so intense and his desire for revenge so great that he reads only "children's books to keep his need for revenge cruel and simple," when he confronts Diana and Rabun at the marina, he only fires his shotgun into the lake, tosses the gun into the water, rushes home, grabs his favorite pillow, sucks his thumb for the first time in 30 years, and wonders just how angry Diana will be with him. Although Lundgren and Diana are reconciled, the narrator underscores the juxtaposition of appearance and reality: "Their marriage didn't immediately return to the Camelot of yore, but then it had never been the Camelot of yore in the first place; and even that lordly kingdom, suspended in the mist between myth and history, had been rife with adultery and violence, albeit of a more courtly quality" (*W*, 256).

A Comic Midlife Crisis, or, "Don't Be a Drag-Ass"

Although Lundgren is Harrison's only true comic hero, he still suffers a midlife crisis that comically bounces his life a few degrees toward wacky. Besides certain loose ends dotting his life, like his failed art career and his first marriage of seven years, the main impetus for his crisis is his inability to find a suitable job since resigning his $45,000-a-year executive position in Lansing, Michigan, where the quality of life is "like owning the very best, most expensive diving equipment and only having a cesspool or a mud puddle to swim in" (*W*, 42). He and Diana flee to northern Michigan's Lake Leelanau Peninsula because Lundgren thinks it still contains the "summer memories of his youth until college: the northland with its crystalline lakes and streams, small villages pervaded by the scent of pine forests that surrounded them, hills, dales, valleys with small marginal farms owned by people not at all unlike their southern counterparts; that is basically small minded and stupid but possessing a specific archaic attractiveness—nostalgia in the flesh" (*W*, 42). However, much to his chagrin, Lundgren has to admit that northern Michigan is "growing daily more and more unlike the north of his dream-bound youth." Stockbrokers and doctors have bought the farms for vacation or retirement homes, the lakes are crowded with people and cottages, the small villages have a "false front, mansard-roofed, Swiss chalet look," and "solvent hippies" have moved in with their "arts and crafts boutiques and health food stores—leather and hokum Indian jewelry, groats and granola and magnum vitamins to counteract their drug ingestion" (*W*, 42). Despite these incursions, and despite the fact that Sunday night television is an evangelical wasteland—Jim Bakker's PTL Club is on one station and Jack Van Impe and his wife Rexella are on the other—Lundgren thinks that northern Michigan is "all still beautiful compared to anyplace else" (*W*, 43).

His midlife crisis becomes more acute when he dreams of seeing his own dead body on the kitchen floor. It was actually the garbage can that Hudley, Lundgren's fractious Airedale, had knocked over; Hudley enjoys humping garbage cans. After this dream, Lundgren decides he must reestablish some meaning and purpose in his life. In fact, Cletis Griscombe, a stable friend, carpenter, bricklayer, hunter, fisherman, and champion street fighter, counsels Lundgren, "Don't you know everyone's life is shit? You're smart enough to do something about your own. Don't be such a drag-ass" (*W*, 72). Moreover, a year earlier, Virgil Schmidt, one of the foundation's trustees and Rabun's friend, had said that Lundgren needed a "trial by fire, a momentous event that would shake the loose shit out of your brain. You don't live in the actual world. You live in an inferior world where you dissipate all your energies making the world conform to your wishes" (*W*, 75).

Lundgren's "trial by fire" begins when Rabun hires him as a private investigator, a job Lundgren believes will change his life. On his first undercover assignment, for example, he even fantasizes that the Mackinac Bridge is a "path over some holy Rubicon" and he is grasping the "future like a chalice," but the bridge, the narrator says, is a bridge downward. The downward bridge symbolizes his association with the nefarious Rabun and his undercover assignment into West Palm Beach's "demimonde," or as Lundgren's father the cop tells him: "It's chocked full of detritus . . . . The place is full of murdering crooks, Cubans and Colombians wholesaling drugs with millions to spend. Your life isn't worth a plugged nickel down there" (*W*, 185). In keeping with the novel's comic tone, however, Florida's demimonde includes Lundgren's comical interludes with Gloria Rabun, the Fardels' "living drama" series and their subsequent hokey Mafia assassination threat, and Lundgren's experiences in the Cockatoo, a mostly rich and mostly gay bar that "held the demimonde, no doubt providing a pressure valve for the swells" (*W*, 209).

All in all, Lundgren's private detective experiences provide the change his life needed. He quits wallowing in self-pity, jogs to get in shape and lose weight, and helps people who have come to depend on him, like Gloria and Ted Rabun, whom Rabun has swindled. More important, whereas Lundgren had been dependent upon Diana, she now needs him, especially when she learns what Rabun did to her when she was drugged by some exotic South American concoction; in fact, she suffers a "modest mental relapse" because in her mind she has "fallen from a high place, an utter dupe" (*W*, 259–60). Lundgren helps her overcome her mental depression and agrees that she should go to medical school, for which he will pay since Gloria and Ted are still paying him, and Feingold, Rabun's lawyer, is still sending him money because Rabun has not told him to stop paying Lundgren's salary. Through his comic blunderings and fopperies, Lundgren recognizes what is significant in his life—Diana, his marriage, and even the fractious, garbage can–humping Hudley. Robert Corrigan notes that in the comic view of life, "no matter how many times man is knocked down he somehow manages to pull himself up and keep going. Thus, while tragedy is a celebration of man's capacity to aspire and suffer, comedy celebrates his capacity to endure."[8] And Lundgren does indeed endure a number of comic but humanizing pratfalls.

Another Hearth Goddess

Like Sylvia in *A Good Day to Die* and Rosealee in *Farmer*, Diana is a hearth goddess whose "pragmatic bent" begins in early childhood on the family farm when she helps her father deliver calves and clean chickens. She makes "childish notes on the progress of eggs" because she wants to know "how things, especially organisms, worked" (*W*, 40). She is "one of those farm girl valedictorians who go through college and into life with the confidence of gaited horses. . . . Such women, Warlock had read in *Ladies' Home Journal*, are usually multi-orgasmic and have a definite edge in marital and public life. At thirty-two she was without a cavity and had only recently confessed to him an IQ superior to his own, after repeated questioning" (*W*, 20). In addition to being the "best surgical nurse in northern Michigan," Diana is an ardent ERA supporter, sexually confident, and sexually liberated. Although she is not promiscuous, she has an occasional affair: "She knew the ways of men and felt it only fair to exercise her own impulses as long as she obeyed the niceties of discretion" (*W*, 40). During a convention of surgical nurses in Detroit, for example, she beds the guest speaker; pushing "this maven from MIT back on his king sized, mirrored vibra bed, [she] solemnly studied his erect penis until he was nervous, let out a long fugal laugh which was her habit before sex, and sat on it. By dawn he was ready to give up his wife, children, a full professorship. She gave him a peck and said don't be silly. This . . . scarcely reflected promiscuity on her part. It was simply that every year or two since she was married she would meet an especially intelligent man" (*W*, 40–41).

Unlike Lundgren, who rages at her for her indiscretion with a Chicago photographer and considers divorcing her because of the Rabun debacle, Diana forgives Lundgren for his indiscretion with Isabella and especially for his fling with Laura Fardel; she even "caromed off the kitchen walls with laughter" at Lundgren's gullibility (*W*, 258). Nor does she neglect Lundgren: their sex, if not "truly magnificent," as on one occasion, is warm and satisfying. More important, not only does Diana provide a stable midpoint for Lundgren during his unemployment anxieties, but she often adamantly tells him "to get his spine back and be happy" (*W*, 20), to quit wallowing in self-pity. "I'm trying to help you, Johnny," she says.

> "You're going mad from self-pity, self-concern, self-indulgence. You begin every fucking sentence with 'I' or 'my.' You say 'I'm hungry,' 'My stomach is upset,' 'I'm horny,' 'My heart is broken,' 'I hate *Kojak*,' 'I hate hamburgers,' 'I hate *Star Wars*.' "I, I, I, I, I, I," she sang as if she were a mariachi singer in a Mexican cantina. (*W*, 154)

Like Lundgren's symbolic trip downward when he becomes Rabun's private investigator, Diana's trip downward results from being attracted to Rabun's intelligence and then agreeing to perform some final scientific tests with Rabun's dildos; she admits that "her reverence for genius had brought her to shame" (*W*, 260). In other words, Lundgren's romantic bent and Diana's pragmatic bent make them Rabun's dupes, and yet theirs is not a tragic fall since, in the spirit of comedy, they reconcile. In the closing scene, they make love in the forest, then dash in opposite

directions to find the car when it begins to rain, each promising to honk
if the first to find the car.

    Compared with Sylvia in *A Good Day to Die* and Rosealee in *Farmer*,
Diana is more intellectual, cosmopolitan, independent, and sexually liberated. Whereas Sylvia is "helplessly feminine" and Rosealee is reticent
about Joseph's predicaments and vacillations, Diana berates Lundgren
when necessary, and more important, she demands her equal rights. Not
only does she have her sexual flings, which she never tells Lundgren
about, but when he rages about her interlude with the Chicago photographer (before they were married), she tells Lundgren, "I'm not an acre
of your property. . . . And stop stomping around like you're the champ
fuck of the world, you Hitler bastard" (*W*, 17). Yet, like Sylvia and
Rosealee, Diana is loving and compassionate and provides a stable, calm
center amid Lundgren's whining self-pity and unemployment anxieties.
Finally, Diana's characterization marks a definite progression in
Harrison's ability to depict the female psyche and thus foreshadows his
equally strong feminine portraits of Dalva (*Dalva*), Claire (*The Woman Lit
by Fireflies*), and Julip (*Julip*).

Setting, Machismo, and Hudley

The setting for *Warlock* is familiar Harrison territory; this time the primary setting is Lake Leelanau. Harrison makes references to Dick's Pour
House, a bar he frequents, and Lundgren's house and its setting obliquely recalls Harrison's own house. As in *Farmer*, civilization's encroach-
ments are evident in the references to the managerial classes who buy
the marginal farms and to the small villages losing their individual grace
and charm as they ape the Swiss chalet look. Whereas in *Wolf* and *Farmer*
Harrison describes the landscape and its people in poetic terms and nos-
talgic tones, in *Warlock* his descriptions, while just as poetic, reflect the
tilt of his comic vision. The thunderstorms and winter snowstorms make
his dog Hudley howl and Lundgren shudder. Not only is Sunday night
television an evangelical wasteland, but the most exciting event of the
winter is the egg-sucking contest on Saturday nights: "Don Schneck, the
local Leelanau Peninsula champion, went through seven dozen one
snowy March evening before projectile vomiting set in, much to the
amusement of his belching cronies" (*W*, 41). Still, like Joseph in *Farmer*,
John Lundgren thinks that northern Michigan is "all still beautiful when
compared with anyplace else." Significantly, too, Lundgren returns to
northern Michigan to reestablish purpose and meaning in his life.

In its satirical image of its hero, *Warlock* parodies the macho point of view. In most detective fiction, for example, the private detective epitomizes the tough, self-reliant male, but as part of its spoof, Lundgren comically bumbles through his secret missions and is detected more often than he detects. Even his alias Warlock—his undercover name and his "alter-ego"—has comical overtones in its origin: it was bestowed upon him by his Cub Scout leader, the high school band director who is a "trifle fey" and eventually is run out of town "after having been discovered in the middle of a sodomic frenzy in a camp privy" (*W*, 6). Even the novel's comical conclusion satirizes macho posturings. Still goaded by macho standards and armed with his macho 20-gauge Fox-Sterlingworth shotgun, Warlock, instead of blowing away Rabun and his wife (the form that macho vengeance takes in *Revenge* and *Legends of the Fall*), fires his gun into the lake and rushes home to wonder just how angry Diana is going to be. As his psychiatrist notes, Warlock is "hopeless and harmless" (*W*, 260).

Hudley emerges as a truly comical foil for Lundgren. The dog is described as being, "for better and usually worse," Lundgren's "Rozinante, though without saddle and snaffle" (*W*, 11). In an article about *Le Feu d'Airedaile*, Lundgren discovers that Hudley is an "individual": "Early in his puberty Hudley had developed an affection for garbage cans as sexual objects. The dog would push a can over and hump it in a hypnotic frenzy" (*W*, 10). Even though Diana punishes Hudley "justly and unmercifully" and Lundgren heaps "love on the dog as some sort of obtuse soul mate," Hudley "adored Diana and only tolerated Warlock" (*W*, 11). Moreover, Hudley often defecates in the middle of sidewalks, barks loudly at passing cars when Lundgren has a head-splitting hangover, and even eats a large bowl of popcorn when Lundgren falls asleep watching television with the bowl in his lap. One of the most comical scenes occurs when Lundgren takes Hudley on his first undercover assignment to Michigan's Upper Peninsula; he has fantasized about getting lost in the forest and Hudley "lop[ing] into the circle of light the campfire cast carrying a young deer. . . . The dog would keep him warm and lead him out of the forest at dawn" (*W*, 120). Naturally, when Lundgren does become hopelessly lost, Hudley bounds off into the gathering darkness and sleeps in the car while Lundgren wonders, "Perhaps he was trying to lead me back to the car? Unlikely at the speed he was running" (*W*, 126).

Reviewers and critics may cavil about *Warlock*'s timing and other faults, but Harrison did what he intended to do in this work—he wrote a comic novel not ruled by irony. *Warlock* is therefore a rollicking, ribald spoof not only of detective fiction but also of people's pretensions, foibles, and humanities. As with his experiments in other literary forms, *Warlock* is innovative and reveals Harrison's adept comic voice, a voice that resurfaces in *Brown Dog* and *The Seven-Ounce Man*.

Chapter Seven

"The Strangs of the World": *Sundog*

In reviewing *Sundog* for the *New York Times*, Michiko Kakutani noted that, like *Warlock*, *Sundog* is a "detective story" about the "mystery of personality"—specifically, the personality of Robert Corvus Strang, who "embodies all the optimism, vitality and raw, frontier values of an older and almost defunct America." Kakutani added that, in turning the journalist-narrator's pursuit of Strang into a "*Heart of Darkness*–like quest," Harrison may have "found a narrative strategy perfectly designed for showing off the gift of epic storytelling that he had used to such effect in his fine novella, *Legends of the Fall*." However, Kakutani then faulted *Sundog* for having characters who are neither "mythic personages resonant with meaning nor the kind of well-rounded figures one meets in the best naturalistic fiction; rather they remain an assortment of cliches—unlikeable line-drawings, rendered with a shaky hand."[1] A. C. Greene claimed that *Sundog* is an "unsatisfying book" because it is fragmentary and "unformed," with "three stories struggling to get out of one slim book." Greene added that the narrator is not a "believable literary figure," but more important, the novel's "paramount" weakness is Strang's characterization: "Strang, as man or god, is never effectively delivered, his supposedly heightened sensibilities and solutions to life are unpersuasive, and his insistent idolizing of an older brother is baffling. It is hard to convince us that a mean, sneering jerk like Strang is charming."[2] Although he praised Harrison's ability in describing the novel's physical setting, Richard Deverson believed that the narrator's "hero worship" of Strang is "never properly subjected to scrutiny. Why *is* there an American need for supermen who stalk the wilderness? Why does Harrison seem at pains to avoid asking the question?"[3]

On the other hand, James B. Hemesath calls *Sundog* a "novel of considerable stature"; its "setting, characterization, and a strong sense of humor are some of the key elements to the novel's success."[4] Terming *Sundog* a "quietly beautiful book" in its "evocation of the grandeur of Michigan's semi-wilderness," the anonymous *Publishers Weekly* reviewer said that Harrison "presents his characters with a careful attention reminiscent of Mark Twain," and that both Strang and the narrator are interesting characters.[5] William Bradley Hooper thought that *Sundog* would increase Harrison's critical esteem and that Harrison's "gritty and elegant" style "achieves a harsh yet lovely evocation of the spirit of a person who made a difference."[6] "Harrison's techniques show him in full control of diverse narrative voices," wrote the anonymous *Virginia Quarterly* reviewer, who concluded, "Humor, long absent from the early novels is here everywhere, in all three narrative voices quite inconspicuous and very efficient."[7]

A Hero Free from Dread: Robert Corvus Strang

When Kay Bonetti asked Harrison where he got the character Strang, Harrison replied: "*Sundog* came out of my conviction that the American literary novel as opposed to a more commercial kind of novel tends to ignore about seven-eighths of the people. The literary novel often concentrates itself upon people in New York or Los Angeles, academic and scientific communities. People don't write about the Strangs of the world because they don't know any of them" (Bonetti, 76). Harrison had met construction workers during his travels and even met a self-educated foreman from Tennessee who was in charge of 32,000 workers on a dam-building project in the Amazon Basin (69). With Senator Bill Bradley's help, Harrison had also toured the Richard Russell Dam project in Georgia as part of his research ("Lake").[8] Harrison accumulated four boxes of notes "ranging from the story line itself to dam engineering to the nature of Third World economics," although "when I drafted the novel, I didn't use that. But it was all there, see?" he said, pointing to his head (Skwira, 14). As Harrison became more interested in construction workers, Strang's "character took shape": "I wanted to create a hero who was free from dread. Dread and irony have gotten to be literary addictions. And I noticed there are people that live without it. So I created this character Strang" (Bonetti, 69).

The novel's central focus is Robert Corvus Strang and his life. In July 1941, when he was seven years old and fishing for perch and bluegills, a sudden, violent thunderstorm developed. Strang and his fishing boat were struck by lightning, he was pitched backward out of the boat, and although he miraculously survived, he thereafter suffered petit mal epileptic seizures. His father, a preacher, took Strang on the revival circuit to testify at tent meetings about his miraculous survival. Strang eventually became a boy-preacher and perfected a "thirty-minute sermon" that he admits he delivered "with a few variations" about "fifty times in two years."[9] After his father's death, Strang, who was only 14 years old, moved in with his older brother Ted and his wife. He helped Ted build tract houses and buildings for three years, and when Ted became a subcontractor for the Mackinac Bridge project, Strang worked on the bridge. When he was 16, he married Emmeline and fathered Bobby and Aurora. About the time when he was between 14 and 20, Strang admits, "I'm not proud of those years. . . . Most of them seem characterized by selfishness and insensitivity. Work was the excuse, an urge to prove myself at the expense of Emmeline" (*S*, 146). During his construction apprenticeship, Strang did indeed prove himself and mastered valuable skills. He read and followed blueprints, operated bulldozers and backhoes, repaired automobiles and heavy equipment, learned plumbing and wiring, and drove shallow wells.

Strang also admits that the Mackinac Bridge "represented the slowly building path to the outside world" (*S*, 147). When he was 20, he left Emmeline and his children to build a school in Kenya for the United Nazarene Mission; that job led to others in Sudan, Uganda, Peru, Brazil, Costa Rica, and Venezuela, and Strang never really returns to Michigan for 25 years. In addition to whoring and having affairs, he marries two more times—Allegria Menquez, an intelligent, beautiful prostitute he meets in San Jose, Costa Rica, and Evelyn, a doctor specializing in tropical medicine for the World Health Organization who treats him for schistosomiasis. Although each wife is different in temper and personality, Strang loves them equally, each of them loves him in return, and each visits him when he returns to Michigan's Upper Peninsula.

As the novel opens, Strang has returned to Michigan's Upper Peninsula to recuperate from two almost fatal mishaps. Because he is too busy drinking and whoring in Caracas to have his Tagamet prescription for epilepsy refilled, he runs out of medicine while working on the Rio Kuduyari dam. He tries a Kubeo Indian herbal remedy made from *Aristolochia medicinalis* to control his epilepsy but takes the wrong dosage; according to Strang, "It can be both insanity and paralysis. It can let up or not" (*S*, 27). Moreover, the dosage causes him to lose his balance and fall about 300 feet down the dam's face; fortunately, he lands on a flume of water that catapults him into the rushing river. Although he cannot move his injured legs, he swims with the current using only his arms and survives. Because of the herbal remedy, Strang's brain often short-circuits, and because of the fall down the dam, his legs are encased in braces and he can walk only with a three-sided aluminum walker. When the narrator first sees Strang, he says, "I knew he was a little older than me, but I had never seen a man who looked so totally 'used' by life" (*S*, 23).

Strang has returned to his cabin in the Upper Peninsula not so much to reestablish purpose and meaning to his life, as Harrison's other protagonists do, as to restore his health through physical therapy. Part of his therapy involves crawling, a treatment prescribed by an Ann Arbor doctor to "repattern" Strang's "brain and body to walk." Despite the excruciating pain and the swarms of mosquitoes and blackflies that even lotions fail to repel, Strang crawls every afternoon. "It's my only chance," he says, "to see the world clearly, you know, to get better. If I just sat here and took all the drugs I've been prescribed, nothing would happen except narcosis" (*S*, 61). More important, however, Strang crawls because "it's the only work at hand and I'm a worker and it's my only chance to get back to my real work. Maybe the treatment is a hoax, even a fatal hoax, but it's the only one I've got to go on. . . . You've got to beat the dread out of yourself or you can't do anything for yourself properly" (*S*, 63). When an orthopedic specialist prescribes swimming because crawling has built "big bunches of compensatory muscles around the injuries," Strang swims as diligently as he has crawled. Ultimately, however, Strang crawls and swims because he sincerely believes that he will be well enough to work on a dam in New Guinea in the winter. He says to the narrator: "I know you've been thinking 'he's never going to make it to New Guinea.' Well, I think I will. Maybe not right away. I've got a little farm up near Nicoya, north of Puntarenas, that's run by one of Allegria's relatives. If I have to, I'll go down there. . . . You might say, I'm not dead yet, and even that might be preferable to stopping my whole life in lieu of illness" (*S*, 215).

As the novel ends, Eulia, Strang's adopted daughter, leaves for Costa Rica to join a dance troupe, both Strang and the narrator are in present time since Strang began recounting his life, and Evelyn arrives to take Strang to Switzerland for her own therapy. "In layman's terms," she says, "it would require at least a year of absolute rest, of semisedation. . . . We need to weaken the muscle groups and restructure them if he's ever to walk normally" (*S*, 227). Before she can take him, Strang drugs her rum drink, makes love to her, and, sometime during the night, leaves his clothes and leg braces on the river bank and disappears.

The novel's ending is inconclusive about Strang's fate. The possibility exists, for example, that Strang, who would surely abhor semisedation— earlier he mentions detesting narcosis—swims down the river and either dies in the river's turbulence and logjams or swims until he drowns and is swept into Lake Superior. Even the narrator says that Strang may have been swept out into Lake Superior and rests "cold and intact in two hundred feet of water" (*S*, 239). On the other hand, while admitting that it is an "extremely unfriendly stretch of water," the narrator believes that such a swim is "not impossible for a man of his capabilities" (*S*, 238). The narrator's theory is that Eulia, instead of leaving, has met Bobby, and the two of them wait at the end of the two-track and help their father out of the water. Then Strang and Eulia go to his farm north of Puntarenas where Strang continues his recovery regimen. When Gregory Skwira asked Harrison about Strang's fate, Harrison replied, "I think he's in Costa Rica on that farm of his . . . until he's feeling better, and he hopes to probably be in New Guinea. . . . I think he'll probably make it, even though he walks like a land crab" (Skwira, 15).

Unlike Harrison's other protagonists, Strang does not find his life knocked out of whack by a midlife crisis. His overdose on the herbal remedy and the dam accident may arguably create a crisis, but they do not force him to reassess his values and realign his life, as do the crises in the lives of Harrison's other heroes. Instead, these mishaps are only interruptions in his life, since he knows, and has always known, that he wants to build dams, and indeed, he believes he will be well enough to work on the New Guinea dam. Unlike Swanson, the narrator in *A Good Day to Die*, and both Joseph and Johnny Lundgren, Strang is a confident, self-taught, self-made man who has charted his life ever since he began working on the Mackinac Bridge. Indeed, his position as a foreman symbolizes his stature and his accomplishments. Although the narrator first doubts whether Strang is "an alpha type, a technological genius, at home in any country" (*S*, 91), by the end of the narrative Strang does indeed represent all of these qualities.

When facing their midlife crises, Harrison's other heroes dread the necessary changes that result and agonize about them. In contrast, Strang's life is free from dread. "You've got to beat the dread out of yourself," he explains, "or you can't do anything for yourself properly" (*S*, 63). He knows, for example, that the herbal remedy he takes for his epileptic seizures may cause insanity or paralysis and that both the crawling and swimming regimens may be fatal hoaxes, but he doggedly crawls and swims because that is all he has to go on and he is not dead yet. These exercises are painful and exhausting, but he is at least active—a better alternative than narcosis or semisedation. In this sense, Strang is like Harrison's other protagonists, who want to be free enough to choose their own courses of action, a choice he certainly makes when he slips into the river rather than opt for Evelyn's semisedated therapy.

While Harrison's other heroes have a certain cautious zest for life despite their dread, Strang is probably the only one who enjoys life in all of its pains and pleasures. Between 1953 and 1983, for example, he never took a vacation; he explains, "My work was my play in that it always gave me tremendous pleasure" (*S*, 35). He even believes that people in America "suffer terribly" because "they live without energy" and so they "can't get anything done" and "lame around" (*S*, 24). Though lamed by his fall from the dam, Strang does not "lame around." As the narrator watches Strang endure the agony of his swimming regimen, he thinks, "O Jesus, give up, you godforsaken bastard, flatten yourself, subdue your spirit, eat the dirt the rest of us eat from the pot of self-pity," but at the same time the narrator realizes that Strang's life "seems full because it 'is' full, and effortlessly so" (*S*, 128–29, 127). Moreover, Strang's zest for life is symbolized in the narrator's remark that Strang "looked so totally 'used' by life," an assessment that the plot seems to contradict in that Strang has not been totally used by life so much as he has totally used life to make his life effortlessly full.

In a 1984 letter, Harrison wrote that Strang "seems to be my first Christian hero."[10] Although Harrison did not explain how or why, plot details support this idea. After his boy-preacher years, Strang rejects formalized religion but remains a humble, compassionate, selfless man, despite his whoring and carousing. He can admit that he is ashamed of his self-centered years with Emmeline, and he tirelessly and selflessly works on construction projects in Third World countries because he believes such projects will remedy hunger and other social evils. "The real goad to working hard in India for some of us," he tells the narrator, "was the hunger you would see all around us" (*S*, 191). Moreover, as Strang reflects about his brother Karl's vengeance on the three who raped Ted's daughter, Strang takes a "peculiar turn into a Tolstoy version of Christian behavior": "What Karl had done to the three young men was horribly wrong, and his own feelings about vengeance in Central America and for blacks and Indians was wrong headed, keeping as it did, the wheel of karma spinning out its usual freight of human guts" (*S*, 213).

Finally, before disappearing on his night swim, Strang, according to Marshall, has "given everything away to wives, children, students, organizations. He wasn't very worldly," Marshall concludes, after which the narrator enigmatically retorts, "I think he probably was" (*S*, 240). Either comment underscores Strang's Christian virtues. Marshall sees an ascetic Strang who disdains worldly possessions and gives them away to people and organizations. In the narrator's eyes, Strang cares so much for the world and for people that he returns to people and the world what he has received from them. In either case, as the narrator learns, Strang's story has been "immersed in love, work, and death; its lack of decor was made up for by the tired . . . saws of wholeness, harmony, and even . . . a modicum of radiance. In short, the mystery of personality, of life itself" (*S*, 210). Rather than being the "mean sneering jerk" that A. C. Greene labels him, Strang is one of those workers who does the work of the world and who does indeed make a difference. In this sense, Strang "embodies all the optimism, vitality and raw frontier values," and this is Harrison's point.

"As Told To": *Sundog*'s Narrator

When Kay Bonetti asked for an explanation of *Sundog*'s subtitle—*The Story of an American Foreman . . . as told to Jim Harrison*—Harrison replied: "That's just to have fun. Like Nabokov. I did that to throw people off the track. It is a little bit myself, but I had to have a contrast to Strang. I had to have somebody coming from way outside, coming into that world. You could say they're almost extremities of the right and left lobes of the same brain" (Bonetti, 70).[11] While the similarities between the narrator and Harrison are minor, the differences are major. Like Harrison, the narrator is a gourmand and a gourmet who suffers from gout. He annually fishes for tarpon in Key West, associates with other writers and with movie stars, and has been to Europe, Africa, and Costa Rica. He drives a four-wheel-drive sports vehicle, and his mother is an avid bird-watcher. He also is a writer of note but is "so weak-stomached about criticism" that he reads only reviews that people assure him are laudatory.

Unlike Harrison, however, the narrator has been divorced twice; his two homes are a New York co-op and a Sag Harbor cottage, both of which he loses in the divorce, or rather, as he says, "not so much lost, but gave them up in an attack of kindness" (*S*, 1). The narrator's father is a botanist, not a rural agriculture agent, but a more important difference is revealed in the narrator's remark about his Michigan roots: "I might have been born up here, but I didn't belong" (*S*, 13). As he had done in previous novels, Harrison used autobiographical experiences—Strang as a boy-preacher, for instance—but transformed them in creating fiction. Harrison told Kay Bonetti, "Strang isn't me" (Bonetti, 69), and neither is the narrator Harrison, though he does provide a contrast to Strang.

Although Strang undergoes no midlife crisis, the narrator does. In the Author's Note, he writes, "I was in Florida for the winter trying to get over the effects of a divorce and declining health. . . . I suffered deeply from gout at age forty-five" (*S*, x). The narrator has a very high pulse rate and blood pressure and is 30 pounds overweight. He feels he does not belong in Michigan, and he says that the Upper Peninsula has blurred his "peripheries," an image that recalls Harrison's other protagonists who sense that their lives are ten degrees out of whack. Similarly, the narrator has to realign his perspective and his life, and his five months with Strang provide the catalyst for doing just that.

While Strang's experiences have taught him to live without dread, the narrator is full of dread. When the novel opens, he is in the posh Palm Beach locker room and Marshall is calling the club members "asshole fops" in comparison to his ex-son-in-law Strang. Marshall points his finger at the narrator, who says that his "temples ached with panic" because he dreads criticism. Marshall says, "I read your books. They're nice enough, but you might try writing about someone who actually does something" (*S*, xi). More important, Strang recognizes the narrator's dread and asks, "You don't seem to know what you're doing up here, do you?" (*S*, 37). After the narrator admits that he does not really know and that he thinks he may do "some journalism," Strang tells him: "Pretty good but you need some nouns in there for fuel. I can tell that you think you're either over your head or under your head. I can tell by the way you ate that you're worried about what you're going to do about food in town, and by the way you look at my daughter I can see you're worried about getting laid" (*S*, 38). Compared with Strang's epilepsy and his medical prognosis, the narrator's dreads are indeed mundane and foppish.

In contrast to Strang's rather serious, philosophical, and determined personality, the narrator's zany, waffling personality results in humorous misadventures that recall some of the zany situations in *Wolf*, *Farmer*, and especially *Warlock*. The narrator's concerns about eating, and eating well, often lead him into humorous situations. For example, after Evelyn chastises him about being in "terrible shape," telling him he could "support an entire African village" with the money he spends on his "gut," she gives him a diet and warns him, "Follow the enclosed diet or you'll never see fifty" (*S*, 4, 5). Even though he thinks the diet is "suitable for someone with a disposition of a Gandhi, a Sister Theresa, a Gautama Buddha—some tiny brown, selfless person," he vows to follow the diet and even skips lunch (*S*, 5). To keep from thinking about food as he drives north, he sexually fantasizes about Evelyn, becomes "heated up to the point" that he reaches for a bottle of Le Bejorce, which weakens his

diet resolve, and swerves off the interstate near Macon, Georgia, for a
heaped platter of barbeque beef and pork ribs at Home Folks Barbeque.
He admits that he has planned "this move subconsciously for an entire
day": "Strangely, Doctor Evelyn seemed to peer up from the glistening
pool of sauce, and I called for a doggy bag" (*S*, 6). The narrator's initial
firm resolve, his waffling spirit, and his speeding off the highway to a
restaurant recall Johnny Lundgren's resolve and waffling will in *Warlock*.

The narrator's worries about sex also give rise to humorous incidents.
He notes, for example, that, "sexually, the U.P. was a sensory deprivation
tank. . . . The moment you left any settlement up here you were smack-
dab in the middle of the forest. In the old days there were nymphs and
bacchantes in the forest, but they seem to have disappeared to better
weather, probably California" (*S*, 137). In one comical scene, he buys six
skin magazines—"fifteen bucks worth of porky rumps with splayed
apertures"—and when he tries to pose as a doctor to get directions to
Strang's cabin, the middle-aged Scandinavian lady innkeeper tells him,
"I've never sold filthy magazines to a doctor. They come up here for the
natural beauty" (*S*, 17). In another scene, he decides to go to the dance
at the bar because there will be a "live band"—"as opposed to a dead
one," he speculates—and also because the "night might hold romance,"
and indeed it does. After returning to his room at three in the morning,
he records on his tape machine, "Wrestled with a woman my own age in
car. She took advantage of me" (*S*, 46).

The humor is also evident in his waffling reserve and lust for Eulia.
"There is a problem," he admits, "of keeping Eulia at arm's length when
it is your narrator who is in modest pursuit" (*S*, 132). His waffling spirit
is especially tempted when Eulia runs out into the rain wearing only bra
and panties, when she does her dance workouts clad in an abbreviated
leotard, and when she sunbathes in a string bikini that the narrator says
could "fit, chipmunk style, in one of my cheeks" (*S*, 61). On one occasion, when she is wearing the bikini and bending over so that her bottom points at him, the narrator rationalizes, "If I can't have it, it must be
suspicious" (*S*, 127). When he takes her to a local beach and she wears
her "half ounce idea of what a bathing suit was," he becomes so excited
that he plans a gourmet dinner and offers a "silent prayer that she would
be thirsty enough to become pliant" (*S*, 172). However, when she borrows his car to run a short errand—she is going to meet Bobby—the
narrator is so depressed that he botches the recipe and then admits that
he "nearly didn't eat dinner" (*S*, 172). When he does make love to her—
she is bent over a chair in his room—his climax sends him "reeling back-

wards like a squid in the general direction of the bed" (*S*, 209), an incident somewhat reminiscent of Swanson making love to the girl in the
alley, falling backward, and landing on the bottle cap.

Despite his clownish misadventures, waffling spirit, and dreads, the
narrator does lose 15 pounds during his five months with Strang and
even manages to realign his life. Both he and Strang, in fact, help each
other metaphorically to get better. The interview process, for example,
repatterns Strang's brain as he recalls his past, and he even tells the narrator, "You got me started again, though I'm not sure my heart is in it. I
walked better than ever yesterday and this morning, and I'm not sure
why. . . . I know you've been thinking 'he's never going to make it to
New Guinea.' Well, I think I will" (*S*, 215). Moreover, after asking,
"We've become friends, haven't we?" Strang makes the narrator promise
to see the Delta Project when he goes to Europe in November and to
take care of his dog if anything happens to him. "Naturally I agreed to
both," the narrator claims, "and, to my minimal credit, fulfilled both
vows" (*S*, 224). "That afternoon," he tells the reader, "was the rather
nagging and painful beginning for me of a long voyage back toward
Earth, however simpleminded might be my arrival" (*S*, xi–xii).

"Textural Concretia": *Sundog*'s Structure

Perhaps more so than in Harrison's previous novels and novellas,
Sundog's form is technically innovative in its use of three narrative voices—Strang's, the narrator's formal voice, and the narrator's taped voice.
Harrison explained: "What the narrator was finding in Strang is maybe
what I found in the left side of my brain. And the taped device amplified
it which is fun, because you have the more formal narrator, then you
have the narrator off-the-wall. And some of the inserts have the narrator
wondering what he's going to eat, wondering how he's going to get laid.
Textural concretia, the 'thinginess' of life. That's an old rule I have on
the wall. Make it vivid" (Bonetti, 72). Rather than being "fragmentary"
and "unformed," to use A. C. Greene's phrasing, *Sundog* is unified and
complete, and each narrative voice complements the others as it
advances the plot line.

The narrator's story proper begins linearly as he poignantly describes
his journey north, on which he will do "something truly different." This
journey will become his metaphorical "long voyage back toward Earth":
like Strang, he is returning to the region of his youth not only to realign
his life after his midlife crisis but also to recover his somewhat poor

health (gout, high blood pressure, and excess weight). The linear plot development continues as he interviews Strang and worries about sex and food. Once he meets Strang and the interview begins, the voyages of the two men dovetail and move forward until five months later, in early autumn, Strang ends with, "That's all there is to say," and the narrator realizes they have arrived at the present. "What do we do when we arrive at the present?" he asks (*S*, 224).

Technically, the narrator's formal and off-the-wall voices supply not only part of the novel's humor but the "thinginess" of "textural concretia" in that they report what is occurring in the present while Strang is telling his story. For instance, when Eulia runs out into the rain in her bra and panties, the narrator says, "I must interrupt Strang's tale. The most extraordinary thing just happened" (*S*, 49). Furthermore, both voices of the narrator comment about Strang suffering from but enduring his crawling and swimming therapies. If Strang were to talk about his pain and trials, he would sound like a self-serving martyr, but the narrator's objective, albeit sympathetic, account enhances Strang's stature and underscores his story of death, love, and radiance. Not only do their lives dovetail, but Strang's crawling, swimming, and talking about his past are also therapeutic for the narrator. "Only later," the narrator says, "when I neared bankruptcy due to this project, did I regain my health" (*S*, x).

The novel's subtitle is *The Story of an American Foreman*,[12] and Strang's is the central narrative voice because of the narrator's initial fascination with Marshall's comment on writing about "someone who actually does something." The narrator's initial idea that Marshall's comment is the beginning of a "long voyage back to Earth" is also true for Strang, since his recollections move linearly from past to present, from childhood and adolescence to manhood, middle age, and end, as he relates the story of his accident, signaled by, "Here's what happened." The linear movement is also evident in Strang's frequent identification of time frames. For example, he either mentions historical figures like Eisenhower, Churchill, Nehru, and Amin or refers to his own age and dates—"When Karl returned in December of my twelfth year, in 1947," or, "I was a twenty-year-old stripling who had only been out of the U.P." (*S*, 107, 155). His narrative, like the narrator's, also contains textural concretia in that he explains the knowledge and insights he has gained from his experiences and the interesting things he has seen (for example, the king cobra incident in India) and done (for example, his encounter with the transvestite whom he innocently thought was a female prostitute).

There is not only a linear progression from the past to the present in Strang's narration but a circular progression as well. Strang left Michigan only to return 25 years later, and in the novel's conclusion, he may have taken the road south to the outside world again, as he did 25 years before. More significant, however, is the progression in Strang's therapy. While his crawling and swimming regimens have strengthened his body, talking about his past has cleared his mind, even though, as he says, his mind often short-circuits. That talking about his past has been therapeutic is evident when he tells the narrator: "From all my reading done in construction camps throughout the world, the main point or challenge is to stay as conscious as possible, absurd as that seems. Talking to you now I'm getting back some of that vividness" (*S*, 154). Although he may not have recovered fully, the extent of Strang's redux is apparent when he tells the narrator:

> That's all there is to say. And now I'm here. Five months in the hospital and four months here. Do you realize how unspeakably grand it was to come up to this cabin, the area of my youth, after that long in the hospital, which is so often—and I thought it would be for me—the house of death. That's why I refused all those drugs after a while. I had to be conscious. That's all. How could I bear not being conscious? Last night I was swimming in the dark in my dreams and it was wonderful. (*S*, 235)

Harrison told Gregory Skwira that writing *Sundog* was therapeutic in helping him see that he had decided to "work hard all my life whether I get any money or not. My pleasure in life is just work itself, not the reward. Just like Strang and his dams. . . . I don't know if the novel's any good, but it was the very best novel I could write at the time. And that's a very peaceful thing to know, that I gave it my best shot" (Skwira, 15). Although generally overlooked by critics and scholars, *Sundog* merits close scholarly analysis. In its innovative three narrative voices, its intricately dovetailed stories, and its rendering of Michigan's Upper Peninsula, it is a finely crafted novel. Indeed, time may prove that *Sundog* is just as grand as *Farmer*, *Legends of the Fall*, and Harrison's next novel, *Dalva*, another of his critically acclaimed works.

Chapter Eight
"*Dalva* . . . Near Killed Me": *Dalva*

Although some reviewers have noted the technical and stylistic flaws in *Dalva*, most have praised the novel for its portrayal of Dalva, for the Northridge journal sections, and for its three narrative voices. John Clute wrote, for example, that *Dalva* is a "failed novel" because Dalva's characterization is "at times rather difficult to swallow"—"as a lover she is flamboyant and generous; on horseback she is superb; she cooks well and knows wine; she drives like a man. She is rich." Although he admired Harrison's crafting of the Northridge journals, Clute thought that his "paucity of invention" becomes evident when he "allows Dalva and the other Northridge descendants unquestioned moral hegemony" over the journals, resulting in Harrison's reliance on a "congested assertiveness, wheezily poetical, clearly uneasy." Clute did say, however, that Dalva is a "remarkably charismatic protagonist for a failed novel, and no failure of strictures should blind one to Harrison's success in making one wish to believe in her."[1] "The interpolated fragments of Northridge's journal are the best thing in this scrappy book," asserted Roz Kaveney. "Harrison is a fine writer of novellas; his problem as a novelist is that here at least he is not writing a novel—he is writing three novellas of varying qualities and shuffling the pages together. The general effect is patchy—he has to rely on effects like the gaudy image of Dalva's dying lover riding his horse into the sea." Yet, Kaveney concluded that *Dalva* is a "powerful and inspiring book even though on many pages we want to take the author and shake him for his sentimentalities and laziness."[2]

More laudatory is Michael C. M. Huey's praise for the three distinct narrative voices of Dalva, Michael, and J. W. Northridge: "As different as the writers/speakers are, they have one thing in common. Writing offers them a quiet medium for confronting the boundaries of their lives." *Dalva* is a "festival of life's poetry."[3] Similarly, Jonathan Yardley found *Dalva* "moving, interesting and satisfying"—Harrison's "most ambitious" work to date—and believed that it "should bring him a substantial and appreciative readership." He noted that Michael's narrative "runs a bit off course," since his voice differs from Dalva's, but thought that Northridge and his journals are interesting and that Dalva is "far

and away the book's most interesting figure. . . . She is that rare fictional creation, a character whom the reader would dearly love to meet. That
she is the creation of a man makes her all the more interesting, for
Harrison took a great risk in attempting to put himself into the mind of
a woman."[4]

C. Lynn Munro likewise asserted that *Dalva* is Harrison's "most
ambitious" novel, not only because it covers a "multigenerational family
history," but also because "two-thirds of the novel is told from a
woman's perspective" and thus indicates Harrison's ability to "transcend
the masculine point of view and enter into a world that, according to the
majority of critics, he has never even conceptualized."[5] Louise Erdrich
also praised *Dalva* for its "fascinating mixture of voices that cut through
time and cross barriers of culture and gender to achieve a work in cho-
rus"; furthermore, Erdrich claimed, "There is no putting aside the book
until the time-bombs go off, the identities are revealed, and the skeletons almost literally tumble from closets. *Dalva* is rich in language and
characterization, exploiting the possibilities of its form."[6]

What does Harrison say about *Dalva*? He has admitted that he did
not intend to write about Dalva but rather about J. W. Northridge.
Dalva, however, metaphorically dominated his imagination and forced
him to write about her. The sequel, tentatively entitled *Earthdiver* (a
Native American term for "someone who belongs to the earth"), will be
about Northridge. In fact, Northridge records in his journal on 13 May
1871 that the Sioux call him "earthdiver" because he is "forever digging
holes and inspecting the root systems of trees."[7] Portraying the female
psyche took a great deal of "emotional energy," Harrison said; indeed, in
a type of "Buddhist process," he had to "totally abnegate" his own personality to become Dalva.[8] Moreover, the physical toll was exacting:
"*Dalva* fucking near killed me. By the time I finished *Dalva*, I had an old
thyroid inflammation and both my eardrums were broken because I had
had different kinds of flu and viruses, and I ignored them totally until I
was about dead. But I guess it was worth it" ("Lake"). Harrison also
admits that he never "knew from one day to the next what [Dalva] was
going to do," that she would probably make him very nervous if he ever
met her," and only after finishing the book did he have her under control.[9] If Harrison had trouble writing about Dalva, Russell Chatham
spent a year trying to paint her picture; Harrison told him, "I invented
the woman I wanted to be in love with" (Julia Reed, 506). In "From the
Dalva Notebooks," reprinted in *Just before Dark*, Harrison describes his
concentration-consecration talisman: "Hot tip from Taisen Deshimaru on

writing this book, 'You must concentrate upon and consecrate yourself wholly to each day, as though a fire were raging in your hair' " (*JBD*, 286). Finally, regarding his reentry after *Dalva*, Harrison notes in "From the *Dalva* Notebooks": "Postscript. Finished the novel in July and have since driven 27,000 miles to get over it. Perhaps it is easier to write a novel than survive it" (*JBD*, 289).

The Central Focus: Dalva's Midlife Crisis and *Hanblecheyapi*

As the novel opens, Dalva is 45 years old, has been living in Santa Monica, California, for seven years, and counsels troubled teenagers. When she loses her job, she begins to wonder about the son she gave up for adoption the day he was born; Dalva decides to return to Nebraska and her roots to make peace with the ghosts of her past and thus make sense of her life.

Two of the ghosts from her past are her father, who was killed in Korea when she was nine years old, and Duane Stone Horse, her half-brother and the father of her son. He committed suicide by riding his buckskin horse out into the Gulf Stream. Because of her ghosts and her son, Dalva's life has been a series of moves as she searches for meaning and purpose:

> All my moves had been radical—New York City and Los Angeles had alternated with remote regions of Montana, Minnesota, Michigan, and Nebraska. There had been short unsuccessful attempts to live in foreign countries—France, England, Mexico, Brazil—but I was so thoroughly an American that my homesickness led to a premature return; out of forty-five years well over forty-three had been spent in New York, Los Angeles, or in areas so remote that my friends in those cities found them laughable. (*D*, 73)

As Ruth reminds her, "You need neutral territory to live in. Ghosts make you old" (*D*, 74).

Dalva stays in Santa Monica for seven years because of the "trees and the ocean"—"the landscape helped me to let problems float out through the top of my head, through my skin, and into the air" (*D*, 17). Despite the trees and ocean, this landscape is peppered with urban-sprawl violence. She notes, for example, that someone has spray-painted the word "MENACE" on the Palisades Park benches, on the steps leading down to the ocean, and on an overpass: "I stopped counting at twenty," she writes.

"Fortunately most lunatics don't have the vigor of Charles Manson" (*D*, 6). Another menace is the coastal highway, where a girl in a green bathing suit is "hit seven times before the last car tossed her in a ditch. The autopsy said California speedball" (*D*, 3). A more dehumanizing and deadly menace is Guillermo Sandoval, who so brutally sodomizes Franco, his nephew, that Franco's anus bleeds profusely, soaking through the paper towels Franco has stuffed down his pants. Dalva asks, "How could all this happen when there was an ocean?" (*D*, 14). When she decides to talk with Franco's mother, she discovers that the mother has run away with a pimp; Guillermo begins cursing and slapping Dalva until some barrio teenagers lash him with automobile antennas that tear his clothes and scar his hands and face. When the police arrive, Guillermo escapes, begins stalking Dalva, and is finally arrested in the parking garage of her apartment building, where he is hiding and carrying a .38 Ruger, a sharpened car aerial, and a piece of rope. Although she says that the Pacific and the trees tug at her heart when she leaves to return to Nebraska, she also admits that at age 45, her "tolerance for cities was waning" (*D*, 82).

Dalva's crisis is symbolized not only by her desultory wanderings but by her emotional anxieties, which are manifested in recurring pains in her chest. Before she moves from Santa Monica, she feels a "tremor of loneliness" that is replaced with a "vertiginous notion" and a "sharp pang beneath" her breastbone (*D*, 72). The pain is also evident when she returns to Nebraska and has to deal with her past: "It is nearly thirty years ago and I still feel the pain of that October and November so that my heart aches, my skin tightens, and I can barely swallow" (*D*, 33). The pain returns, for example, when she calls Andrew to find out about her son; she describes her feelings as "far beyond rationality, above or below it." "I had involuntarily thought so much about the subject that it had reduced itself to a knot, a lump of coal beneath my breastbone" (*D*, 266). In an effort to purge herself after she learns that her son is alive and his foster mother will talk with her, Dalva rides Peach, her mare, and begins to yell, "Goddamn the world who gives me no father and no son. No husband" (*D*, 268). As she yells, the ache, she says, continues "upward from my stomach to my heart to my throat and into my head and back down for another circle" (*D*, 268). The pain symbolizes her *Weltschmerz* or world-hurt, and she must first let go of the worry and the pain if she is to realign her life.

Rachel, Duane's mother, tells Dalva about an Oglala-Sioux word, *Hanblecheyapi*, a reference to a "rite of 'lament'"; the word describes "a period where you expressed all your anguish, then received a new vision of life to keep you going" (*D*, 249). Although Dalva's "Goddamn the

world" outburst certainly expresses her anguish, three key scenes symbolize her letting go of her anguish and reentering life's pattern. First,
after her initial outburst, she and Peach swim in the creek, make a circle,
and come out on the far bank near Duane's tepee circle and the hanging
deer skull, where she rolls in the sand and then rolls over and over back
into the creek. Whether the sand-wallowing and the creek immersion
are metaphorical baptisms is arguable, but afterwards, Dalva "realized
that my stomachache was gone and with it the pain beneath my breastbone and in my throat and head" (*D*, 268). Subsequently, she agrees to
counsel bankrupt farm families, because "I was goddamned sick of simple dangling" (*D*, 290).

Another part of her *Hanblecheyapi* is evident when she admits that she
has "begun not to drift": "It was as if I had made my decision, gradual as
it was, to come home," a notion implicit in the title of book 3, "Going
Home" (*D*, 292). The second stage of her reentry occurs as she drives
through the Buffalo Gap National Grasslands and thinks about Fort
Robinson as the "Sioux equivalent of the Warsaw Ghetto" (*D*, 293). She
becomes so angry that she speeds around three slow-moving campers
and then pulls onto the left shoulder to avoid an oncoming car. Because
her heart is racing and she is frightened, she stops and walks off into the
"ocean of grass," where she assuages her anguish:

> "What I am trying to do is trade in a dead lover for a live son. I'll throw
> in a dead father with a dead lover and their souls I have kept in the base-
> ment perhaps. Even if I don't get to see the son I have to let the others
> go. . . . I'm a crazy woman. Why didn't I do this long ago? I'm forty-five
> and there's still a weeping girl in my stomach. I'm still in the arms of
> dead men—first Father then Duane. I may as well have burned down the
> goddamned house. Whether I see the son he is at least a living obses-
> sion." (*D*, 293)

Sam Creekmouth, Dalva's new love and a descendant of her great-
grandfather's friend, obliquely tells Dalva to abandon the past when he
tells her about his horse that was stolen when he was nine years old.
Twenty years later, Sam's father, who is dying in a VA hospital, says,
"Sam, it's time to stop thinking about getting that mare back" (*D*, 294).

After her immersion in the sea of grass, Dalva must perform a final
rite before she can surrender the past and have a "new vision of life." As
suggested in her comment about the souls she has perhaps kept in her
metaphorical basement (that is, in her own mind and heart), she must
now visit the Northridge subbasement: "I pretty much knew what it
held but I also realized it was terribly important to resolve the whole

thing by actually seeing it" (*D*, 282). In the subbasement, she sees the skeletons of the three soldiers, the skeletons of the "five warriors in full regalia," and a trove of "tagged and labeled artifacts from the tribes of the Great Basin" (*D*, 298). Dalva sits in the subbasement and thinks about anything except what she sees. More important, while she sits, "My father and Duane seemed to be with me, then went away as did the weeping girl I had felt in my chest. She went out an upstairs window where she had sat watching the summer morning, the descent of the moon" (*D*, 298). Finally, Lundquist, her grandfather's friend and handyman, becomes worried that Dalva has been "swallowed up," and he calls her name; they climb the stairs to the kitchen, where Dalva notes that the sun shines brightly and that she "could swear there was a hollowness in my chest where the weeping girl had been" (*D*, 299).

Not only has Dalva made peace with the ghosts of her past—she says that by entering the subbasement she released the "souls of Duane and my father" (*D*, 297)—but her *Hanblecheyapi* is complete. Later, as she looks at a picture of James Dean on her bedroom wall and feels herself being "drawn ceaselessly back into the past" that she wishes "to emerge from," she says, "I had come to know only recently that one *could* emerge without forgetting, and that to remember need not be to suffocate" (*D*, 307). Her Uncle Paul tells her that "country life" has "improved [her] appearance in little more than a month" (*D*, 322). With the family picnic at the Northridge house, *Dalva* ends with affirmative images. Not only are Frieda, Lundquist, and Michael there, but so, of course, is Dalva, who, after one of "those great sleeps," has metaphorically returned home. For that matter, Naomi, Paul, Ruth, and Luiz have returned, and so has Dalva's son. As the novel closes, Dalva and her son sit in her upstairs bedroom and look at pictures of the past, including ones of Duane and his buckskin horse. When they hear music, they look out the window to see Michael roasting the chickens, Frieda setting the table, Paul and Luiz standing by the tire swing, Naomi and Ruth sitting at the picnic table, and Lundquist wandering "around in the groves of lilacs, among the gravestones . . . playing his miniature violin, as if he were at the same time serenading the living and the dead" (*D*, 324). As if to underscore the title of book 3 and the homecoming of Dalva and her son, the novel's last sentence is, "We went down to join them" (*D*, 324).

"And a Dipshit": Professor Michael's Section

Russell Chatham says that *Dalva* is about "a woman, an old man, and a dipshit" (Julia Reed, 506). The "dipshit" is Michael, a Stanford University history professor whose sabbatical, generous foundation grant, tenure, and perhaps career depend on a scholarly book about J. W. Northridge's journals. Michael's section, entitled "Michael's Workbook," provides comic relief and resolves his midlife crisis.

Before his life begins unraveling at the seams, Michael has struggled toward success. From an Ohio Valley, Protestant, "marginal farm-factory" family, he won a scholarship to Notre Dame, did factory work in the summers, spent a year in Northwestern's writing program, "with a failed, awful novel to show for it," and endured "long and arduous graduate work at the University of Wisconsin and Yale, ending with a Ph.D. in American studies [and] a couple of nonscholarly books" (D, 62). Michael's indiscretions during his undergraduate and graduate years gradually ignite his midlife crisis.

At Notre Dame, he pilfers some rare books, but the charges are dropped; at the University of Wisconsin, he picks up three drunk driving convictions; in Seattle, he is "institutionalized under psychiatric care" for six weeks because his wife divorced him (D, 219). His academic career is also fraudulent. He claims that his Ph.D. dissertation, *Bitter One: The Life and Death of an Ohio Steeltown*, passed "muster with flying colors," was published by a university press, and has been "well reviewed in academic circles," but he confesses that it is "shot through with fraudulent details [and] faked if plausible interviews" and fears that, "like a tax cheater," someday he may be "found out" (D, 127). "I had written the whole mess under the influence of booze and Dexedrine, with my blurred and electric peripheries avoiding any hard work. . . . My travel grant back to the Ohio Valley was dissipated on Chicago high life" (D, 127). He has even lied to the Stanford leave committee, telling them he has obtained permission to study Northridge's journals. Other factors contributing to his midlife crisis are his divorce—which he attributes to having been "simply too stupid to seek help"—and mounting debts. Dalva decides to help Michael because he has fallen so far. When she sees him in San Francisco, for example, she says that he looks "as battered as the front end of his car" and that his "destructive behavior" may be equivalent to the "weeping used by women." His life is a "sorry mess" and reminds her of a "more grotesque version of parts of my own life, and the lives of many of those I knew" (D, 81, 63). More important, as she tells Naomi later, "I didn't want a boring scholar who would only produce a boring work of scholarship" (D, 220). Just as Dalva receives a new vision of life when she returns to Nebraska, Michael's sojourn in Nebraska and his study of Northridge's journals reshape and revision his life's "blurred and electric peripheries," even though his reshaping will be more comical. Like Harrison's other comic foils—Swanson, Johnny Lundgren, *Sundog*'s narrator, and Brown Dog—Michael means well, but he often causes his own comical predicaments.

As an outlander in Nebraska, his bumblings are indeed comical. The geese are hostile on his first morning, and when he helps Dalva and an old horse trader unload four horses, one of the horses yanks its lead rope, jarring Michael's shoulder, and the other bites his shirtsleeve and begins to back away. "It was," writes Michael, "a medievalist's vision of torture, and the shirt began to give way" (*D*, 128). His shouting further excites both horses but brings Dalva and the old man to his rescue. Michael says, "The old man cuffed the bejesus out of the horses, which offered me minimal satisfaction" (*D*, 128). As Dalva laughs, Michael shambles off to the bunkhouse, wishing he had some whiskey and planning to "sneak into the house for a few hits of [Dalva's] precious brandy, a small recompense for my tattered shirt" (*D*, 129). Later the four horses charge the corral fence when they see him, as if they want to be friends with him, but he says, "I told them we were going to have to work this thing out" (*D*, 131).

Another comical interlude occurs when Frieda, the Northridge cook and housekeeper, wakes Michael at dawn because Dalva has suggested that he might like an early breakfast and early morning hike, another comical fiasco. He trudges through dense windbreaks and alfalfa fields, becomes lost, and rests on a rock pile in the center of a field, where he dozes, dreams that the rock pile is an Indian burial mound, and awakes screaming and surrounded by sunning blacksnakes. "There was a loud noise that turned out to be my yelling, which I managed to do while running backward. Son of a bitch, I almost dumped in my pants! I am not by inclination a nature buff, and this experience cinched my dislike of its tooth-and-claw world" (*D*, 115). Attempting to hike back to the farm, he steps on and breaks a pheasant egg—the pheasant unnerves him with a "bowel-shaking squawk"—and he gets mired in a muddy creek bank and loses one of his "handmade brogans." Mosquitoes plague him, his muscles are sore, and he injures his foot. When "mounted cowboys and farmers in bib overalls" gallop toward him, he thinks he may be hanged for trespassing, but they are a rescue party sent by Naomi. Dalva comforts Michael: "Don't worry about getting lost yesterday. They're all quite pleased and they'll talk about it for years. They think that's what happens to brilliant professors. There might be a small item in the weekly newspaper, 'Scholar Loses Shoe'" (*D*, 122).

In the "dismal outback," as Michael terms Nebraska, he—like Swanson and *Sundog*'s narrator—is concerned about food and drink (both preferably imported from gourmet New York and California shops) and sex (preferably with Dalva). These preoccupations give rise to some hilarious incidents as well. One of the most comically orchestrated of them involves Michael and Karen Olafson, a sexually aware high school senior with model-and-starlet aspirations, who confesses that her dream is to "pledge either Pi Beta Phi or Kappa Kappa Gamma" and become the homecoming queen (*D*, 163). Michael's fopperies shine when she interviews him for a high school journalism project. Not only does he plot a "campaign like Rommel about to enter Egypt" or "Timoshenko before the maps of war," but he also uses a "sliver of a British accent, affecting a Noel Coward weariness but an actor's intensity": "I acted worldly, troubled, morose, so sophisticated that my answers tended to streak off into airy tangents" (*D*, 162). When he blathers about her need for direction and guidance and she begins to cry, Michael looks out the window, pretends to be lost in thought, but is actually thinking about lunch—"Maybe a friatta with anchovies, eggs, shallots, fontina" (*D*, 164). Sensing that Karen has "stewed in her banal juices" long enough, he offers to help her modeling career and asks her to undress so that he can better judge her potential. Making calipers of his thumbs and forefingers,

> I kneaded the buttocks a bit as if searching for problems, then scrambled around to her front, not wanting to lose this particular angle of vision. I had, sadly, used up all my terms, being short on the sciences, so muttered a few cooking and food terms in French. "Fine *ris de veau*," I said, a flick of the tongue away from the pubis; "*bagner de Bourgogne*" to her belly button, and "*tête de veau*" to her ample titties. At that point I had to turn away in unrestrained anguish. I was overrevving like a runaway diesel. (*D*, 165).

As he persuades Karen to do sit-ups, his "weiner" becomes a "wisdom-toothache" and there is a "roaring" in his ears—which turns out to be Frieda roaring into the yard in her big Dodge Ram. The interview ends. Michael persuades Karen to return later that night and to bring some candid photographs to send to his California modeling contact. When she returns, they have oral sex because, she says, "I'm straight with my boyfriend but maybe it wouldn't hurt to do the other thing." As Michael recalls, "Some call it sex. A twinge of angina and a blur in the vision. . . .

Even at thirty-nine I'm getting on in years for this sort of thing" (*D*, 177, 178).

Michael's indiscretion with Karen becomes another comic pratfall. When he and Dalva attend the hometown horse show, Pete Olafson, Karen's giant of a father, shows Michael one of Karen's nude photographs and breaks Michael's arm and jaw. When Dalva sees Karen's photograph, she laughs out loud; when a "Jap" photographer and a woman arrive to photograph Karen, Frieda says, "Poor Professor Michael getting his head broke to help that slut. She gets famous and he gets a headache" (*D*, 264). Significantly, Michael suffers this time for his faux pas, and it begins to change his life. For that matter, his sojourn in Nebraska and study of Northridge's journals also reshape his life. After confessing about his fraudulent dissertation, he cautiously emphasizes, "The point is that I have resolved to play this one straight, or as straight as possible" (*D*, 127). Moreover, he becomes so engrossed in reading the journals that he "barely" remembers "to smoke and forget[s] altogether to drink the beer in the refrigerator." Later he says, "I had been so grotesquely involved in my work I had forgotten the food packages of the day before! Anyone who has known me would find this unbelievable" (*D*, 131, 135). Dalva's therapy of limiting his food and alcohol intake causes him to lose weight despite the drinks he sneaks and his beer-drinking sprees with old Lundquist. Finally, and more important, Dalva writes about Michael, "I felt sorry for him. All the suffering had leavened my own at the time, and had helped explain my family's character to me" (*D*, 282). Yet Michael is still Michael; he has not radically changed, as is evident when he confesses to being unfaithful to Dalva with one of his nurses, who is "inelegantly" called Debbie, comes from Iowa, and brings him a "quart of homemade beef broth with plenty of garlic in it" (*D*, 276).

The "Indian Disease": *Dalva*'s Native American Theme

In "From the *Dalva* Notebooks," Harrison recalls that Bernard Fontana warned about "getting the 'Indian disease,'" the point being that it "takes a great deal of discipline not to shatter into fragments" (*JBD*, 287–88). This metaphorical "Indian disease" is surely Harrison's interest in Native American culture and history, evident in his essays and articles in *Just before Dark*, as minor themes in *Wolf*, *A Good Day to Die*, and *The Man Who Gave up His Name*, and as a secondary theme in *Legends of the Fall*. In *Dalva*,

however, the Native American theme is more comprehensive, complementing the setting and the characterizations. In talking with Kathleen
Stocking about *Dalva* and this theme, Harrison observed: "This nation has
a history, but it also has a soul history, and that's what I was interested in.
Our original sin in this country was the desecration of Indians, followed by
the importation of slaves. Underlying this is greed. . . . Because without a
moral vision, there is no future. Without vision, you die" (Stocking, 19). In
Dalva, the greed, desecration, and moral vision reside in J. W. Northridge's
journals and life, both of which reveal his own Indian disease—his understanding of and compassion for Native Americans.

Because Michael skips around in the journals, the dates of the journal
entries are not sequentially arranged in the plot; historically,
Northridge's journals range from 1865 and 1866, through 1871 to
1877, and conclude with entries for 1889, 1890, and 1891. After reading the 13 May 1871 entry about the friendship between Northridge
and He Dog, Michael is awed and notes that "this little passage alone
meant that J. W. Northridge was truly in the thick of things" (*D*, 124).
In other words, from the end of the Civil War through the Indian wars,
Northridge recorded those events that shaped and changed the nation
and its people, especially the Native Americans. Michael realizes how
"difficult [it is] to imagine actually living through that period on a firsthand, intimate basis, as did Northridge: from the end of the Civil War to
the massacre at Wounded Knee in 1890, the Great Plains were in a state
of historical convulsion" (*D*, 137).

Northridge's Civil War entries record the horrors he witnessed at
Andersonville when he was imprisoned and his moral indignation about
the government's policy in Georgia: "It is unthinkable that the gov't let
General Sherman burn and pillage Georgia, and now wishes to starve
the survivors" (*D*, 151). His journals about the Great Plains, the Sioux,
and the "Indian Question" chronicle even more tumultuous changes. In
the 22 May 1866 entry, for example, he thrills to his first sight of a vast
buffalo herd, but his entry for July 1874 reveals that he has written "the
President, many Senators, also General Terry on [the buffalo's extinc-
tion] but none have deigned to answer in a year's time" (*D*, 191). On 3
September 1874, he notes that a "family of bone pickers . . . drew nine
dollars a ton at the railhead for buffalo bones." He somberly adds, "The
bones in the fields block the coulters & moldboards of the steam plows.
The bones are used for combs, knife handles, the refining of sugar, and
ground for fertilizer. It is indeed a melancholy use for these grand beasts"
(*D*, 129).

In other 1874 journal entries, Northridge writes about meeting Crazy Horse, Sam Creekmouth, Captain William Ludlow, One Stab, George Bird Grinnell, and Lieutenant Colonel Custer, who stops "barely short" of calling Northridge a "meddler" (*D*, 193). His journals also chronicle other ominous events. The 7 March 1874 entry is about They Are Afraid of Her, Crazy Horse's daughter, who has whooping cough, a "disease" that Northridge says is "often survived by white children but almost never by the Sioux"; later he wonders if Crazy Horse will "make war again on us who brought this pestilence to his country" (*D*, 157, 158). On 29 May 1875, Northridge gives Aase Jensen, his betrothed, a "large Black Hills gold nugget"; the 1876 entries concern the massing of the Great Plains tribes and the battle of the Little Bighorn; the entries from August 29 through September 5 1877 detail the internment of the Sioux at Fort Robinson, their impending relocation, and Crazy Horse's death; and the 1889 and 1890 entries allude to Wovoka, the Ghost Dance, and the Wounded Knee massacre, which, at Black Elk's insistence, Northridge witnessed through his telescope.

Moreover, Northridge's journals record the political fiascoes and unconscionable greed that came into play in solving the Indian Question. He alludes to the numerous broken treaties between the U.S. government and the Indians, and he particularly abhors and detests Senator Charles Gates Dawes, the sponsor of the Dawes Act, also called the General Allotment Act, which stipulated that communal landholdings would be split and the Indians would be taught to farm, thus making individuals out of tribal people. Northridge writes on 23 March 1886, "Before the fire I feel an anger I have not felt in a sorry decade. I have written many articles, traveled to Washington & have bribed Congressmen & Senators only to be betrayed. In the fire I see I must murder Senator Dawes. I howl into the fire and begin to weep" (*D*, 305).

The culmination of Northridge's abortive attempts to champion the Native Americans' cause occurs at the Mohonk Conference on the Indian Question. In his journal for 17 July 1886, he writes that although at first he is cordially welcomed, the other participants shy away from him once they realize he is "utterly serious" about creating an "entire Indian Nation" in parts of the Dakotas, Montana, Wyoming, Colorado, Arizona, and New Mexico. "No matter that it is just," he writes, "this plan is viewed as madness by these folks who are said to be the conscience of our Nation, both religious and political. Dawes is not here and is said to be vacationing, perhaps from the rigors of chicanery" (*D*, 309). Even more absurd is that only he and two others out of the 80 participants have lived among the Indians, "an item," Northridge emphasizes, "that ascribes us no particular authority as we are said to be blinded by this contiguity" (*D*, 309).

"My downfall came on the afternoon of the third day": Northridge and his two colleagues are completely shunned—these two "take to drink out of despair"—and Northridge realizes that he will not be permitted to present his recommendations. When Mohawk and Iroquois dancers entertain the luncheon guests, Northridge refuses to "witness this humiliation" and walks off into the woods to pray, but he confesses, "My prayers . . . stuck in my craw and I returned for the afternoon guest address determined to seize the lectern" (*D*, 310). During the afternoon session, Reverend Gates, president of Amherst College, explains how Indians can benefit "from the use of property": "We have, to begin with, the absolute need of awakening in the savage Indian broader desires and ampler wants. In his dull savagery he must be touched by the wings of the divine angel of discontent. . . . Discontent with the 'teepee' and the starving rations of the Indian Camp in winter is needed to get the Indian out of the blanket and into trousers—and trousers with a pocket that aches to be filled with dollars!" (*D*, 310). Hearing this "blasphemy," Northridge runs to the lectern, shakes and hurls the "fool" into the audience, attempts to address the audience, but is restrained and arrested. After five days in jail, he is put aboard a westbound train and forbidden to return to New York. As he sadly notes, "I have failed thoroughly as John Brown with not a corpse to my credit" (*D*, 308).

Northridge's journals chronicle not only his marriages—first to Aase, who dies of tuberculosis, and next to Small Bird—but his abandonment of both organized religion and his white heritage. He writes zealously in 1865 that he will become a missionary and a botanist and help the Indians "make the inevitable transition from warriors to tillers of the soil, an occupation toward which I am advised they have no disposition" (*D*, 115). He "shall hide the preacher" in order to show these "captives of the void that befalls a conquered people" "how to feed themselves without buffalo"; for his own part, he will "walk north into summer" to "avoid the stink of trains" and the "freight of living and dead" (*D*, 115). These comments foreshadow what will happen to his faith in his religion and heritage.

His gradual loss of faith begins in 1866 when, having decided to spend the Sabbath reading his Bible, he notes that it "reads less well in the wilderness" (*D*, 70). Moreover, in 1871 he confesses that he does not "have a single apple or convert to show for myself in five years"; in 1874 he writes, "My thoughts have been troubled by a loss of faith & the doom of the Sioux brought about by the extermination of the buffalo"; and in 1886 he finally admits, "I have brought neither Christ nor agriculture to the Sioux who desire neither" (*D*, 179, 191, 305). Two other incidents mark Northridge's loss of faith. When he is hunting during a bitter Nebraska winter and becomes exhausted, he utters a Sioux prayer and kills an elk. Another time, He Dog tells Northridge how to rid himself of his Civil War nightmares, and Northridge writes, "I did as he advised in defiance of science & my religion and my nightmare was gone" (*D*, 179).

Also bruising his religious faith are the hypocrisies and lack of compassion he detects in men of the cloth. For example, his 20 May 1876 journal entry describes his meeting in Scotts Bluff with the "new Director of Missions," a "porcine Reverend from Cincinnati who cannot mount a horse and finds carriages not to his liking, so is never found more than a block from the railroad" (*D*, 184). During the "short half hour" conference, the director asks about the rumors that Northridge has "'gone over' to the Indians," because he has not yet built the "simplest church." When Northridge replies that he must first teach the Indians to grow food before presuming to build a church, and that the Indians are "anyway nomads & it would be difficult to locate a church," the director of missions says that the Sioux will be relocated and confined in the southern part of the Dakotas and that Northridge should worry about saving their souls because they are "dying of our diseases so quickly (including hunger)" (*D*, 184). Not only does the news about the confinement shock Northridge—"it is in defiance of all previous treaties"—but his disgust with the director of missions and with Christianity becomes apparent when the director reminds him that Northridge is the "last of the church in concourse with the worst of the Sioux" and that the "brethren all pray for [his] safety with little confidence. . . . I thank him for his prayers & make retreat to escape the heaviness of his talcum" (*D*, 184).

When self-serving politicians and army generals ignore him and self-righteous Christians misunderstand and rebuff his efforts to help the Indians—he writes in 1874 that the "Antichrist is Greed"—Northridge becomes a pariah and is "widely considered in the West to be a total lunatic" (*D*, 198, 312). The two events that finally turn him away from both his religion and heritage are the Mohonk Conference and the Wounded Knee massacre. After the conference—attended by the supposed keepers of the nation's religious and political conscience—Dalva

reports that her great-grandfather returned home, set up a "small fief-
dom supporting as many as fifty charges, including a miniature army of
a dozen headed by He Dog and Sam Creekmouth," and "literally"
became an Indian, "or a version thereof" (D, 311). In his 3 April 1890
journal entry, Northridge writes that he has begun to experiment with
peyote and even perform the Ghost Dance. After the Wounded Knee
massacre, during which the bullets sliced the Indian children "to rib-
bons," Northridge is arrested by the army "during his maddened efforts
to bandage back together what was left of the children" (D, 319).
General Miles orders his release, but Northridge is forbidden to return to
the Dakotas or to have anything more to do with the Sioux, an order he
willfully violates. He also hides "escaping chiefs and warriors including
Kicking Bear," as well as cherished Indian artifacts, from the government and collectors: "After Sitting Bull's death some businessman had
offered the army a thousand dollars for his body in order to display it for
profit" (D, 318). Ironically, in abnegating his Christian and white roots,
Northridge becomes revered by the Sioux. Dalva explains: "Despite his
sense of his own abysmal failure, the Sioux thought of Northridge as a
holy man in his many roles as one who fed them, who taught them to
grow things no matter that they despised it, and who had become a
capable if amateur doctor over the years" (D, 314).

Northridge's journal and story climax with the entry on 21 June
1891. During his missionary years among the Sioux, his path often
intersected with that of a former Cornell classmate whom Northridge
refuses to name, out of respect for the classmate's father, a prominent
Chicago businessman and Quaker who paid Northridge to serve in the
Civil War in place of his son. Even so, the son, whom Northridge
describes as "headstrong, impetuous, and a drinker," abandons home
and family, goes west, and eventually becomes an army lieutenant.
Northridge first meets his ex-classmate at Fort Robinson the day after
Crazy Horse is murdered. Arrogantly snide, the lieutenant not only
admits that he has no sympathy for Northridge's "efforts among the
Sioux whom he will continue to help destroy," but smiles as he offers
condolences about the deaths of Crazy Horse and Small Bird's mother.
Northridge writes that later in the evening he feels like a coward for not
shooting the lieutenant: "Before I sleep I find I cannot ask forgiveness
for this impulse so opposed as it is to my waning faith" (D, 209).
Moreover, Northridge's impulse to murder the lieutenant is whetted
even more when he learns that the man ordered Crazy Horse's legs to be
"broken in many places so he could be jammed into a small wooden cof-

fin" (*D*, 313). On 21 June 1891, the ex-classmate, now a lieutenant colonel, comes to Northridge's ranch, demands food and shelter, to which he is entitled by law, begins drinking, and turns mean and abusive. When he spitefully throws a child's doll into the fire, Northridge shoots the lieutenant colonel in the head, the sergeant in the heart, and the private, who runs to the door, twice in the back. Northridge drags the bodies under the basement and turns the army horses loose across the Niobara. An army search party later finds the horses in the possession of "two petty criminals who are summarily executed for the murder of the three men" (*D*, 320). As Dalva writes, "Except for twenty years of farming and planting trees the story of Northridge ended" (*D*, 320).

Technically, if Northridge's experiences with the director of missions and with the Mohonk Conference participants represent the dark side of religious greed and arrogance, then his experiences with the lieutenant represent the dark side of military power and arrogance. Regardless of whether they want to save the Indians' souls or to civilize them, each faction's solution to the Indian Question is ultimately to exterminate the Indians. In contrast, of course, is Northridge's solution to the Indian Question, which is ultimately more feasible, more humane, and more Christian in that he lives among them, learns their language, respects their traditions and religious beliefs, and above all, treats them as human beings.

Setting and Technique

Dalva's primary setting in northwest Nebraska is a place Harrison has visited and knows. He has gleaned resonant images from his Nebraska visits and drive-throughs—he told Julia Reed that "virtually everything of consequence in *Dalva* got done on solo driving trips" (Reed, 506)—and he has driven the routes mentioned in the book, such as Route 12, where the "rolling prairie stretched endlessly," or Route 20 outside of Chadron, which had been a "buffalo path" in the time of Crazy Horse, Sitting Bull, He Dog, and Little Big Man (*JBD*, 185, 181). Harrison has visited Fort Robinson and the Sturh Museum of the Prairie Pioneer in Grand Island, Nebraska, a museum, he says, that "will deeply satisfy anyone with an interest in how we used to live and, consequently, why we live the way we do now" (*JBD*, 177). With so deep a knowledge of the place, Harrison can vividly describe its landscapes, even down to the "windbreaks and shelterbreaks" (*JBD*, 177).

Somewhat like Strang's Upper Peninsula cabin, the Northridge land is idyllic, a haven to which Dalva returns to heal her personal world-hurts—as do, by extension, Naomi, Ruth, Dalva's son Nelse, and Michael. For that matter, like William and Tristan Ludlow in *Legends of the Fall* seeking solace from their Montana land, Northridge retreats to his land after 25 years as a missionary, especially after the Mohonk Conference and Wounded Knee. Whereas in Harrison's previous works the main characters usually act upon and thus create the landscapes, in *Dalva* the landscapes acquire depth because they are so suffused with the region's history and with the epic, tragic fates of the Native Americans, particularly the Sioux. In *Dalva*, therefore, not only are the characters' lives shaped, defined, and identified by the landscapes, but so, too, are the novel's conflicts and themes.

While Northridge's journals are chronicles of the Great Plains and the Sioux, they also record his personal history and the history of the Northridge family. Although initially written so that her son would know something about her, Dalva's journals are also her personal history, a history of the Northridge family, and an extension of Northridge's chronicles in providing additional information about her great-grandfather, grandfather, father and mother, her sister Ruth, and her son—four generations of Northridge history. Whereas Northridge's journals are from the past, Dalva's journals weave in and out of past and present. In the first section, present-time events are about the Sandoval incident, Michael obtaining his sabbatical and grant, Dalva initiating the search for her son, and her departure for Nebraska. In the present-time section of book 3, Dalva resolves the Michael-Karen indiscretions, decides to counsel bankrupt farm families, is attracted to Sam Creekmouth, talks with her son's foster mother, visits the Northridge subbasement, and finally is reunited with Nelse, her son, at the July family reunion picnic.

When Dalva's journals record the past, however, they reveal the painfully tragic details clouding both her past and present life. She recalls her father and grandfather, but her central focus is her ill-starred love for Duane Stone Horse, a story that begins: "Here is how it happened to me, how I had my child early in my sixteenth year" (*D*, 19). She begins with August 1956, when Duane arrives unexpectedly at her grandfather's farm. She recalls also when her grandfather gave Duane the buckskin horse; when Duane fights the football players who insult Dalva; when they first make love; and when he disappears—"That was the last time I saw Duane for fifteen years" (*D*, 31). Duane, who is not even aware that Dalva is pregnant, leaves her when he learns that she is his half-sister; only when he is dying from his Vietnam wounds, and right before he commits suicide, does he marry her so she will benefit from his GI disability benefits. Other past-time references are about Dalva's efforts to find Duane, her meeting Rachel, and giving birth to and then giving her baby for adoption. At the end of book 1, she recounts meeting Duane in Florida and his suicide in the Gulf Stream; she concludes: *"I was not well after that and Uncle Paul came from Arizona to get me. Months later . . . I buried an empty coffin like my father's in our cemetery in the middle of the lilac grove"* (D, 106–7).

Harrison has probed the female psyche and point of view through Sylvia (*A Good Day to Die*), Rosealee and Joseph's mother (*Farmer*), Diana (*Warlock*), and Laura (*The Man Who Gave up His Name*), and each work marks the progression in his ability to portray heroines. As critics and reviewers have noted, however, his consummate portrait is Dalva. While combining the hearth goddess virtues of Harrison's other heroines, she personifies his idea that women should have the same prerogatives as a man. Dalva emerges, therefore, as a stronger and more independent heroine. Her sense of freedom and independence begins when she receives a turquoise Ford convertible with a white top, a 17th birthday present from her grandfather. "What happened," Dalva writes, "is that this car equaled freedom to me, and naturally a longer-range freedom than that of walking or horseback. . . . Perhaps this is less true of women than men, but in my upbringing the differentiation wasn't emphasized" (D, 65).

Her independence is also evident in other plot details. She abandons formal religion when a righteous Methodist minister asks her to pray for God's forgiveness because she has had a baby out of wedlock. Her various jobs also reflect her independence: "I have always worked because nothing whatsoever in my background had prepared me to act like a rich person, a notorious nonprofession" (D, 249). Just as she never flaunts her affluence, she never flaunts her beauty—she says her attractiveness sets her "aside" and brings "notice when none was desired"— and so she refuses to become a cheerleader because she would rather take care of her horses. In her affairs, Dalva decides with whom she will bed, and when, and she is equally adept at dealing with macho posturings. When the son of the Northridge family doctor gives her a ride home from school and tries to rape her—he is a senior and she is only 13—she breaks one of his fingers, even though "he forced my face close to his penis which erupted all over me. I was so shocked I laughed. He held his broken finger and began crying for forgiveness" (D, 23). Dalva's disdain for machismo is evident in her repartee in "gutter Spanish" with a barrio teenage tough when she goes to talk with Franco's mother:

"Did you come to fuck me, beautiful gringo?"
"You have some growing to do, you miserable little goat turd."
"I am already big. Do you want to see?"
"I forgot my glasses. How could you be my lover when you spend
your days playing with yourself?" (*D*, 15)

    Dalva is filled with Harrison's trademarks—the lyrical prose, the landscapes, the layers of meaning—all of which recall his previous works. Ultimately, however, *Dalva* is one of Harrison's major achievements not because of his trademarks, but because of the epic proportions of the Northridge journals, and especially because of Dalva, one of Harrison's most dynamic, endearing feminine portraits.

Chapter Nine

"Always Worth a Look": *The Woman Lit by Fireflies*

Eleven years separate *Legends of the Fall* from *The Woman Lit by Fireflies*, another Harrison three-novella collection containing *Brown Dog*, *Sunset Limited*, and *The Woman Lit by Fireflies*. Michiko Kakutani observed that *Brown Dog* would be familiar to Harrison's readers since it features "another one of those macho men of the wilderness who are fond of solitude, alcohol and women (in more or less that order)." However, Kakutani liked *Brown Dog* because Harrison "conjures up life in the Michigan wilderness in strong, authoritative prose" and is "equally adept at satirizing the ecological-minded yuppies who arrive there intent on writing dissertations about Indian burial mounds and local story telling customs . . . [The incidents are] smoothly knit into the narrative, lending it both suspense and a heightened sense of legend." Terming *Sunset Limited* a "well-observed account of a 'Big Chill'-like reunion" that turns into a "moralistic fable about guilt and redemption, revolutionary zeal and liberal piety," Kakutani faulted the ending because Zip's rescue "is not only tricked up in the worst movie-of-the-week fashion, it is also delineated in such badly manipulative terms that the reader is never able to forget that Mr. Harrison is behind the scenes, pushing and pulling his characters hither and thither to illustrate his own thesis." Similarly, Kakutani did not admire *The Woman Lit by Fireflies* because of its contrivance: "Like *Dalva*, it attempts to give a portrait of a middle-age woman as she searches her past for clues to her identity. . . . In the end, Clare, like Mr. Harrison's other two protagonists, finds fulfillment and a measure of redemption in moving on to the next chapter of her life. The reader is ultimately less satisfied, finishing with decidedly mixed feelings."[1]

According to Joseph Coates, Harrison "writes the kind of bedrock Americana that Hemingway might have turned out if he had come home from the Great War, moved up to Michigan and stayed there, with occasional side trips to Key West, Idaho and other points west." Harrison's "poetic attentiveness to detail" and the "commonplaceness" of his life, emphasized Coates, give Harrison's work a "genuine mythopoeic quality that is rare, if not unique, among contemporary American writers." Coates called *Brown Dog* hilarious, described *Sunset Limited* as *The Big Chill* "played for keeps," and admired *The Woman Lit by Fireflies* for its poignancy; he believed that the meanings of all three tales reside in the metaphor of *Brown Dog*'s "sunken Indian"—"something painful, unfaceable is brought to the surface of a half-lived life, and recognition of it allows life to resume being lived as it should be."[2] While noting the humor in *Brown Dog*, as well as Harrison's skill in describing the Michigan landscape, John Baron found *Sunset Limited* a less successful narrative, "really just a higher-minded" *Big Chill*; however, Baron believed that *The Woman Lit by Fireflies* is a "tour de force" that proves "just how good" Harrison is in depicting women: "Cross-cutting between her 'survival' tactics in the field and scenes from her past life, Harrison brilliantly shows how Clare came to be the kind of woman who would flee from her husband."[3]

In a retrospective glance, Robert Houston wrote:

> A dozen years ago, Jim Harrison published a collection called *Legends of the Fall*, which may well be the best set of novellas to appear in this country during the last quarter-century. But if *The Woman Lit by Fireflies* . . . doesn't move at the break-neck speed of its predecessor, there's no cause for Harrison's fans to become alarmed. No writer who tries to extend his range, as good writers must, can allow himself to repeat effects only because they worked well the first time. *The Woman Lit by Fireflies* demonstrates, in fact, a powerful talent in search of its limits.

Houston noted the "hard narrative drive" that propels the action of *Sunset Limited*, somewhat as it does the stories in *Legends of the Fall*, but found that the not "terribly credible action-movie ending" mars the story: one of the characters is "blown apart by an AK-47" but dies smiling—"Actors, one imagines, are much more likely to die smiling than real people who are torn to shreds by assault rifles." Houston claims that *The Woman Lit by Fireflies* not only proves that Harrison can "handle a woman's point of view," but also rejects the "inane argument that a writer must stick on with his or her own sex, race, religion and so on."[4]

In a similar vein, Judith Freeman said that Harrison's works have always demonstrated great narrative strength, a "compelling sense of movement and beautifully eclectic euridation, ribaldry and humor." Freeman also noted that "something else has graced the work, a tender, almost androgynous understanding of the human condition, which allows him to write convincingly in either male or female voice, widening even further the range of his work." Although she found *Sunset Limited* the least successful of the three narratives, Freeman praised the collection for its distinctive voices—*Brown Dog* for its male voice, *The Woman Lit by Fireflies* for its female voice, and *Sunset Limited* for its mixture of voices. Freeman concluded by affirming that each story in *The Woman Lit by Fireflies* is so engrossing that one cannot stop after reading the first sentence: Harrison "creates appealingly vulnerable characters who inhabit palpably real worlds. His passion for food and wine, his affection for animals, connect us to the sensual. These three accomplished novellas are remarkably different. What they have in common is Harrison's greatest strength, a rich and nourishing sense of pleasure."[5]

In another retrospective glance, Arthur Krystal wrote that *Warlock*, *Sundog*, and *Dalva* are "in certain respects successful and in certain respects flawed" and lack the "clarity, sureness of phrase and cumulative power of the novellas" in *Legends of the Fall*. Continuing, Krystal noted that although *The Woman Lit by Fireflies* is different from *Legends of the Fall*, each collection has the "enviable quality of gaining in depth as the novellas proceed." Krystal faulted *Brown Dog* for the "triteness of B.D.'s persona" as well as the "predictability of his relations with women." *Sunset Limited* is a "slightly more believable, though slicker, tale," and in *The Woman Lit by Fireflies*, Harrison "adroitly manages to get inside a woman's mind—no small feat for the burly, rough-looking guy on the dust jacket." Krystal concluded: "However one feels about Harrison's evolution as a writer, he is always worth a look. . . . Like Thomas McGuane, Barry Hannah and Richard Ford, whose work is alike only in the dissimilarity to the slick fiction by and about urban professionals, Harrison has a narrative voice that fairly defies the reader to ignore it."[6]

"A Kind of American That Never Gets into Fiction": *Brown Dog*

According to Harrison, "There's a kind of American that never gets into fiction that I try to get in. It's people like Brown Dog. . . . There's a literary prevalence that *poor* means depressed and miserable. Well, not always, let's face it" ("Lake"). Harrison said that many of the people who live in Michigan's Upper Peninsula are unique and interesting because they "know things"—how to do their own plumbing and wiring, how to repair automobiles and engines. Because of his roots and experiences, Brown Dog also hunts, fishes, cooks, cuts wood, and knows about deep-sea diving and engines. At the same time, his life is neither depressing

nor miserable. He is a woodsman who lives close to the land and is probably one of Harrison's more resilient and self-reliant protagonists. His
crisis begins with a dead Indian.

"JUST BEFORE DARK at the bottom of the sea I found the Indian . . .
sitting there on the ledge of rock in about seventy feet of water" are the
words with which B.D. (a.k.a. Brown Dog, the Anishinabe name that
David Four Feet's mother gave him) opens his first-person narrative.[7] His
narrative is, in fact, the therapy that Shelley Newkirk, his inamorata and
a University of Michigan graduate anthropology student, has prescribed
so he can understand his past life and actions. "The main reason she is
helping me write this," B.D. reports, "is so I can stop lying to myself and
others, which from my way of thinking will cut the interesting heart right
out of my life" (*BD*, 4). Rather than reflecting a life gone seriously awry,
B.D.'s journal reveals a life thrown off balance, first as a result of finding
the murdered Indian in Lake Superior, and second because of Shelley's
pseudo-psychological attempts to cajole him into disclosing a burial
mound site and to make his life conform to the modern world's standards, both of which attempts will metaphorically cut the "interesting
heart" out of his life.

The novella opens in mid-October as B.D. recalls the events that cul-
minated in his arrest and Shelley's appointment, to quote him, as his
"legal guardian and semi-probation officer" (*BD*, 3). In June, B.D., a
diver for the Grand Marias Salvage Corporation—a "fancy name for a
scavenging operation," he admits—found the chief in Lake Superior,
which is "so cold near the bottom that drowned bodies never make it to
the surface" since they never "rot and bloat like in other fresh water"
(*BD*, 3). When he and Bob, an ex-navy SEAL and his diving partner, try
to sell the chief's body to Avakian, a Chicago nautical artifacts dealer, for
$20,000, they are arrested, but not before some very comical scenes
occur. In his journal, B.D. records other unsettling events—for instance,
meeting Shelley two years before in a bar, which he says is a "downfall of
sorts." Shelley and her cousin Tarah had attempted to wheedle out of
him the location of a Chippewa burial mound that he has promised Old
Claude, a 77-year-old Chippewa, not to reveal.

At 42, B.D.'s midlife crisis results from finding the chief and from
Shelley and Tarah's conspiring attempts to find the burial grounds. He
often speaks of feeling out of balance; for instance, he says that Shelley's
"potty mouth" is incongruous for "such a high class girl. . . . I never ran
into this before in a woman and it threw me off balance" (*BD*, 44).
Learning that Shelley wants to lure him to Marquette so that her two

male colleagues can search for the Chippewa mounds, B.D. remarks, "I'm not talking about feeling betrayed because I saw that coming, but the idea that far too much had been happening in the past four months for me to get my balance back" (*BD*, 48). Similarly, after Tarah pinches his penis, he writes, "After I thought it over later I can't say I didn't enjoy myself though I never got my balance back after Tarah's pinch." Later, when he sees Shelley and Tarah in bed nude, he says again, "The world was moving too fast and I had to get my balance back"; it is "time to take stock" (*BD*, 62, 65, 66). In a wry twist, however, his journal-writing therapy enables him to "take stock" and reclaim his balance.

Although finding the chief's body definitely upsets the balance in B.D.'s life, it, too, will help restore his balance. In the "crime of the century" (not much has happened there since the state "closed down the nut house" [*BD*, 47]), B.D. steals an ice truck in Newberry to transport the chief's body to Chicago. After wrapping the 300-pound chief in a gill net and towing him to Little Lake, B.D. puts the body in the ice truck and ties it to an easy chair to keep the chief from "sliding around in an undignified way." B.D. notices the chief's driver's license, which identifies him as Ted Sleeping Bear, and while tying the chief in the chair, he also finds what he thinks may be a bullet hole in the chief's head. As B.D. and Bob drive toward Chicago, the hot air and the truck's bad exhaust nauseate B.D., and he decides to ride in the back with the chief's body. After admitting that he is not afraid of the body, B.D. adds: "To be truthful, while riding back there in the cold dark I got to thinking he might be my dad. Of course I was half drunk and sick, also afraid of being caught, so my mind was a bit crazy. This is what the court called 'delusional.' There was nothing to say the Chief wasn't my dad. . . . Of course Shelley has pointed out just about any man near sixty years or older could be my dad" (*BD*, 52). When Bob is arrested in a very comical scene, B.D. drives off into the woods, or "deep into bug hell," as he phrases it. When too many mosquitoes begin to plague him, he gets in the back again and dozes on the arm of the easy chair; whether he dreams it or not, B.D. says the chief talks to him:

> *B.D., my son, you haven't exactly panned out but then you didn't start with much. To whom the Lord gives much, much is expected so you are not on the hot seat in regards to gifts. . . . Your greed got you into this. Beware of women with forked tongues. . . . Don't rely on alcohol so much for good times. . . . Remember when you were so good at square dancing in the seventh grade? . . . Well, don't come tromping into the Halls of Death, but live your life with light feet. Before I forget, bury me in the forest where I belong, not with the fish. (BD, 56)*

The chief also sings some beautiful nursery rhymes, an act that strikes B.D. as probably "what fathers do for sons who are hurt or grieving" (*BD*, 56). Significantly, however, B.D. admits that he feels "pretty strong" after his talk with the chief and resolves to bury the chief in the forest and then surrender to the police. A half-mile past the burial mounds, B.D. digs a well pit-sized grave and, before burying the chief, puts his arm around him, listens to the whippoorwills and coyotes, says, "Goodbye, Dad," almost cries, and then buries him.

Ironically, the chief's advice is insightful: B.D.'s life has indeed not been all that bad to date, and so he is not in the "hot seat in regards to gifts." Shelley and Tarah are the ones with "forked tongues" in that they are conspiring to trick B.D. into revealing the burial mound site. One of B.D.'s realizations, in fact, is that Shelley and Tarah are probably using sex so that Shelley can become a famous anthropologist by discovering the early Hopewell site and writing about her find. Nevertheless, B.D.'s greed causes the body-selling fiasco, and it is his lust for Shelley (another form of greed) that initially prompts him to show her the site, or as he admits, "That was a downfall of sorts as I took her out to the burial mounds to impress her in order to screw her" (*BD*, 44). Greed also motivates the interest Shelley and her two colleagues have in the site, even though they claim to admire, respect, and love Native Americans. Finally, the chief's advice about living with "light feet" is exactly what B.D. has been trying to do and what he does do once he gets his balance back.

In contrast to the chief's assessment that B.D.'s life is only slightly awry, Shelley's pseudo-psychological, pseudo-psychiatric analyses—what B.D. calls her "probings"—sound ominous. His journals, however, record only normal rites of passage. For instance, he and David Four Feet sell illegal fireworks; another time B.D., David, and David's brothers jacklight a deer, and a game warden pursues them up a two-track dead end and simply waits until they come out. "Shelley didn't think this was too funny," says B.D., "as it betrayed an early start in the life of 'petty' crime" (*BD*, 70). When a spiteful deputy sheriff kills Sam, B.D.'s cantankerous, chicken-stealing bear hound, B.D. burns down the deputy's chicken coop after letting the chickens escape. He admits, "I hoped it would make me feel better but it didn't. You can't compare a chicken coop to a dog" (*BD*, 21). A more telling rite of passage occurs when B.D.'s grandfather gives him a heavy punching bag for his 15th Christmas. B.D. works out diligently and begins winning bare-knuckle fights in his area. At 19, however, his career ends when he beats a huge, beered-up pulp cutter by repeatedly punching him in the lower stomach and then the throat. When the man's five-year-old son hugs his father and then hits B.D. over and over on the legs with a stick, B.D. says, "I never knew my own father but if I had I sure wouldn't want to see him get beat up. The whole thing was awful. I never fought again except on the rare occasions when I was attacked by surprise in a bar" (*BD*, 22).

The truth is that, like Harrison's other comic heroes, B.D. means well but his good intentions are often waylaid. Still, despite the trouble he finds himself in, he is neither petty nor mean; as he says, "I never intentionally hurt anyone" (*BD*, 71). His code is to enjoy life's beauty and gifts daily, never to hurt anyone intentionally, and above all, to not "Doggett"—a term he and his grandfather developed in reference to Lester Doggett, a second cousin from Peshtigo, Wisconsin, who, because his grandparents died in the "great Peshtigo fire" 70 years before, would always "piss and moan about the likelihood of a forest fire" (*BD*, 25). "'Don't Doggett' was what Grandpa said to me when I whined, complained or expressed any self-pity. It still means to stand up and take your medicine, though it doesn't mean you can't get even" (*BD*, 25). His "Don't Doggett" code is not only what prompts him to surrender to the police after burying the chief but is also the basis of his redemption: "Don't Doggett, I thought. . . . Take your medicine and reform yourself, however that is done" (*BD*, 71).

Because he does not whine or wallow in self-pity, B.D. is very resilient. For example, during one of her probings, Shelley berates him with, "You think each day is a fresh new start, which it isn't" (*BD*, 75). Actually, for B.D. each day is exactly that. For instance, when he sees Shelley and Tarah in bed nude, he decides to make love to them, thinking, "Let bygones be bygones. A bad night had passed and now it was a new day, also it was hard to think of anything more purely beautiful than those two bottoms" (*BD*, 67). Indeed, B.D.'s whole life is pleasure-filled:

> When Shelley probes me she can't get over what she calls my "prefer-ences" and "life choices." For instance, my favorite thing is just plain walking in the woods. I can do it days on end without getting tired of it. I mix this up a bit with fishing and hunting. Of course I like to make love and drink. That goes without saying. Before I started diving for Bob I sometimes had to cut pulp which is hard work. When I cut pulp my favorite moments were drinking cold water, making my dinner, then falling asleep because I was bone tired. (*BD*, 48–49)

In other words, B.D.'s life is simple but fulfilling: "I never felt I did all that badly at life, at least for up here. I'd say half the men I know are worse off one way or another, either from drink or jail or because a tree fell on them while cutting pulp" (*BD*, 16).

The novella's positive ending underscores B.D.'s optimism and resiliency. As part of her probings, as well as of her efforts to end the relationship, Shelley and B.D. visit Escanaba and Bark River, where B.D. was raised. Shelley says the trip will "complete the circle," but B.D. remarks that "it started what I hoped was a new part of my life" (*BD*, 69). Since his favorite fishing stream has silted up because the road has been widened, David Four Feet's house has burned down, and David himself has been killed in Jackson Prison, it seems at first that B.D. may not be able to go home again. However, when he and Shelley get to his old homestead, David's mother, sister Rose, and Rose's son Red and daughter Berry are living there. Still attracted to Rose, his childhood love, B.D. asks her if he can visit later; she replies, "Suit yourself," as she pinches his ass. "Later at the hotel," B.D. admits, "I checked out the red spot and it made me feel good" (*BD*, 74).

Although the purpose of the trip is ostensibly to complete the circle and end their relationship, Shelley's real purpose is to bribe B.D.—"The upshot was that either I told her where my burial mounds were or I was facing three to five years in the prison down in Jackson for the crime of arson, added on to the other stuff" (*BD*, 75). When she offers him $1,000, he agrees to take it because he is "suddenly . . . tired of the whole damn thing" (*BD*, 75). B.D.'s optimism is evident the next morning when he begins "memorizing" Shelley's body: "another one that fine was not likely to pass [his] way again" (*BD*, 80). He sadly notes: "I said I never cried but I think I was getting close by the time I got the job done. . . . Also I remembered how the Chief told me to keep my feet light. Luckily other emotions took over and by the time she fully awoke she was making yodeling sounds like Judy Canova on the *Louisiana Hayride* program" (*BD*, 81).

Two other concluding incidents highlight *Brown Dog*'s positive ending. As Shelley drives away and leaves him standing in the Sunday morning snow with his toothbrush in his pocket and an envelope with the $1,000 in his hand, B.D. thinks about hitchhiking to Marquette to get his van, musing, "Worse things have happened" (*BD*, 82). When he hires a taxi to take him to Marquette and the old driver asks him if he is the one who fought the pulp cutter in "Iron Mountain twenty-five years ago," B.D. thinks, "It wasn't the biggest thing on earth but it made me feel life was holding together somehow" (*BD*, 83). On the way out of Escanaba, B.D. decides to buy some chickens and take them to Rose and her mother, who may just cook Sunday dinner while he and Red ride to Marquette to pick up his van. B.D. ends his journal with: "And that's what I did. A pinch and a 'suit yourself' wasn't much to go on but it didn't hurt to try" (*BD*, 83). Still traveling on "light feet," still feeling that life is "holding together somehow," the redoubtable B.D. is off again on a new day's adventure; more important, he has regained his sense of balance despite the incursion of the anthropologists and yuppies on his life and world, and despite Shelley's "probings" into his past.

Yuppiedom and Satire in *Brown Dog*   In *Dalva*, some of the humor resides in Harrison's oblique satire about yuppies, as evident in Michael's clothes, BMW, alcohol/drug binges, his daughter's private school education, and even in Karen Olafson's aspirations. In *Brown Dog*, not only is yuppiedom more fully satirized, but the satire complements the plot's comedy.

Shelley's two male anthropologist colleagues, whom B.D. names Jerk and Jerkoff, wear $100 tennis shoes, and Shelley and Tarah dress in yuppie vogue, from their Patagonia clothes to their "great big hiking boots." Shelley's expensive Land Rover, with its calfskin seats and "big tires"— "In the U.P. it's the car that doesn't get stuck that gets the admiration," muses B.D.—is another yuppie status symbol, as are Shelley's and Tarah's cocaine toots; according to B.D., they have been "tired and sad from their problems so they bought a bunch" (*BD*, 61). In fact, a very comical scene occurs at a fashionable dinner party hosted by Dr. and Mrs. Fred. Before, during, and after dinner, everyone, B.D. reports, keeps "glugging drinks and disappearing into the bathroom for reasons I guessed President Bush wouldn't approve of" (*BD*, 63). B.D. does not like cocaine because when he tried it, "I got real excitable but my weenie wouldn't stand up so I got drunk. The idea of paying a hundred bucks for a half-master is beyond me" (*BD*, 61).

In Tarah's characterization, Harrison satirizes yuppie "empowerment" ceremonies and vision quests.[8] B.D. learns, for example, that Tarah is not her real name but rather a name she was given at an empowerment ceremony in Taos, New Mexico. In one comical scene, Tarah holds her own empowerment ceremony for Shelley and B.D., which includes making some tea from "secret Indian herbs" ("I can't say I felt anything different from the tea," B.D. says, "but I had high hopes, sobriety being a tough row to hoe"); spreading a velvet cloth and placing a crystal in the middle of it (B.D. calls it a rock); and then in a soft, whispery voice, saying, "You are more than you think you are" (B.D. thinks, "I didn't exactly

take to this as good news because what I already was had gotten my ass
in enough of a sling") (*BD*, 25–26). When Tarah begins speaking in
what B.D. terms a "bunch of what sounded like nonsense symbols," he
candidly admits, "I wasn't concentrating too well as Tarah was sitting
cross-legged like an Oriental and you could see up her crotch past her
shorts to where we all come from" (*BD*, 26). The ceremony's purpose is
to get B.D. to reveal the location of the burial site. When he lies about
becoming a huge condor feeding off a dead buffalo (an image he remembers from Chicago's Field Museum), she says, "That's truly wonderful,
B.D. It means your spirit wishes to soar far above your current problems.
Your spirit wishes to use your condor being and blood to help you. In
order to do this you must not deny the proud heritage of your people.
You must let us help you rediscover your heritage" (*BD*, 27).

The satire continues when B.D. takes Tarah on a zigzag course to the
burial mounds. As she lies on the mound, she mistakes a lost baby bear's
cries for an Indian spirit and becomes hysterical. B.D.'s "therapy" is to
strip off her clothes, bite her on the leg "to get her attention," throw her
headfirst into the river, and shake the "living shit out of her" while
screaming, "In the name of the sacred coyote, get the fuck out of here,
demons. . . . I used coyote because I couldn't think of anything else at
the moment but raccoons and woodchucks and they didn't seem right"
(*BD*, 34–35). The comical aftermath occurs after their lovemaking,
which he justifies with: "Then she grabbed hold of me so legally speaking it was more her fault than mine, not that I was exactly a victim
though this girl was as strong as any" (*BD*, 35). Later, when Shelley
accuses him of tricking Tarah by throwing his voice and making love to
her, both of which acts cause Tarah's "nervous breakdown" since she has
never gotten an "out-loud response from the spirit world before," B.D.
replies: "I said I couldn't throw my voice like Edgar Bergen did to
Charlie McCarthy and Mortimer Snerd, but she had never heard of these
people, which shows the difference in generations," so "I had to
stonewall it by saying Tarah was 'delusional' just like they'd said about
me at the trial" (*BD*, 60–61).

Just as Michael's pretensions cause his comic downfall in *Dalva*,
Tarah's "empowerment" pretensions cause hers. She erroneously believes
that the Taos empowerment ceremony made her one with herself and one
with nature, yet she cannot identify the sound of a bawling bear cub, nor
has she ever received an "out-loud" response from the spirit world.
Conversely, B.D. knows animals and their sounds and, more important,
knows that communication, if any, from the spirit world is likely to be

either dreamlike, as when the chief talks to him, or emotional, as when he and Tarah arrive at the mounds and he notices that the "light was too clear, the clearest I had seen, and the area was full of ravens whirling and croaking." Somehow he knows better than to lie face down on one of the burial mounds: "I don't have an ounce of superstition in me but . . . I wasn't going near the mounds this time" (*BD*, 34).

Another yuppie satirized in *Brown Dog* is Brad, Tarah's paramour and a health food and triathlon devotee. B.D. recounts, for instance, how Brad arrives and immediately unloads a "thick-tired bicycle" that cost $1,000; goofily dressed in shiny stretch shorts, an odd-shaped helmet, goggles, and special shoes, he rides off at "top speed" down the dirt road while "farting like a bucking horse" (*BD*, 25). On returning from his 30-mile bike ride, Brad swims out to Lonesome Point and back, a distance of three miles, even though the temperature is in the lower forties. B.D. is also astounded by the amount of food Brad can eat: for his all-day ride, Brad's lunch consists of 12 apples, a bag of carrots, a head of cabbage, and a jar of honey. His all-day ride, however, results in his comic pratfall. As he rides around a bend on a deer path, he crashes into the Golden Age Dirt Trackers—senior citizens who ride three- and four-wheel ATVs—and suffers a spiral leg fracture when he flies through the air and almost crushes an old man. Like Tarah, Brad is out in but never one with nature, as evidenced when he returns from his 30-mile ride to the Hurricane River and B.D. asks him if he saw the moose that hangs around the Hurricane. "I see nothing but the road," Brad replies (*BD*, 28).

Also satirized are Shelley's "probings" to help B.D. discover and confront his past and thus become one with himself. Although he claims that Shelley is a "fine young woman" who saves him, B.D.'s more candid remarks underscore the satire. He says that her methods for "digging up the past" come not from her "university training" but from her "troubled youth" (*BD*, 9). Because her Uncle Nick made her play with "his weenie on camping trips," and because her father, a Detroit gynecologist, is "overfamiliar with women" and thus acts "remote and impersonal to Shelley," she has gone to psychiatrists, therapists, and psychologists. According to B.D., Shelley has been "probed from eight to eighteen at who knows what costs," and so not only is she "at one with herself and the world," but she can adjust his brain as well with "high horsepower energy" (*BD*, 9, 10). While Shelley's probings are just as chic as Tarah's empowerment ceremonies, B.D.'s insights heighten the humor in the satire. Regarding the once dysfunctional but now functional relationship between Shelley and her father, B.D. remarks, "They're in fine shape now. He gave her a new 4WD made in England when she got her master's degree. I'd call that a top drawer relationship for a father and a daughter on a certain level" (*BD*, 9). Sometimes during Shelley's probings, B.D. confesses, "her voice gives me a boner but I'm out of luck because this business does not allow a quick time out, sad to say, for fucking" (*BD*, 10).

In short, being "probed from eight to eighteen" does not make Shelley an authority on therapy, psychology, or psychiatry, and therefore her professional questions, her ideas about "honest confrontations" with the past, and her analyses of B.D.'s past actions (for example, that his episode with Beatrice and the church money "established a pattern of failure as a self-fulfilling prophecy") are metaphorically, like Tarah's empowerment chants, "nonsense symbols" to B.D., especially in light of her real motive—to become a famous anthropologist. Indeed, during their argument in a hotel dining room, he angrily retorts to her comment about his thinking each day is a new start, "I don't get why you and your friends are always doing run-downs on people. You're always taking people apart in pieces, especially me" (*BD*, 75). Ironically, both B.D.'s "Don't Doggett" philosophy and his grandfather's witticisms are far more practical and reliable than Shelley's probings or Tarah's empowerment ceremonies. Furthermore, B.D.'s life, though hardscrabble, is more satisfying than theirs: "I never owned a house but my van is free and clear, though it's a '78 Dodge and could use some work. I rent deer cabins real cheap to keep a roof over my head. . . . Sometimes I live rent free if I do some improvements" (*BD*, 16).

Brown Dog, B.D., and Comedy

Like Johnny Lundgren's comic exploits in *Warlock*, B.D.'s exploits often end in rollicking humor, as when he transports the chief's body and faces "meltage," or when he attends Dr. Fred's chic dinner party. One extended comic piece is about B.D.'s stint, on scholarship, at Chicago's Moody Bible Institute, where he must deal with the world, the flesh, and Satan. He becomes obsessed with Beatrice, a part black, part Italian, "bubble-butted" waitress at a diner where he eats breakfast and "spring[s] a hard-on just watching Beatrice wipe off a table" (*BD*, 11). Because of his spartan food budget, all he can order is a 30¢ bowl of oatmeal. "I have always had a weakness for catsup," he says, "but it didn't go too well with oatmeal. I tried it once and it wasn't a popular move at the diner. For days afterward other customers would look at me and shake their heads" (*BD*, 11).

As he sits in his room in the "Christian rooming house (no smoking or drinking)" and lusts for Beatrice, the comedy escalates. So as not to "exhaust" himself with "unclean thoughts," he opens a letter that he thinks is just another support letter from his home congregation; instead, it is a check for $390 that the church treasurer has sent to him instead of directly to the institute. "The possibilities hit like lightning so I dropped to my knees and prayed for strength which did not arrive" (*BD*, 11). Off to the diner he goes, sits in Beatrice's section, orders the T-bone steak special, and flashes his wad of bills. Beatrice, who earlier called him a "snot-nosed little Bible thumper," smiles. "I had become handsome between breakfast and dinner," B.D. concludes (*BD*, 11).

After making a date with Beatrice, B.D. returns to his room, where the comical battle between heaven and hell rages anew: "There was a sense in my small room that I was wrestling with Satan and I somehow knew I was going to lose to His power. . . . I prayed and almost wept and even gnashed my teeth" (*BD*, 12). He tries to complete a term paper about Nicodemus but confesses that the "bubble-butt of Beatrice seemed to arise from the page and smack my nose. . . . Forbidden bubble-butt fruit is what I was dealing with. Years later when President Carter spoke of lust in his heart I sure as hell knew what he was talking about" (*BD*, 12). Off to Beatrice's apartment he goes: "We started slow but soon enough we were on the fast track, me to perdition, and for her, business as usual" (*BD*, 13). After five days in "Beatrice's school of love," B.D. is out of money; Beatrice, whose "professional standards" permit no "freebies," serves him a single meatball (she is cooking spaghetti for her boyfriend) and shows him the door. Although B.D. is locked out of his room for back rent and ends up bumming in the park, he is resiliently philosophical: "It is hard for me to admit that I didn't turn her head one little bit. But still, a wise man would do well to go looking for a woman who's half black and half Italian. There's no point in searching the U.P. because the population is too scant for such a combination" (*BD*, 15).

Those "Who Drive These People Crazy": More on Satire and the Native American Theme In "Poetry as Survival," Harrison obliquely describes himself as a "shy observer" when visiting Indian reservations, not wanting to be "confused with anthropologists and spiritual shoppers who drive these people crazy" (*JBD*, 298). While Tarah personifies the "spiritual shoppers" ("I want to commune with these people, not dig them up," she says), Shelley typifies those anthropologists who not only drive Native Americans crazy with probings and questions but violate burial mounds by destroying them in order to study them.

That Shelley is certainly no "shy observer" is apparent when she, Jerk, and Jerkoff enter the Dunes Saloon and she immediately intrudes on the conversation between B.D. and Old Claude, a Chippewa herbalist in his midseventies whom Shelley wants to interview. When Claude announces that it is his birthday, she blathers about "how wonderful" that is, asks how old he is, and without waiting for an answer informs him they have driven 350 miles to see him. Claude stares at the three anthropologists for a full minute and then bolts out the door. "You missed your cue," B.D. explains, "When Claude says it's his birthday you're supposed to ask if you can buy him a drink" (BD, 5). Undaunted, Shelley then decides to talk with B.D.; "unconsciously using her breasts to lead," she asks, "Are you related? I mean are you an Indian?" (BD, 5). Shelley blunders because she is unaware of the Native American custom of offering gifts—in this case, the birthday drink—and having polite conversation before asking questions.

In B.D.'s conflict with Shelley, Jerk, and Jerkoff, the satire becomes more evident. Jerkoff "walks around being sincere about everything" and even gives B.D. a book of poetry—perhaps to further Shelley's cause—but B.D. says the book is written by a "fruitcake Arab by the name of Gibran that I couldn't understand, so I gave it to a tourist girl and it made her horny as a toad" (BD, 47). B.D. discovers Shelley surrounded by a pile of books for her research into the question of how Indians preserve herbs to use in the winter; he suggests, probably with greater accuracy than will be reflected in her paper: "They hung them out to dry after they picked them" (BD, 29). Shelley insists, despite his repeated denials, that B.D. is part Chippewa, basing her argument on two facts: he is ashamed of his roots, and he refuses to talk about them. B.D. wryly concludes: "I've been tempted a few times but then was worried about being caught out. After all, all these [anthropologists] know more about Indians than any Indian I ever met, except what it is like to be one. I never saw David Four Feet's family having all that much fun" (BD, 28).

Although B.D. may be a rogue in some respects, he does attempt to protect the burial mounds after promising Claude that he would—"My word is not too reliable in most matters but this one is important" (BD, 20). His promise, of course, results in the comical incident with Tarah and his sabotage of Jerk and Jerkoff's campsite when he burns their tent, with their expensive camping equipment and field notes inside, flattens their Toyota's tires, and traces on the dusty side of the vehicle a skull that he says looks "more like a schmoo" (*BD*, 54). He later admits that he did not enjoy torching their camp since "mine was the original sin of taking Shelley out there in the first place in my pussy trance" (*BD*, 54). Although neither Tarah nor Shelley learns anything from their interest in and study of Native Americans, B.D. learns much from Claude and the chief, whom he honors by burying him in the forest where he belongs. Finally, whereas B.D. transcends his initial greed in attempting to sell the chief to Avakian, Shelley does not transcend her greedy desire to become a famous anthropologist.

In *Dalva*, Northridge's journals chronicle the greed as well as political and religious hypocrisy that inevitably destroy Native American culture and life. In *Brown Dog*, B.D.'s journals record the insensitivity and greed of contemporary anthropologists who destroy artifacts and burial mounds. Moreover, just as the U.S. government condoned the atrocities Northridge recorded, Shelley's lawyer and a state police detective condone her actions. In *Dalva*, the Native American theme is rendered in tragic proportions; in *Brown Dog*, this theme is given a lighter, though still serious, touch.

"What Would the Rest of the Gang Do?": *Sunset Limited*

The seminal idea for *Sunset Limited* began when Harrison wondered what Russell Chatham, Tom McGuane, Guy de la Valdene, and he himself would do if one of them got into trouble in South America. Russell Chatham, for example, is "liable to get into trouble really because he leads with his chin," and "I can think of three who would do anything to get him out—myself, Guy, and Tom." As an afterthought, Harrison includes Bob Datilla, since he "knows things," an obvious reference to Datilla's Sicilian ancestry ("Lake"). Out of these real-life suppositions Harrison imaginatively spins an exciting story in *Sunset Limited*.

The tale is about the Wild Bunch—or the Pacifist Wild Bunch, as they call themselves—five radicals who met at the University of Colorado. Gwen Simpson, Theodore Frazer (a.k.a. Zip), Billy Creighton, Patty, and Sam, galvanized by the fiery Zip, trashed a local draft board in 1968 by pouring glue and cow's blood into the files, were arrested, served their sentences, and then pursued different lifestyles. After unhappily marrying a university mathematician, Gwen Simpson, at 41, has retreated with her adopted daughter Sun to the family ranch in Arizona between Mule Junction and Guthrie. At 42, Billy Creighton is an affluent international lawyer for his family firm, Creighton & Creighton, with offices in Los Angeles, Hong Kong, London, Paris, Bonn, São Paulo, and Buenos Aires. Patty is a vice president at a movie studio and has risen to prominence by saving movie moguls "from the mistakes the imperial purple is heir to" and turning down box-office flops like *Heaven's Gate*, *Ishtar*, and *Rhinestone*. A former Green Beret medic in Vietnam, Sam is medically discharged after he tries to "duct-tape back together some children who had been blown to pieces" (*SL*, 131), an image that recalls Northridge's attempts to bandage Indian children after the Wounded Knee massacre. After earning a master's degree in game biology at the University of Oregon, Sam studies grizzlies, runs afoul of the Department of Interior about using phencyclidine on the bears, and eventually receives a grant to study coyotes in northern New Mexico. Zip is still a radical; he has tried to organize workers in Cuba, Panama, Costa Rica, Guatemala, and Mexico, and the "right wings of a half-dozen countries" wish to assassinate him even though he is, to quote Mathias Arndt-Guerrez, the Mexican consulate, an "old-style Don Quixote radical." The plot's suspense and conflict begin when Zip is arrested in Mexico and faces a 50-year sentence, during which he may be killed.

Judith Freeman wrote that *Sunset Limited* "started out as a treatment for a screen play," a possible explanation for why "it feels slightly staged and why its characters seem to act out roles" (Freeman, 1).[9] In fact, one such staged scene in *Sunset Limited*, somewhat reminiscent of John Sturges's *The Magnificent Seven* (1960) or Sam Peckinpah's *The Wild Bunch* (1969), is the introduction and gathering of the old Wild Bunch before they leave for Mexico. Then Lawrence Kasdan's *The Big Chill* (1980) is recalled when the Bunch assemble at Gwen's ranch, renew friendships, reminisce about the past, and celebrate with a dinner that vacillates between "giddiness, melancholy, silence, laughter," while Sun plays 1960s music like B.B. King, the Allman Brothers, an Otis Redding-Carla Thomas duet, Janis Joplin's "Get It While You Can," and Grace Slick's "White Rabbit" (*SL*, 141). Other staged scenes include the Bunch's first meeting with Zip; the meeting between Billy, Gwen, and Virgil Atkins, a CIA operative who says, "I'm here to see your scumbag friend get put away for life" (*SL*, 150); and finally, the big escape scene when the Federales captain and the American agent plan to blow Gwen's Cessna out of the sky with two AK-47s. Even the narrative reads like stage directions: "Billy, Gwen and Patty rush to help Sam push the Cessna out of the pole barn," or, "Then Billy runs out and gets one shot off before the AK-47 blows him along the ground" (*SL*, 173, 174).

Throughout these scenes, the characters act predictably. Gwen is as stalwart and understanding as she was when she helped Patty endure their time in prison and when she slept with the policeman, at Zip's request, to learn why they were caught vandalizing the draft board (Sarah, Billy's girlfriend, overheard their plans and told Billy's father). Patty, the "weak sister" in prison, initially abandons the others—because it is "too late in life for her to go back to prison because of a 'fucking lunatic'"—but returns the next morning on the pretext that she "couldn't leave until she at least said goodbye to Zip" (*SL*, 148, 151). Sam is the wily, tough ex-Green Beret who likes the "way things are getting less vague in favor of something down and dirty" (*SL*, 155). Predictably, too, Billy not only rebels against his domineering father—who admires Billy's courage and even offers his help—but redeems himself (he is partially responsible for their being caught trashing the draft board) in the closing scene when he sacrifices himself so the others can escape. Although Zip is an "old-style Don Quixote radical" and has become, says the Mexican lawyer, a "harmless nitwit who was being pursued because certain as yet unknown authorities had nothing better to do at the moment," he still prefers to be assassinated for a cause (*SL*, 146). Finally, even the minor characters act out their roles. Billy's daughter, Rebecca, and Sun admire the Wild Bunch, and Virgil Atkins, the Federales captain, and a shadowy American operative are consummate villains.

"The Primacy of Friendship": The Theme   *Sunset Limited* is suspenseful, indicating Harrison's skill at spinning a taut tale, but as usual this Harrison plot goes deeper than the surface suspense. In an authorial intrusion that begins chapter 7, Harrison writes, "It's time to pause a moment at the beginning of the last and longest chapter of our fable." After referring to Milton's *Paradise Lost*, the Catholic Church's "position paper" on the Holocaust, and the Sonoran ranchero song about "Two horses, two friends, and two guns," Harrison then observes, "It's all part of the old school of 'nobody gets out of here alive,' the reflection, whether in mirror, lake or coffee cup, most often vanishing in seconds, that something is terribly wrong" (*SL*, 136–37). He concludes:

> To give up, to abandon Ted Frazer, a.k.a. Zip, finally would be to abandon their own pasts, to say that the vibrancy of the time they spent together, no matter that it ended badly, meant nothing, or meant an insufficient amount to divert the courses of their lives for a few days.

> Within the mythology of our culture back to the early explorers, the
> mountain men, the Indian fighters, the cowboys, through a half-dozen
> wars, the notion of the primacy of friendship runs like a national spinal
> column. The fact that it was more talked about than adhered to does not
> make it less a motivation. Most often, no one threw themselves on that
> live grenade to save their friend. (*SL*, 137)

These comments provide certain clues for interpreting *Sunset Limited* as
more than the thriller suggested by the staged sequences and characters.

If fables record the exploits of legendary persons, then *Sunset Limited*
is no fable since, however notorious their exploits, the Pacifist Wild
Bunch is no collection of living legends. They are not even very wild,
since they only did what thousands of other hippies and radicals did in
the 1960s—read radical literature and authors, grooved at Grateful
Dead concerts, smoked marijuana and dropped Dexedrine spansules,
and protested at antiwar demonstrations. Even their most aggressive
action, vandalizing the draft board, is not very notable 20 years later. If,
however, a fable emphasizes a cautionary or edifying point, then *Sunset
Limited* is certainly such a tale with its theme about the primacy of
friendship. Not only does friendship bring them together at the
University of Colorado and sustain them all during their zany times in
the sixties, but friendship reunites them 20 years later when Zip is in
trouble. As the stalwart, understanding one, Gwen contacts the others
because, during Zip's stay at her ranch, she realized that after 20 years
he had become a "fatigued gadfly rather than a revolutionary," that he
was "ignored and avoided by his fellow revolutionaries," and that he had
"nothing meaningful on his record" in over ten years (*SL*, 138). He is no
longer the firebrand radical full of "zip," but rather someone who is not
important, who is *zip, zero, zilch, nothing*. He is also simply a friend in
trouble. When Gwen first talks with Billy and he hesitates, Gwen
reminds him, "This isn't a cause but a friend. . . . I'm not sure when a
friend stops being a friend, are you?" (*SL*, 107). Similarly, when Patty
does not want to be involved because she suspects Billy is responsible for
their draft board arrest, Gwen responds, "This isn't about you or Billy or
me but about a man who's going to be killed. We both used to love him,
didn't we?" (*SL*, 116).

The author's comment that "nobody gets out of here alive" (*here*
being life and the world) and "something is terribly wrong" underscores
life's brevity and the world's injustices and evils. In counteracting the
"something" that is "terribly wrong," the Wild Bunch's friendship tran-

scends the local and international machinations, Virgil Atkins's personal vendetta against Zip, and the Bunch's own petty differences, since to abandon Zip is to "abandon their own pasts" (*SL*, 137). They may indeed be out of their depth and not know what they are doing, but at least they are reaffirming their friendship and thus refuting the idea that friendship is "more often talked about than adhered to." And Billy's death is the ultimate reaffirmation: "Most often, no one threw themselves on [a] live grenade to save their friends" (*SL*, 137).

"All Those Tricky Things": *The Woman Lit by Fireflies*

Harrison's explanation of the scene in *The Woman Lit by Fireflies* in which the fireflies whirl about Clare's head in the thicket was revealing: "I've seen it before, an intensity of fireflies with their lights. . . . I do all of these tricky things that are largely unnoticed. Like my first novellas were written in suites almost like the poetry formula—three sections of 33 pages with a page of epigraph and stuff like that" ("Lake"). The idea for *The Woman Lit by Fireflies* came when Harrison and Dan Gerber stopped at a rest stop, and Harrison began thinking, what if a woman climbed the rest-stop fence and walked off into a cornfield ("Lake"). The novel is about Clare, Harrison's 50-year-old protagonist who literally walks away from her husband Donald and their 30-year marriage by climbing a fence at an Iowa Welcome Center on Interstate 80 and spending the night in a cornfield. During the night, Clare has an imaginary conversation with her daughter Laurel, recalls incidents from her past life, and finally decides to break free of her stultifying marriage and to reestablish purpose and meaning in her life. The plot's suspense and conflict are heightened not only by Clare's assessment of her life and the incidents that brought her to the night in the Iowa cornfield and her epiphany, but also by all those "tricky things" Harrison uses to tell Clare's story and to capture the female psyche.

Like Harrison's other protagonists, Clare experiences a midlife crisis when she finally realizes that her marriage is no longer happy or fulfilling, a realization she had had seven years before but failed to act upon. Her smoldering crisis is suggested when Clare tells Laurel goodbye that day and Laurel says, "I love you, Mom, but I can't understand why you don't leave that asshole" (*WLF*, 178). If Dalva must let go of the past to experience the next order of fulfillment, then Clare must let go of the present, that present being anchored in her eroding marriage.

The narrative power arises from Harrison's analyses of how a marriage can sour. Toward the end, Clare recalls their early happiness. Although an assistant office manager, Donald still wore lumberjack shirts in the evenings and on weekends. They still associated with their politically active friends from Michigan State, enjoyed eating at inexpensive Greek, Chinese, Polish, and Italian restaurants, and saw the "wonderful movies of those times: all of Bergman, Fellini and the early Antonioni" (*WLF*, 219). They also marched with other civil rights protesters, shook hands with Martin Luther King Jr., who told Donald to "keep up the good work, brother," and commiserated when Kennedy was assassinated in Dallas. Clare was attracted to Donald because he was her "act of rebellion, a left-wing political science major who wore lumberjack shirts, the only son in a working-class family from Flint, who intended to be a writer or labor leader. On dates they read John Dos Passos's *U.S.A.* trilogy to each other" (*WLF*, 183).

Clare recalls the evening when she and Donald invited all of their friends over for dinner and to listen to blues and jazz on their new stereo in celebration of their imminent move into the Bloomfield Hills home that Clare's mother had bought and redecorated; she muses that "perhaps that evening had been the beginning of the end" (*WLF*, 220). Clare was embarrassed when her mother sent over a "little something from the club"—a "huge prime rib, a Smithfield ham, side dishes including six dozen oysters, a mixed case of French wine and two cases of imported beer" (*WLF*, 220). Although their friends ate, drank, danced, and laughed—"without a single negative comment"—the next morning she and Donald had "the first serious argument of their marriage" about one of James Baldwin's novels and a newspaper profile about Malcolm X. When they moved into their new home, Clare noted, "things were never the same again, nor were meant to be," because although he "jokes about work Donald had become a well-concealed predator, a skilled manipulator, something he had learned as a political activist" (*WLF*, 220).

In his essays and other works, a Harrison motif is that greed is killing the life-soul of the country; Donald's obsession with money and affluence smothers the life-soul of his marriage. Clare recalls when Donald Jr. was born and Donald, wearing his "first tailored" suit, arrived late at the hospital and gloated about being elected a member of the Detroit Athletic Club: "[Clare] remembered looking closely at Donald, a long pause where she waited patiently for him to mention the birth of his son" (*WLF*, 221). She remembers another incident that may have been the "beginning of the end"; it occurred five years before the present time, when Donald Jr. graduated from the University of Michigan. Clare and Zilpha, her best friend and confidante, had planned to join a Detroit Institute of Arts tour of the museums of Moscow and Leningrad. Zilpha's visa arrived promptly, but Clare's did not—because Donald had "jinxed the visa with a phone call to a friend in the State Department, the sort of favor that is due a major Republican fund raiser like Donald" (*WLF*, 199). When she confronted him, Donald affected a "minor breakdown, saying he couldn't have borne up under the strain of his beloved wife's visiting the 'evil empire'" (*WLF*, 199). "Untypically, Clare thought of shooting him while he slept" (*WLF*, 199).

As *The Woman Lit by Fireflies* opens, Donald has evolved into a business-obsessed executive who is totally oblivious to Clare and her needs, an idea underscored in the Harrisonesque image-evoking opening sentence: "She had not yet accepted as real the quiver in her stomach and the slight green dot of pain in the middle of her head that signaled the incipient migraine" (*WLF*, 177). As Clare endures the pain, which will be the catalyst that sends her over the rest-stop fence—"I knew the pain was coming and I lost my good sense," she tells Laurel—Donald plays *Tracking the Blues*, a tape described as the "witless drone of a weekly financial lecture"; he has played it three times to get "'fair value' for his money" (*WLF*, 177). So money-oriented is Donald that when he buys Clare a copy of Faulkner's *A Green Bough* for Christmas, he tells a friend that the book of poems cost him "an arm and a leg," and when he buys her cases of either Chambertin or Meursault, he jokes out loud, "Here goes three shares of General Motors," to which the old store clerk smiles "his mask of a smile knowing it was Clare's money in the first place" (*WLF*, 199, 181–82). During a European vacation, Clare has to listen to his "incessant business prattle"; when they are in the nave of Notre Dame, he wants her to remind him to "make a call"—"as if he ever forgot," she thinks to herself. At the Uffizi, he keeps repeating, "I wonder what that would bring at Parke-Bernet" (*WLF*, 214). As they travel toward the rest stop where Donald will make his daily call to his broker, Clare suddenly realizes "that Donald didn't feel really good about making money unless others were losing theirs, which made it all, to her mind, a silly game to spend your life on rather than the grave process with which he was totally obsessed" (*WLF*, 179). When they meet at a Des Moines Best Western after her night in the cornfield, Clare notes the day's *Wall Street Journal* and a "notepad covered with numbers" and concludes, "He was the same Donald" (*WLF*, 246).

While Donald's obsession with business and money smothers the life-soul of his marriage, he is neither vicious nor villainous, simply myopic in that he thinks all about him is fine, especially his marriage. Clare even recognizes his good qualities and asks, "But how could you blame Donald for so fulsomely taking on the colors of the workaday world?" (*WLF*, 215). Later, when thinking about their first house, she regrets "her mother's gift of a house so soon after they were married. Money tended to derange people when it arrived so abruptly, and the house wasn't, ultimately, fair to Donald" (*WLF*, 223). Typically, when they meet at the Best Western in Des Moines, Donald says, "I can't say I didn't see this coming, but I'd hoped we'd carry on," to which she replies, "I don't have anything left to carry on" (*WLF*, 246). That Donald still does not comprehend what has happened is evident when he says, "[Laurel] said you were tired of the life you were living and wanted to do something else. Is it as simple as that?" Clare responds that it is indeed "as simple as that" (*WLF*, 246). Ultimately and ironically, Donald is unaware that he has "disfigured himself beyond recognition and [bears] no resemblance to the man she in innocence had been proud to love" (*WLF*, 237).

"My Husband Has Been Abusing Me": Clare's Revolt Before climbing the rest-stop fence and walking off into the cornfield, Clare leaves a note in the women's bathroom: "I am in a small red car driving east. My husband has been abusing me. Do not believe anything he says. Call my daughter" (*WLF*, 184). Although Donald has never physically abused Clare, he has unwittingly been emotionally abusing her with his obsession about making money. Not only are his jokes about General Motor shares and his comment about the cost of the Faulkner book emotionally abusive, but so are his actions in the novella's opening section. When he replays *Tracking the Blues*, for example, he cuts off Stravinsky's *Histoire du Soldat*, which Clare has always enjoyed. With the onslaught of another migraine, Clare realizes that instead of driving she should be "sitting with her eyes closed listening to music . . . but she drove to avoid reading to him, which is what he required when he drove" (*WLF*, 177–78). "What he required" is definitely given more importance than what she prefers or needs. During her imaginary conversation with Laurel—who says that Clare is the "center" of Donald's life, "with making money a close second"—Clare rightly observes, "I'm the center like a prized possession. Remember when I wouldn't go to any more fund raisers after I was introduced as a 'prominent Republican wife,' with no name attached. It seemed to stand for something quite out of focus" (*WLF*, 202–3).

During another part of her imaginary conversation with Laurel, Clare explains why she has not left Donald before: "I had my friends, my books, dogs, garden, my children" (*WLF*, 202). More important, however, she has been drifting through life: "Of the seven women who had been in her tennis group (the A class) a decade ago, four had been divorced in the past few years and none of them were doing very well, but then it was so easy to be smug about her own passivity, the way she let the years float gently by, relying on Zilpha's natural ebullience, two long walks a day with Sammy [her female Labrador], hours of reading and cooking, the latter more for herself than for Donald who ate everything she cooked him with equal gusto" (*WLF*, 204). Significantly, she loses two mainstays within two weeks when both Zilpha and Sammy die—Zilpha from lung cancer, Sammy from fibroid cancer. That these deaths are part of the catalyst for her revolt is evident when she tells Laurel, "Strangely, I couldn't have done this if they had still been with me. It was a pleasure to give so much to them because I loved them. They were gone and I had to do something" (*WLF*, 203). When Laurel reminds her that she can still return to the rest stop, Clare responds, "No thanks, dear," an indication that she intends to break from the present and move to the next order of fulfillment. Ironically, however, she knows that her acquaintances and neighbors in Bloomfield Hills will misinterpret her revolt and "were bound to prate 'nervous breakdown' or 'depression' during countless phone calls and lunches. . . . The probable cause in her case would be obvious to all—the deaths of Zilpha and Sammy—but her marriage which was considered to be improbably solid, would not be questioned" (*WLF*, 217).

Among the novella's clues that Clare has decided to free herself from her suffocating marriage is her profanity, which at first is as untypical as her thought about shooting Donald while he slept. After she slides down the muddy bank into the Guernsey, "an inadvertent baptism by immersion," she returns to her campsite, decides that she is flexible whereas Donald is not, and then recalls that Zilpha often swore and Laurel swears constantly. In contrast, although she has never learned how, she whispers, "Fuck you, Donald, you jerkoff, but the oath was froth" (*WLF*, 207). Later when she walks until she becomes sleepy, she again thinks of Donald and their neighborhood and swears more adamantly, "*Oh, fuck Donald. . . . I am here because he isn't*" (*WLF*, 225). When she returns after her walk, she feels a "lightness in her body" because "she did not give a flat fuck if she ever saw her brother or Donald again. It was as simple as that. She repeated the phrase 'flat fuck' with an avowed intent to take up swearing as a pressure valve" (*WLF*, 231).

Another symbol of her revolt is her tan beret, which she first bought "thirty years before on Rue St. Jacques and had never worn" (*WLF*, 183). As she thinks about leaving Donald, she takes the beret out of her bag, puts it on, and laughs "softly to herself. It was so easy" (*WLF*, 183). Once she walks about 100 yards into the cornfield, she feels so silly in the beret that she takes it off, but significantly, "the moment the hat came off the [migraine] pain became so excruciating she fell to her hands and knees and retched up her lunch of iced tea and a club sandwich" (*WLF*, 184). By suggestion, the beret is a talisman that gives her courage and confidence, but once she removes it she becomes retchingly ill, an idea later confirmed when she empties her purse and arranges her "compass, address book, the beret, the empty juice can . . . and the passport . . . like talismans" (*WLF*, 196). During the night, she puts her "beret on tight for extra comfort" (*WLF*, 216). As *The Woman Lit by Fireflies* closes, Clare has left Donald and gone to Paris. Although feeling a "little lost," she decides that "she felt less lost than before her night in the thicket, and when the afternoon cooled she would write letters to Dr. Roth and Laurel. If it rained, she would wear the beret to dinner" (*WLF*, 247).

Like Harrison's other works, *The Woman Lit by Fireflies* ends cautiously yet affirmatively in that Clare admits she is a "little lost"; she realizes now what Camus meant by "'terrible freedom,' that once you decided not to commit suicide, whether physically or figuratively, you assumed the responsibility of freedom" (*WLF*, 235). Indeed, Clare's marriage is and will be a figurative suicide if she continues to "let the years float gently by." Two incidents underscore not only her marriage's malaise but also the "terrible freedom" she faces if she leaves Donald. In the first, she recalls the health spa near Tecate in northern Sonora; after Zilpha acutely observes that "we're all the same here," Clare admits it is true:

> Other than a dozen men there were nearly ninety women, between the ages of forty and sixty, but a concentration around fifty. More than age, the women seemed to be fighting a malaise of fatigue and dissociation, of free-floating anxiety so deeply ingrained as to be invisible to the bearer. The regiment of a vegetarian diet and relentless exercise in a lovely setting far from home, the source of the gray-area angst, worked quite well, and within two days spirits were lifted. It was a break, not a cure, a shifting into a pleasant neutral where the body's exhaustion supplanted the brain's dreary machinations. (*WLF*, 234)

While *malaise, dissociation*, and *neutral* typify her eroded marriage, *anxiety* and *gray-area angst* typify, and may very well cause, her migraine headaches with their green dots of pain.

In the second incident, Clare watches a possum play dead in the corn-field and draws "certain parallels . . . if you played dead long enough the act of coming back to life was questionable" (*WLF*, 204). In the denoue-ment, instead of drifting through a soured marriage as one of Donald's "prized possessions," and instead of visiting health spas for a "break, not a cure," Clare chooses the "terrible freedom" of divorce (that is, the ques-tionable "act of coming back to life") and thus redeems herself. She may still be a "little lost," but she is not as "lost as before" her soul-awaken-ing night in the cornfield.

Some "Tricky Things" and Clare's Journeys

As Clare climbs the rest-stop fence, Harrison writes: "She wobbled and the wire cut into the soles of her tennis shoes. On the other side . . . she hurried off down between two corn rows, toward the interior, wherever that may be" (*WLF*, 184). "Toward the interior" recalls Marlow's voyage in *Heart of Darkness*, and one of Harrison's "tricky things" is to make Clare's journey a separation, initiation, and return. She will literally travel into the corn-field's interior, but at the same time she will metaphorically journey into her own psyche in order to assess her life and reestablish some purpose and meaning.

Clare's literal separation occurs when she climbs the fence that will separate her from the world (the traffic on Interstate 80) and from Donald and her marriage. She further separates herself from the world when she hears a police siren, imagines Donald "explaining himself to the police," and then moves deeper into the cornfield, while "her flayed brain began to play the rest of the Stravinsky Donald had truncated" with his *Tracking the Blues* tape (*WLF*, 185). Her separation from life's daily routines occurs when she trips, sprawls in the dirt, looks at her dirty hands, and realizes that "for the first time in her life she did not know where her next shower was coming from" (*WLF*, 186). For that matter, she must also wonder about finding food, water, and shelter for the night.

That Clare will journey metaphorically into her psyche is evident in her imaginary "phantom" conversations with Laurel. Rather than talking with Zilpha, who might "further loosen" Clare's "tenuous grip" on reali-ty, or with Donald Jr., a "more cynical version of his father," Clare choos-es Laurel because she was "matter-of-fact even in the cradle" and because, as Clare says, "Laurel, you little bitch, this is partly your idea. What do I do now?" (*WLF*, 222, 194). At the same time, Laurel has backpacked a great deal, loves hiking and animals, does not think

money is the be-all and end-all, and has even sent Clare a book about
camping. If in *Sundog* Strang and the narrator are two sides of the same
brain, then Laurel represents the practical side of Clare's brain. One of
her tasks is coaching Clare about surviving the night. "For Christ's sake,
Mother," Laurel says, "you're going to have to toughen up. You said you
read that book on camping I sent. You're going to have to get some
water in your system to avoid hypothermia. . . . It's important that you
crawl into that thicket to stay dry" (*WLF*, 195). Laurel also tells Clare
about rolling ears of corn in clay and laying them close to the fire to
cook. In short, if Clare cannot adjust physically to her new environment,
then she may not be able to break away from her marriage. As she tells
Laurel: "I'm sitting here in the dirt and I don't know what to do. Like
most people I'm only prepared for the life I've already lived, none of
which included this sort of thing" (*WLF*, 194–95). That she will adjust
to the cornfield and to her new "terrible freedom" is evident when she
rejects Laurel's reminder that she can always go back to the rest stop.

Underscoring Clare's redemption are two religious allusions: her
immersion in the muddy creek, and the fireflies that whirl about her.
Her accidental plunge into the Guernsey is an "inadvertent baptism by
immersion"; she resurfaces laughing, but more important, "the world
that had been so narrowed by her physical and mental anguish became
quite suddenly larger" (*WLF*, 200). Clare's baptism figuratively washes
away her physical anguish—the migraine that has physically dominated
her—as well as her mental anguish—her sense of guilt about leaving
Donald. After walking herself sleepy, she returns to the thicket; as she
drifts off to sleep, her body is "sweet, warm, deadened, giving itself up to
the bed of leaves and grass, the green odor transmitting a sense she
belonged to the earth as much as any living thing. *I don't need to change.
I'm just this*" (*WLF*, 237). When a rabbit startles her awake, she sees the
fireflies whirling about her and the thicket: "The countless thousands of
fireflies stayed just outside and within and above the thicket and she felt
blessed without thinking whether she deserved it" (*WLF*, 239).

Harrison explained the baptism and the fireflies: "Consciously I put
that in when she slides into that muddy creek. It's sort of a baptism . . .
and then the fireflies and the epiphany. You know those old myths keep
coming out because that's true of human experiences. There's nothing
created about breaking down and putting yourself back together. That's
her time in the wilderness" ("Lake"). Both the immersion and the fireflies
conclude her initiation and its attendant insight into existence; afterwards Clare moves on to the next order of fulfillment: "It was pleasant

to know she had no idea what she was going to do other than wear a beret in Paris on at least a single walk, she hoped on a rainy afternoon. Barring small children most women in her neighborhood in broken marriages ran afoul of sheer idleness. Clare knew she was bright enough to make herself useful somewhere" (*WLF*, 241–42). After this epiphany, Clare falls into a "pure, deep dreamless sleep" and awakens at dawn to "more birds than she ever heard at one time. It was as if she were *within* the birds. . . . She heard whippoorwills, mourning doves, the resurgence of the red-winged blackbirds from the marsh beyond the creek" (*WLF*, 243). She returns from her journey by walking east toward the farmhouse and the world she left, and also toward the rising "burnished orange sun," while thinking that "in the future any place she lived would have to have a clear view of the east" (*WLF*, 243).

After her descent into the Northridge subbasement, Dalva experiences "one of those great sleeps" after which "everything you look at is lucid and sharp-edged" (*D*, 321). Similarly, after her descent into her own haunting psyche, Clare's "pure, deep, dreamless sleep" presages her rebirth into a new self-image and a new world. The literal night in the wilderness and the figurative night in the mazes of her psyche (for instance, as she moves among the corn rows she wonders whether "maize" and "maze" are connected) give way to light images, as symbolized in the birdsongs and the rising sun. Finally, her continued rejection of old life is evident when she hugs Donald goodbye in the motel room and sees "herself hugging him in the wall mirror, with a wave of claustrophobia sweeping through her body" (*WLF*, 246).

The novellas in *The Woman Lit by Fireflies* equal Harrison's achievement in *Legends of the Fall*. Just as each story in *Legends of the Fall* is different in tone and purpose, so, too, is each story in *The Woman Lit by Fireflies*: *Brown Dog* in its guffaw-humor, *Sunset Limited* in its suspense, and *The Woman Lit by Fireflies* in its poignant insights into the female psyche. One of Harrison's "tricky things" is to spin a tale from a "what if": What happens when a character finds the body of an Indian chief at the bottom of Lake Superior? What happens when a good friend is in grave trouble in Mexico? What happens when a woman climbs a rest-stop fence to escape a dead-end marriage? Therein lies true narrative skill and power—as well as the basis for understanding *Julip*, Harrison's next collection of three novellas.

Chapter Ten

"No Reason to See Life as Tragic":
Julip

In praising *Julip*—another collection of three novellas, *Julip*, *The Seven-Ounce Man*, and *The Beige Dolorosa*—David Lyons asserted that Harrison "once again proves himself to be an astute observer of the world at large as he casts a wry and well-calibrated eyeball at relationships between younger women and older men, political correctness in academia, and life at the bottom of the human food chain." Lyons believed that the plot of *Julip*, the title story, is a "vehicle" to probe "victimization, consensual sibling incest, and other psychobaubles of our dysfunctional society, with subtle detours into more serious matters such as dog training, sport fishing, and casual sex"; nevertheless, Lyons thought that Harrison was "at his best when commenting on the sexual quadrangle between Julip and her aging lovers." Lyons found that the title of *The Beige Dolorosa*, "freighted with reference to Christ's journey between Pilate's court and Golgotha, fits Caulkins [the protagonist] snugly," and that, in switching from a present to a past time frame, Harrison subtly "exposes the ludicrous charges university professors must often face in these trying times, including sexism . . . anti-Semitism . . . [and] a trumped-up rape charge by a Generation X co-ed." Lyons concluded: "If the pendulum of social sensibility were at another point in its swing, *Julip* would be a candidate for the bestseller list. Like a frat boy gone wild at a dairy farm, Harrison tips over nearly every sacred cow in sight, making that a most unlikely possibility."[1]

Werner Trieschmann said that the title story is a "tragic/farcical account" of Julip's experiences as she attempts to get her brother out of jail; that Brown Dog, the hero of *The Seven-Ounce Man*, "would easily fit into the pages of a Charles Portis novel"; and that while it may recall the movie *City Slickers*, "with a desolate, defamed English professor replacing Billy Crystal's burned-out urban dweller," *The Beige Dolorosa* concerns a "much larger issue: essentially how one who is completely lost rediscovers and renames the world." In all three novellas, Trieschmann wrote, "at every turn Harrison stretches for a meaning or moment that seemingly lies beyond his grasp. He finds the mark almost every time."[2]

In David Dawson's eyes, Harrison uses a pen to reveal the "grander realities beneath the surface of life's unremittingly mundane events, helping to free us from 'the average messes' that we seem to create for ourselves." Dawson claimed that in *Julip* Harrison "proves himself to be a mature, visionary writer whose tales are guaranteed to elicit profound reactions." He described *The Seven-Ounce Man* as "more of a character study than the other stories," thus lacking the "emotional punch of Harrison's other tales," but found that Julip's methods of saving her brother Bobby "betray a graceful cynicism that is a joy to behold." Dawson's highest praise was for *The Beige Dolorosa*, which is "one of the most profoundly moving tales of personal redemption that I have encountered. Taken with the two other stories, it reveals a powerful, challenging source of refreshing deep waters."[3]

In "The Macho Chronicles," her review of *Julip*, Jonis Agee said that all of the novellas work because of Harrison's "voice, expressed via a curiously old-fashioned, ironic yet earnest narrator who acts as a kind of moral and ethical guide through the shorthand of the sharp cinematic moments of the plots." Agee also believed that Harrison, who often depicts "individuals facing the uncertainty of the future with sheer will in a natural setting," may have been "saddled by the critics with Hemingway's ghost"; *Julip* "recasts such myths of male initiation and redemption" as Harrison exorcises Hemingway's ghost to become a "genuinely comic writer." Agee concludes: "The puniness of our lives, which Hemingway could only accept by creating yet another myth, is really, in Mr. Harrison's view, an opportunity for making do, for creating out of nothing something that is authentic and individual. As his characters discover, there's no reason to see life as tragic."[4]

"It's Always Been a Mystery": *Julip*

In our interview, Harrison told me that he once said to Russell Chatham and Guy de la Valdene, "What do some of these young girls really think about us?" He laughingly added, "Here's these lumbering guys in their late forties, and it's amusing to look at human sexuality in the sense of a sexually active girl because it's always been a mystery. [William] Styron came close to it, but it was too morose with Peyton Loftis in *Lie Down in Darkness* . . . but [Julip] isn't suicidal; she's just looking at it. . . . She observes all these things. It's sort of written in the Japanese style—the third person, just her observations" ("Lake").

Although *Julip* probes the female psyche and female sexuality, the narrative has neither the emotional range nor the tone of either *Dalva* or *The Woman Lit by Fireflies*; it takes a lighter approach to female sexuality, despite the ominous overtones of its opening sentence: "Julip got her name, a mixture of a flower and a drink, by her parents' design in the first flower of a somewhat alcoholic marriage."[5] The novella's opening section sketches her parents' marriage and subsequent life. Her father was a dog trainer and breeder, and her mother was from an affluent Ashland, Wisconsin, family; their marriage "was, and still is, considered to have been a bad marriage for Julip's mother." Ironically, the glut of shopping malls caused her mother's family business to crumble, even as Julip's parents were pictured on the society pages of Milwaukee and Chicago newspapers. Julip's father, an alcoholic, supposedly committed suicide in Minnesota, or as her mother told her, "He did himself in." Julip's mother cooked for rich clients at a quail plantation and neglected her husband and two children, Julip and Bobby. "Margaret was totally without talent or instinct for motherhood due to a panoply of neuroses that would never be unraveled, but was a genius in the kitchen" (*J*, 4).

Julip had "a schizophrenic upbringing, and if it were not for an interested teacher in each place she would not have been saved" (*J*, 5). Also ominous is the transitional sentence into the novella's central plot: "But to the degree Julip was saved Bobby was shattered, both by the reality of their situation and by an imagination so errant it boggled the clinical psychologist after the shooting" (*J*, 5). In defending his family's and sister's honor, Bobby shoots Julip's three middle-aged lovers, who he believes have defiled his sister; he is sentenced to seven to ten years at Florida's Raiford State Prison. While the "bad marriage," the father's alcoholism, the mother's lack of wifely and maternal interest, and even the brother's shooting of the three lovers may recall the Compson family in *The Sound and the Fury*, *Julip* is relentlessly comic in that Julip gains insights into the world around her. "In her quest to understand the truth about the death of her father, about the shootings that her brother is jailed for, about her own fall into the world of love and loss, Julip takes on comic and often truly heroic stature" (Agee, 41).

"An Old Fashioned Moral Tale"   Despite its opening portents, *Julip* becomes comic once 21-year-old Julip Durham, also a dog breeder and trainer, decides to have her brother Bobby transferred from Raiford

State Prison to a mental hospital where, after evaluation and counseling, he will be released in a year or less. To accomplish Bobby's transfer, Julip seduces Sam Hinkley in Starke, Florida, and convinces him to reopen the case. Next, not only must she convince Bobby to plead insanity—a strategy he rejected during the first trial, much to the dismay of his lawyer and the trial judge—but she must also persuade Charles, Arthur, and Ted, the shooting victims (whom she calls "the Boys"), to agree to Bobby's transfer.

Julip's "midlife" crisis results from Bobby's plight, which forces her to deal with two unresolved issues in her life: her father's apparent suicide, and her affairs with the Boys. Julip tells Dr. Wiseman, Bobby's clinical psychologist, "It's been nearly two years, and every day I think about my dad committing suicide" (*J*, 29). She explains that her father had fled the alcohol rehabilitation center and was accidentally killed when drunken teenagers drove over him while he was in his sleeping bag at a picnic area in Fergus Fall, Minnesota; his blood-alcohol content was .05. Wiseman (his name is symbolic) subsequently pinpoints the cause of Julip's mental turmoil: "This all should make you feel better. . . . What I mean is, it's very difficult for a young woman to get over her father's death. And it's very important for you to give up any idea that you could have saved him" (*J*, 29–30). She feels a cathartic "*tonic* of rising anger [emphasis added]" against Bobby for not telling her the truth about her father's death, then screams "'Motherfucker!' a dozen times," an utterance that "at least was different from her ordinary sadness over her family" (*J*, 30). Once back at her motel, Julip finally resolves her inner turmoil over her father's death when she learns that he had become a "traffic fatality" (*J*).

The next part of her quest is to have Bobby transferred. When Julip calls her mother to ask whether she and Mr. Stearne, her parents' employer and later her mother's lover, will pay for Bobby's mental rehabilitation, Julip learns other facts about her father's death. Her mother denies having said he "did himself in" and explains that she committed him to an alcohol rehabilitation center because "Mr. Stearne couldn't keep him unless he dried out. He pitched over on the dinner table in front of the governor. It was easier on you not to be there" (*J*, 36). Not only does their conversation begin to heal the rift between them, but afterwards Julip falls into a "deep, unbelievably sweet sleep" during which she has a "lovely dream": "Her piglet the Labrador had eaten, had become half piglet and half the bear that died under the porch, wonderfully alive in a blueberry marsh in Wisconsin. When she looked at the animal closely its eyes were her father's. What good luck, she thought" (*J*, 37). Like Dalva's "great" sleep with "rich and varied dreams" (*D*, 321) and Clare's "pure, deep dreamless sleep" (*WLF*, 243), Julip's sleep symbolizes her acceptance of her father's death and her readiness for the next stage in self-discovery.

Julip is about female sexuality, and part of Julip's self-discovery depends on her experiences with love and loss. Unlike her cousin Marcia, who admits she is "stupid and aimless" and "must have fucked a hundred morons," Julip has made love to only six men (she does not count Sam Hinckley): Johnny, her high school "first love"; Frank, her kennel worker (Julip tells Marcia that they made love "when he broke his foot, to make him feel better"); a county agent ("I seduced him"); and the Boys (although "they didn't know about each other until after the trial," Julip tells Mildred Wiseman) (*J*, 49, 26). Among these, Julip's lost loves are the Boys, especially Charles, and Johnny.

When she is a high school junior, Julip and Johnny are inseparable, but when she goes south with her family in the fall, Johnny impregnates a girl Julip detests and is "married in the snap of the fingers, in the fashion of the local German Catholics" (*J*, 16). Because she is angry and hurt, the spring of Julip's senior year is "truly dreadful—her season in hell, in fact," as she begins drinking, smoking marijuana, and using vulgar language. Julip matures when she accepts the saving advice of two of her teachers: to "subdue the Iago in her [and] search for her higher self in Emily Dickinson," and to remember that "to ninety-nine out of one hundred men she would always be simply a piece of ass [and] the challenge for a girl was to find number one hundred" (*J*, 18, 17). Moreover, when she thinks about Edward Curtis's prints of Two Whistles and Bear's Belly and remembers that, when scolded or hurt, she wished to hide in Bear's Belly's bearskin robe, Julip realizes she cannot adopt a "hurt child" attitude: "It was certainly the way to ruin a potentially good bird dog during training. Life and bird dogs required a firm hand" (*J*, 19). In rejecting the "hurt child" syndrome, she can store Johnny in her memory's "cool dark place," and more important, she can deal with men on the make, like the "fungoid" Tallahassee desk clerk, the bass fisherman on Jackson Lake, Jim Crabb (the "lamest dickhead she had ever met"), and especially the Boys.

Soon after her father's death, Julip falls in love with 45-year-old Charles, who has brought back a headstrong setter for retraining; her "instincts" warn her "to stop the brief affair." However, Charles calls her daily and buys her a new Subaru station wagon with a dog screen; when he sends her a plane ticket to Key West, Julip says "in the bathroom mirror to her eventual regret, 'What the fuck, why not?'" (*J*, 21). Her "eventual regret" becomes evident when she also becomes involved with Arthur and Ted because Charles does not want her to be faithful. As he explains when she meets him on the pier near Martello Towers, "I was married and it didn't seem fair to you" (*J*, 62). Julip angrily replies: "It's not normal. I loved you and I didn't want to be handed away. . . . I felt like a throw-away, you know. A real expensive toy. You paid for the tickets. That's a lot in some places. And the car, which is a lot more. I got the feeling you didn't want any responsibility for me" (*J*, 62). When Charles asks her to run away and marry him, Julip says, "I guess we wore out the chance to run away. . . . You're already married. And I'm too young for you. . . . I don't want to get married and run away. I want my free will. I just want to love someone and not get fucked over" (*J*, 63). Julip wants to love and be loved in return, a virtue neither Johnny nor the Boys understand.

The Boys have, for that matter, unwittingly made her one of their "house fräuleins" or "lust slaves" and thus not only have used her like a "real expensive toy" but have literally and metaphorically "fucked [her] over." Julip's status becomes apparent when she eats lunch at the Dennis Pharmacy and notices a girl who may have been "one of Charles's previous girlfriends. . . . Or was it Arthur's or Ted's? It was hard to figure out, but the same girl had congratulated Julip in the Full Moon Saloon, on her first trip two years before, for being that year's 'lust slave.'" (*J*, 55). Ironically, Julip never questions the "fact that the Boys were heels, slobs, whiners, perverse, or simply 'jerk-offs,'" because they are not "mean-minded like so many of her dad's clients." She admits to Bobby that she had affairs with the Boys because they were "more interesting than young guys I knew. I got to go places" (*J*, 32, 43).

Just as Julip uses a "firm hand" in training dogs, she uses an equally firm hand in persuading the Boys to agree to Bobby's release and in ending her affair with each of them. Because they are easier to manipulate individually, she schedules to meet each of them on the pier near Martello Towers: Charles at three o'clock, Arthur at four, Ted at five, and Charles again at six for a "wrap-up" that includes her last lovemaking fling with him—"I just wanted to get the job done," Julip tells Charles (*J*, 71). To make the Boys more pliable, she wears a sleeveless blouse, white shorts that are "tight across her bottom," and a dab of lavender on her neck. "The outfit and scent tended to send all of them into a hormonal trance" (*J*, 55). In fact, they all react as she knew they would:

"Did you wear that outfit to torment me?" Charles asks. "Boy, what an outfit," moans Arthur. "I'd give a king's ransom to stick my face in your ass.... Once again I've been victimized by my love." And Ted complains, "I see you're wearing those shorts to torture me"(*J*, 61, 64, 67).

Julip's last night with the Boys ends comically and amicably with a "fine goodbye dinner." Ted returns from his marriage license quest happily intoxicated and, after signing the release form, falls instantly asleep on the couch. Sated and happy, Arthur falls asleep next, and Charles stumbles to his Barcalounger. As she massages his neck before he falls asleep, Julip ends their affair when she tells him that she will still train his dogs. When Charles asks, "That's it?" Julip replies, "That's it" (*J*, 80). As the scene closes, Julip glances at all three of them—"they looked like petrified babies suspended in dreamless sleep"—and returns to her motel, where she "slept the sleep of the righteous" (*J*, 80). After taking Bobby's release form to the judge's office, Julip drives north, "eager to get back to the dogs" (*J*, 82).

Julip ends affirmatively as Julip transcends her "schizophrenic upbringing," her father's death, her "fall into the world of love and loss," and especially her experience being one of the Boys' "lust slaves." In her journey to self-discovery, she refuses to adopt the "hurt child" attitude and also resists becoming a "throw-away," a "real expensive toy." What saves Julip is what saves Harrison's other heroes and heroines—strong ties to the land. For example, after scheduling her meetings with the Boys, she has what she thinks is her first "out-of-body" experience. As she stands outside the Florida motel in the dawn light and hears the water birds and watches a "flock of crows fly westward," she is "swept away to Wisconsin where on cool summer mornings before the heat gathered in the woods she'd run a dozen bird dogs at once with whistle, quirt, and pistol to honor a point and flush" (*J*, 53). Consequently, Julip decides "that her home and dogs were enough to fill a life. If something else good came along, that was well and fine. If not, not. The weight of her father, brother, mother, seemed to have gone westward with the crows. Also the weight of the Boys waiting in Key West" (*J*, 53).

Bobby and the Boys and Comedy   Despite the ominous overtones of the phrase "after the shooting," the actual shooting is more comically absurd than tragic or psychotic. Supposedly outraged at the three playboys who have defiled his "baby sister," Bobby dons various disguises to stalk the Boys—he says he is a "hero with a thousand faces," while Ted describes him as "some weirdo in a number of disguises." After Charles takes Julip to the airport, Bobby waits atop the bridge to Garrison Bight and begins "bapping away with his .22-caliber semiautomatic." The Boys' wounds are "minuscule"; only Ted's wounded knee requires "any serious medical attention." Bobby's trial also underscores the absurdly comic details of the shooting. "The not so subtle and inadmissable factor was that if you really intended to kill someone, you didn't shoot them repeatedly below the crotch with .22 shorts. . . . There was a lackadaisical attempt among the defense lawyer, prosecutor, and the judge to get out of the impasse but it was made impossible by Bobby, who said he would shoot the men again if they didn't behave" (*J*, 13).

Rather than being either another ineffectual, doomed Quentin Compson or an unconscionable pyschopathic killer, Bobby's delusions are as absurdly comic as the shooting. Dr. Wiseman notes, for example, "Sometimes your brother tended to be playfully delusional and it was difficult to separate fact from invention" (*J*, 24). The comedy also is compounded when Bobby's delusions become entwined with what he reads or hears and his "relentless gift for self-drama" (*J*, 9). For example, when a male Labrador kills and eats the pet piglet and Bobby blames his mother, he tells Julip, "Mother must be sacrificed by pushing her off a cliff," a ritual Julip attributes to Bobby's affinity for reading "books about ancient times from the school library" (*J*, 24). Moreover, when he tells Julip that he will swear on his "Modern Library Giant edition of Friedrich Nietzsche" not to shoot the Boys again, Julip recalls, "Bobby's capacity to find fresh bibles to live by had been going on a long time. If pushed, she thought, she could remember a dozen or so figures, including Ayn Rand, Hesse, Hemingway, the New Testament (a brief phase), and a Tibetan by the name of Trungpa" (*J*, 43).

Similarly, Bobby's "relentless gift for self-drama" is evident when he dons numerous disguises and especially when he stands atop the bridge, "bapping away with his .22-caliber semiautomatic" (*J*, 56, 58). Likewise, his motive, to shoot the men who "defiled" his sister, is part of his "self-drama"; Julip even wonders "just how he had come up with the word 'defiled,' whether it was from TV or perhaps something he had read" (*J*, 8). As Julip learns later, Bobby had indeed heard the word *defilement* from the prosecutor, who, quoting Dr. Wiseman, had said that Bobby's delusions "were caused by the death of his father, abandonment by his mother, the defilement of his baby sister by some rich playboys" (*J*, 81). When she asks if he used the word during the trial, the prosecutor says, "Yes. Probably. I like the word, don't you?" (*J*, 81). When Julip reminds the prosecutor that she is one year older than

Bobby, he replies, "Where I come from in Greenville, Mississippi, you're still the baby sister" (*J*, 81).

As part of the comedy, the Boys are caricatures of Guy de la Valdene, Russell Chatham, and Harrison. The Boys are avid sportsmen who have been tarpon fishing in the Florida Keys for over 20 years, and their professions mirror those of Valdene, Chatham, and Harrison—Charles is a photographer, Arthur is a painter, and Ted is a writer. They are also prodigious eaters and drinkers and often gloat about the "collected loss of over a thousand pounds in their dieting." On the anniversary of Bobby's attack, the Boys are boating out of Garrison Bight but are not feeling well because the night before "they had eaten massively, and drunk the same, in pursuit of three secretaries from Cleveland" (*J*, 38). Charles deliberately stalls the engine so the outgoing tide will carry them under the bridge from which Bobby ambushed them. Once under the bridge, Charles yells "Bang," and Arthur and Ted curse him, but Charles says, "It's the anniversary of our near-death experience. . . . I thought we should lighten up" (*J*, 39).

Another source of comedy is the Boys' awareness that they are growing older. In one scene, for example, Ted ruminates that deer would probably "kill themselves" if they knew they were either going to be hunted in the fall or starve to death in the winter; he grimly adds, "Just in case you guys don't know it, at our age we're living in November. It's all over but the bad part" (*J*, 58–59). Besides their "near-death experience," there are other reminders of their mortality. In rejecting each of the Boys' proposals, Julip reminds them of the age differences—"when I'm thirty, you'll be almost sixty," she tells Arthur" (*J*, 65). One of the three secretaries jokingly calls Ted "Gramps," whereupon he goes home "in a snit where he did two medicinal lines of coke and drank a half bottle of whiskey watching the late movie" (*J*, 38). The deaths of three former "lust slaves" over the "past twenty years" are a memento mori symbolizing the fact that the Boys are "living in November."[6]

Their carpe diem attempts to hold on to their youth result in comic pratfalls, especially when pursuing younger women. In one such scene, Charles and Arthur return "home in exhaustion at four A.M., maintaining that they had 'sort of' gotten laid but were too bleary to sort out the details" (*J*, 38). In another scene, when their fishing has been rained out and Ted and Charles are at the supermarket, Arthur tries to seduce the "scruffy maid" by waving the Boys' bag of cocaine at her; later she steals the cocaine "hidden inexpertly in the freezer under a pile of ginger and Chinese sausage" (*J*, 79, 58). On another occasion, the Boys' tarpon-

fishing day becomes torturous: the "involved Oriental meal" they prepared the evening before for two Atlanta schoolteachers has left them
parched with thirst. "The teachers got very drunk," the narrator quips,
"and they all went nude swimming after a few lines of their postdinner
wake-up powder, cocaine. But then one of the teachers . . . kept shriek-
ing 'You guys are wild!' and puked in the bushes. Her friend took her
home. The friend promised Arthur she would return but hadn't done so"
(*J*, 57). In sum, though the Boys may "rail against the dying of the
light," Julip knows that they are "mostly nice" and are "mostly harmful
to themselves" (*J*, 37).

In *Julip*, Harrison adopts traditional literary themes (female sexuality,
family relationships) and traditional literary characters (an alcoholic
father, a less-than-devoted mother, a defiled daughter and sister, her
defilers, an avenging brother) but once again twists literary perspectives
to provide comic rather than tragic insights into the pitfalls of twentieth-
century American life. Family relationships are neither as dark nor as
doomed as first suggested: the father is less than tragic, and the mother,
though zany, is caring; no one takes advantage of the daughter/sister
unless she wills it; the brother is less than menacing; and the defilers are
simply aging affable fops who are "mostly harmful to themselves." Like
Harrison's preceding novels and novellas, and like *The Seven-Ounce Man*
and *The Beige Dolorosa*, *Julip* is about self-discovery and redemption
unaccompanied by any need to see life as tragic. As Harrison emphasizes, *Julip* is "an old fashioned moral tale."[7]

The Seven-Ounce Man: Brown Dog's Further Misadventures

The Seven-Ounce Man continues the misadventures of B.D. (Brown Dog),
after he decides in *Brown Dog* to buy some chickens and beer hoping not
only that Rose and her mother will cook Sunday dinner for him but also
that he will fulfill his boyhood dream of making love to Rose; as he says in
closing his journal in *Brown Dog*: "A pinch and a 'suit yourself' wasn't
much to go on but it didn't hurt to try" (*BD*, 83). In *The Seven-Ounce Man*,
B.D. again suffers comic pratfalls from which he resiliently rebounds, at
times by his own wits, at times by what he himself calls "Fortune . . . a
boon, a blessing, a gift probably not from heaven" (*SOM*, 112).

In *Brown Dog*, B.D. lists his "life choices," or "preferences," as walking
in the woods, fishing, and hunting; he also likes "to make love and
drink. That goes without saying" (*BD*, 48). Indeed, in *The Seven-Ounce*

Man, it is B.D.'s sexual desires that lead to his comic pratfalls as well as to his self-discovery—especially when, after 25 years, he "rediscovers" Rose and hopes to fulfill his boyhood dream. The narrator, however, intimates that B.D.'s dream will be shattered: "Rose had never offered a single gesture of affection in their youth, and she wasn't overly forthcoming in the present. To think of her as a sweetheart at all would be a far reach, in sailing terms. She was born mean, captious, sullen, with occasional small dirty windows of charm. The pail of pig slop she had dumped on Brown Dog's head when he was the neighbor boy might have been a harbinger for a sensible man, but as a sentimentalist he was always trying to get at the heart of something that frequently didn't have a heart" (*SOM*, 87). By the time B.D. returns from retrieving his 1978 Dodge van in Marquette, Rose has drunk 10 beers out of a 12-pack and eaten most of the two chickens; he remains sentimentally hopeful. "Still it was a homecoming . . . and when he stepped outside to quell his anger (and hunger) in the cold air he was amazed that Fate had brought him back, with her peculiar circuitry, to the small farm where his grandfather had raised him. It was a pretty good feeling that after the real threat of prison he had arrived back here even though the home was no longer his" (*SOM*, 87–88).

When Rose poutingly asks him to buy more beer, B.D. tries to impress her further by flashing the $900 he has left from accepting Shelley's bribe. After a spree at Wally's Discount Palace—where he buys a new television complete with a remote, a sewing machine for Doris, bikes for Red and Berry, and an army cot for himself—making a down payment on a satellite dish, and buying a case of beer and a half-gallon of butterscotch schnapps at a liquor store, B.D. has $37 left. Around midnight, he fulfills his boyhood dream of making love to Rose, but the consummation is more comical than romantic. During foreplay, for example, Rose channel-surfs between the Jay Leno and Arsenio Hall shows, and during intercourse, B.D.'s trousers are down around his ankles, thus "allowing limited movement," but he manages to pump "away in unison to her burgeoning snores, his orgasm seemingly timed to when Leno changed to Letterman and her eyes popped open. 'You should know I love only Fred,' she said, and then slept" (*SOM*, 93). Later Rose agrees to let B.D. make love to her for a final time if he pays her $30 so that she can send it to Fred to get his truck repaired.

B.D.'s self-discovery and resiliency are apparent as he reflects on his boyhood dream of making love to Rose: "It rarely is, but it can be a blessed event when a dream dies. The bigger the dream, the bigger the vacuum when the dream slips off into the void. . . . He had finally achieved the dream of making love to Rose and the feeling was much emptier than the pocket that had held the money that morning" (*SOM*, 93, 94). As he prepares to sleep in the pump house, he suddenly misses his deer cabin in Grand Marias and Shelley's "dainty undies" and mourns about his "move up in the world and his plummet back to his original home." But his essential optimism surfaces: "He dismissed his melancholy into the sound of the wind. He might be B.D. dragging along the earth but he actually was a lot lighter in the mind than nearly everyone else, save a few sages and master adepts sprung from the Far East" (*SOM*, 94–95). Moreover, after recalling when he and David Four Feet spied on Rose and Ethyl swimming nude, B.D. reflects: "Now, just over thirty years later, he had fondled [Rose's] bottom, albeit in a much larger state, and felt a sure and certain accomplishment though this was joined to the perennial problem all artists feel on finishing a work— what's next? Not to speak of the fact that he had nothing to show for his efforts except the lincaments of gratified desire" (*SOM*, 95). Finally, after his last lovemaking bout with Rose, B.D. realizes that this "thumping set-to" has given him a "back spasm," and so he sleeps in the "painful cold of the pump shed quite happy that love has died" (*SOM*, 96).

B.D. suffers another reversal when Rose totals his van; he confesses that he "broke down": "It seemed to be the last of Grandpa because I bought the vehicle over ten years ago when he died and I sold the house to a realtor who sold it to Doris after her house burned down" (*SOM*, 117). B.D.'s dark mood is evident when he walks off to his cabin and says to himself, "Fuck the world that takes my last possession from me," and then spends three days and nights isolated in his cabin, or what he calls "down in a mind hole" (*SOM*, 117, 118). At the same time, B.D. reaffirms, "I can't say I feel sorry for myself, I just don't believe in the world for the time being." On the fourth day, he decides that "it's time to stop the grief about my stone-dead vehicle" and to resume his affair with Marcelle Robicheaux, a waitress at Shorty's whose husband is a black belt in karate but is on temporary duty in Somalia.

Marcelle is the "what's next" after his dream about Rose dies. When she intimates that she may be interested and suggests that he "check" her tomorrow, B.D.'s spirits soar: "He fairly pranced the first block toward his van. This was the promise of American life. You wake up wishing you were back in the cabin near Grand Marias. You have your ups and downs. You're down in the cold dumps of the employment office. You shovel snow after being slandered in the newspaper. You have

a hot pork sandwich and love strikes you deep in the gizzard, besides
which blessing your disappeared nine-hundred dollars is just another
burnt-out bulb" (*SOM*, 105). Typically, B.D.'s affair with Marcelle results
in more comedy. After B.D. baits Fred, who is visiting Rose, into collid-
ing with a mailbox, B.D. is staying at a cheap motel on Route 2 next to
a bowling alley where Marcelle bowls in a ladies' league: "Fortune struck
true, a boon, a blessing, a gift probably not from heaven" (*SOM*, 112).
B.D.'s comic fall from grace occurs, however, after his hiatus of three
days and nights in his cabin. Gretchen Stewart, the employment office
clerk, asks him to paint the inside of her house even though Karen, her
artist-roommate, is upstairs painting. "The real problem started,"
records B.D., "when I went into the bedroom which I shouldn't have
done because the door was closed, though not locked" (*SOM*, 126). The
art posters of "naked women hugging each other," Karen's lingerie
smelling of lilac, and a Polaroid of Karen and another girl "buck naked
on a tropical beach" excite him so much that he calls Marcelle, who
rushes over on her break. B.D. narrates the comic aftermath: "It was like
setting off five sticks of dynamite under a stump. We just exploded,
doing it like dogs with her waitress skirt up to her waist and her breasts
hanging out. We made about three revolutions of the living room floor
just getting traction with Marcelle real noisy, yodeling and yelling"
(*SOM*, 126). B.D. records the comic aftermath when Karen, who B.D.
has forgotten is upstairs, calls Gretchen, who storms home, calls him a
pig, and threatens to call the police: "Marcelle was up and out of there
in a split second leaving me to face the music. Once again I made the old
trousers-around-the-ankle mistake. When will I learn, I thought, falling
the first time I tried to get up. I covered my face in shame, also because
I didn't want to look Gretchen in the eyes" (*SOM*, 127). Even though he
says his "heart is heavy" afterwards, his spirits lighten when the wind
changes directions and he stops at a bar for two boilermakers. "I can't
say I was proud of myself, but I sure as hell didn't shoot the President.
Sure I made a mistake, but a mistake is not exactly a crime" (*SOM*, 127).

B.D.'s sexual exploits also result in comic pratfalls for Fred, Rose's
boyfriend, and Travis, Marcelle's husband. In true macho form, they
both want to beat up B.D. when they learn of his affairs with their
women, but their machismo becomes their petard. When B.D. returns
from shoveling snow and cleaning out a flooded church basement, he
sees a three-quarter-ton step-side pickup (an obvious macho symbol) in
Rose's driveway. When Fred comes to the door, "filling the frame," B.D.
shines his deer-jacking spotlight in Fred's eyes. "As a man with a plan"

that is "sucking Fred toward disaster," B.D. drives down the driveway, keeping "barely ahead of Fred," then pretends to have trouble shifting gears. "Sensing victory, Fred moved into a sprint, his hand on the locked door, when B.D. wiped him off against the mailbox perched on the cedar post. Not smart. But fun, he thought" (*SOM*, 111).

When Travis returns from Somalia, Marcelle tells him about her affair with B.D. because she and Travis "exchange stories of their sex wrongs to energize their marriage. They like to go into rages, then feel peaceful afterwards" (*SOM*, 115). Not only does Travis now want to thrash B.D., but Fred, back from his father's funeral, is looking for B.D. Regarding the impending battle, B.D. characteristically remarks, "It had been a long time since I'd had a fistfight but it wasn't likely to be the end of the world, just a real expensive way to pay for getting laid a few times" (*SOM*, 137). Knowing that B.D. usually goes to the Buckhorn Tavern on Saturday night, Travis and Fred also show up there, but at different times. Travis arrives first, "sort of dancing on the balls of his feet" and "dressed up like he was God's own commando." When he asks B.D. if he happens to be B.D., B.D. says that he is not, but that B.D. should arrive shortly. When Travis goes to the men's room, in walks Fred, "half drunk with eyes boiling red," and he also mistakenly asks B.D. if he is B.D., but Delmore Short Bear interrupts and says that B.D. is in the restroom. "It was a real barsweeper and enjoyed by all," B.D. writes in his journal. "Fred was more powerful but Travis had all the moves" (*SOM*, 138–39).

As in *Brown Dog*, in *The Seven-Ounce Man* B.D. neither whines nor wallows in self-pity. Each day is a new beginning, and he still enjoys life's small blessings. During his self-imposed isolation after Rose wrecks his van, for example, he says that the "main good thing out here snowbound in his cabin is that nothing is happening. . . . I've got this personal feeling things are not supposed to be happening to people all of the time" (*SOM*, 118). On another occasion, he talks about the dangers but also the benefits of pulp cutting: "What saves the job is that you're outdoors, and if you're troubled in mind you are too wore out at the end of the day to give a shit, period" (*SOM*, 131). He also describes the pleasures of his "big nature day" in late January when he sees a snowy owl kill a rabbit, three deer feeding on popple tops, and the "first bear den blowhole in my life": "I lay down and smelled the strong scent coming out of the hole . . . then put an ear to it and listened to the slow stretched-out snores. I couldn't remember when I felt luckier" (*SOM*, 134–35). More important, he enjoys being with Rose's children, especially Berry, who is retarded because of fetal alcohol syndrome but who can mimic bird and animal sounds. When he takes Red and Berry to Burger King, B.D. experiences a "specific peaceful feeling of being here with the kids like a real father, and the mood lent itself to thinking about his future" (*SOM*, 88).

Despite his blunderings, especially when his ideas and lifestyle clash with those of conventional society, B.D. is never mean-spirited. And he still adheres to his grandfather's "Don't Doggett" code: don't whine, complain, or wallow in self-pity. All in all, in *The Seven-Ounce Man*, B.D is affable and, like the Boys in *Julip*, mostly harmful only to himself, as several characters note. For example, Harold "Bud" Schultz, the Michigan state police detective shadowing B.D., knows that B.D. is not a dangerous felon but rather only a "loose screw representing himself," a "happy-go-lucky pussy chaser"; indeed, "tailing the man resembled following around a stray dog": "The fact that he consorted with Gretchen Stewart, a feminist activist out of Ohio State, Marcelle Robicheaux who was from a family of Louisiana malcontents and small-time dope smugglers, and Vera Hall whose second husband was an auto thief from Duluth, added up to nothing" (*SOM*, 148). For that matter, Lone Marten describes B.D. as not only a failure as a "limo driver and revolutionary" but as "nothing but a pussy-crazed backwoods rooster" (*SOM*, 167). Delmore Short Bear tells Gretchen that B.D. is "just a big baby. . . . He acts so ordinary he can't see anything coming. If you don't help, he'll end up in the Big House" (*SOM*, 167).

Like the conclusion of *Brown Dog*, the positive ending of *The Seven-Ounce Man* emphasizes the comedy in the plot and B.D.'s resiliency. Moreover, both novellas end with a scene between Shelley and B.D. The scene in *The Seven-Ounce Man*, however, is more comically chaotic. Accompanied by Marten, some Wisconsin Red Power braves, Rose, and Fred ("It's time to put aside our petty bourgeois miseries for the sake of the cause," says Marten), B.D. fulfills his promise to protect the ancient burial site. As the Red Power braves terrorize the camp on their motorcycles, Rose and Fred battle Shelley's huge bodyguard, and Marten adds to the chaos by slingshotting cherry bombs and blockbusters toward the camp, Shelley, clad only in bra and panties, sprints toward B.D. screaming, "B.D., you motherfucker." Clad in the bearskin Delmore gave him, B.D. rises from behind a stump and so startles Shelley that she slips down in the mud. "He was on her like a bear," the narrator says, "crawling over her, growling and howling, giving her a wet kiss. 'It's only just me, your long-lost love,' he whispered, before he felt Marten frantically pulling him off" (*SOM*, 181). Violating the "dead chief's advice not to go south of Green Bay, Wisconsin," B.D. escapes to California with Marten, who must get to UCLA to chair a colloquium entitled "Will Whitey Ever See Red?" B.D. remains hopeful as the narrative ends and he thinks about Shelley: "The worm began to turn. He doubted that she would ever forgive him but he knew she wouldn't forget him. They headed west" (*SOM*, 182).

The Native American Theme and Coyote-Type Indians
Unlike the epic sweep and tragic colorings given to the Native American motif in *Legends of the Fall* and *Dalva*, *The Seven-Ounce Man* gives the theme a comic treatment, especially in the characterization of Lone Marten, David Four Feet and Rose's little brother, about whom Harrison said, "I know a bunch of coyote-type Indians, and I really like them. They're a lot like Rose's brother" ("Lake"). Although Old Claude's characterization is tinged with humor in *Brown Dog*, Lone Marten, who lives in Westwood, California, is Harrison's first comic Native American. Although supposedly returning home to help B.D. protect the ancient burial site from the *"wasichus"*—namely, Shelley Thurman[8] and her colleagues—Marten admits, "Actually, I represent a group of investors—a fancy word for dope dealers, I suppose. My first love is film, but my integrity as an artist depends on my becoming *engagé* at times" (*SOM*, 151).

Although a former member of the American Indian Movement, Marten is not a fierce Red Power revolutionary but is primarily histrionic: like B.D., he is mostly harmful to himself. For example, in checking Marten's rap sheet, Detective Schultz learns that he is "small time indeed" and a "chiseler . . . looking for a little excitement" while visiting his mother. Even Doris is pleased that Marten is not violent like David and has "limited his criminal activities to credit cards, dope, and an infatuation with fireworks that had started early" (*SOM*, 166).

Marten's artistic temperament creates much of the humor. His flair for theatrics is apparent, for example, in his disguises; in the three-year-old Lincoln Town Car complete with telephone that B.D. drives so that Marten can be free to think and plan; in the choreographed preparation for and successful attack on Shelley's campsite; and especially in his direction of "The Wild Wild Midwest Show," in which the six Wisconsin Indians attack the fort and shoot B.D. and Fred, who stand in open windows and fall backward on cushions. As a "vicious squaw," Rose rushes into the fort, cuts off "everyone's ears and balls," and emerges with a "full bloody platter," a "real show stopper," says Marten. When B.D. wonders whether perhaps this was "going too far for tourists," Marten

replies that his "integrity" requires "absolute historical verisimilitude," to
which "they all nodded in sage though uncomprehending assent" (*SOM*,
169). Like Harrison's other comic characters, Marten is affable, likable,
and a threat only to himself.

Unlike Marten, Delmore Short Bear (a.k.a. Delmore Burns) has had
no adverse experiences in the white world. He left Escanaba to work in
Detroit's automobile factories, saved his money, and bought a farm
north of Detroit because he detested city life. He became very wealthy
when he sold his farm, which eventually became Detroit's posh
Bloomfield Hills suburb (the suburb where Donald and Clare live in *The
Woman Lit by Fireflies*). When he moved back home, he became a law-
abiding and respected Native American whom Bud Schultz and deputy
sheriffs call "sir" and "Mr. Burns." Delmore is famous for "being the only
rich native anyone had heard of when B.D. was young" (*SOM*, 102). At a
local powwow during which Berry does the crow dance and an old
Indian performs his last bear dance, Delmore—who B.D. says is still a
"pretty big deal among the local Chips"—is introduced and warmly
applauded.

Even though Delmore's third cousins believe that he should have
been a spiritual leader instead of a Detroit autoworker, Delmore never
abandons his Indian heritage. He weeps as he watches the old man perform his last bear dance, and his Indian room holds his totems—a war
club, rattles hanging from a hook, different kinds of turtle shells, snake-
skins, and a full hooded bearskin from a bear he killed as a young boy
near the Fence River, thus taking the bear's medicine. Because he cannot
devote himself full-time to the bear medicine, he abandons it when he
moves to Detroit, but once on his farm, he dreams of "serpents and tur-
tles," turns to them, and "they stood by him" (*SOM*, 130).

Like Ted Sleeping Bear in *Brown Dog*, Delmore Short Bear is a father
figure for B.D., a role closely tied to Native American tradition. When
B.D. first meets him at Shorty's, Delmore says: "I owe it to your grandpa to keep an eye on you. How come you think the judge let you off so
easy and gave your partner time when you stole the ice truck to sell the
body in Chicago? It wasn't just that Republican cunt friend of yours and
her rich father. You've always been up to nothing over at Grand Marias
and I'm here to help you get good at it. . . . You're pussy struck is your
main problem, among hundreds" (*SOM*, 103). Delmore's most significant fatherly gesture springs directly from Native American tradition: he
gives B.D. the full hooded bearskin that traditionally should have been
passed down either to his own son or to his sister's son. His nephew,

however, "had been murdered in a scuffle on a fishing boat . . . after he knocked up B.D.'s grandpa Jake's worthless daughter, who had then run off with Delmore's own son to disappear forever" (*SOM*, 155). In the ceremony, Delmore symbolically adopts B.D. when he has B.D. take a hot bath, then don the plaid shirt he had worn when he killed the bear; when B.D. is dressed, Delmore gives him the bear's gallstones. Delmore has become successful in the white world, but he never forgets his Native American heritage and roots, and thus he represents those Native Americans who make the best of both the white and red cultures.

"One for the Professors:" *The Beige Dolorosa*

Regarding *The Beige Dolorosa*, Harrison remarked, "I got one for the professors this time because I've always loved Christopher Smart and John Clare." The novella's plot is about a "professor who thinks he has Alzheimer's because I thought I had Alzheimer's about two years ago. . . . So I read everything I could find about it because I thought I was becoming stupid. All it was is that I was tired. Once I took a break, I got my brain back." The interesting part about writing *The Beige Dolorosa* was seeing the "mind totally disintegrate," a phenomenon Harrison experienced himself "a couple of times like when you're just on the edge of madness. . . . I dealt with that comically . . . with that professor [Michael] in the middle section of *Dalva* when he's just divorced and his wife leaves him in that car and he just continues talking" ("Lake").

Phillip Caulkins, the 50-year-old protagonist of *The Beige Dolorosa*, endures a midlife crisis that upsets his comfortable, ordered life; like Harrison's other protagonists, he must reestablish purpose and meaning in his life. Perhaps Caulkins's crisis is direr than those of Harrison's other characters, however, since Caulkins believes that he has Alzheimer's disease and his mind may be "melting." During the opening of his first-person narrative, Caulkins says:

> But, oh God, how did I get here from there? I'm about to tell you, and I better hurry because I'm losing interest in myself. During my extended crisis it occurred to me that it must be my personality that makes life disappointing. . . . Besides when you take away the livelihood a man has practiced for thirty years there is suddenly a hiatus wherein it is natural to try to figure out what's left. . . . This sort of thing has become a daily banality in the newspapers but I assure you it's quite different when you're sitting in the lap of the vacuum (*TBD*, 186–87).

As Caulkins explains how he got "from here to there," his narrative
weaves in and out of past and present time, a Harrisonesque narrative
device. Technically, the past time frame, the *there* alluded to in his question, recounts those incidents that result in his "extended crisis." The present time frame, the *here*, relates those incidents that mark his gradual
redemption and reemergence into life's flow and graces—or as his last
name suggests, his recaulking of the broken seams in his being and life.

Caulkins's crisis results when, after 30 years, he loses his tenured, full
professor position teaching English literature at a southern Michigan college. Before his crisis, his life has been pleasant. He had achieved tenure
when he was 30, based primarily on his book, *The Economics of Madness in
English Poetry*, an in-depth analysis of the lives of Christopher Smart and
John Clare. At 35, he was promoted to full professor, lived on the town's
outskirts in a "fine house on three acres," and received offers from
Berkeley, Princeton, and the University of Texas. "I chose to stay put out
of timidity," he admits. "I did not have another book idea to keep pace
in the upper reaches of the academic world and, as Marilyn elegantly
stated, I was better off being a big frog in a small pond" (*TBD*, 190).
Caulkins has even overcome the trauma of his divorce ten years before
from Marilyn, who had been having an affair with Ballard, the English
Department chairman soon after promoted to dean of science and arts.
After 18 years of marriage, "Marilyn said to my very face that she loved
me but that I was of insufficient interest to last a lifetime" (*TBD*, 186).
Despite his divorce, and despite being only a "big frog in a small pond,"
Caulkins admits, "Life passed on rather sleepily for years," a comment
somewhat reminiscent of Clare's in *The Woman Lit by Fireflies* that she "let
the years float gently by" (*WLF*, 204).

Inevitably, however, a series of totally absurd incidents upend his
tenured position and his sleepily drifting life. "It all started," Caulkins
recalls, "on the first fine day in early April when I errantly went into my
Milton class and said, 'Good morning, you ladies are looking lovely
today.'" He is subsequently called into Dean Ballard's office to justify his
politically incorrect "sexist comment" (*TBD*, 191, 192). Other equally
absurd incidents compound his predicament and inevitably erode his 30-
year teaching career. In a course entitled "English Poetics: From *Beowulf*
to Auden," for example, he is accused of anti-Semitism when he quotes
Ezra Pound because, though "an admitted fool and anti-Semite, [he] had
some wise things to say about poetry" (*TBD*, 193). On another occasion—what he calls the "Earth Day assault charge"—Caulkins attempts
to retrieve some books from his office on a rainy day and accidentally

strikes one of the student mimes who have surrounded him: "I'm a bit of a claustrophobe and when they got so close that I could smell their breath, I attempted to shield myself with the umbrella, the point of which supposedly struck one of the mimes, who collapsed screaming. Another mime summoned a nearby campus policewoman and I was duly charged" (*TBD*, 193–94). The charges are dropped when the injured girl goes to New York City, allowing Caulkins to regain his "balance for a couple of weeks" (*TBD*, 200). Other bizarre incidents plague him. After his officemate Bob tells him that Dean Ballard has been seen "smooching" with a coed named Elizabeth in a Chicago jazz club, Caulkins drinks his six Watneys too fast, attempts to drive the five blocks to his home, but nicks the rear end of the basketball coach's automobile; the coach calls the police on his car phone, and Caulkins barely passes the breathalyzer test. Later that evening, he accidentally locks himself out of his apartment while wearing only his underpants, the police are called (the same ones who gave him the breathalyzer test), and Caulkins talks himself "out of an assortment of charges, including drunk and disorderly and indecent exposure" (*TBD*, 200).

The most damning incident occurs later when Ballard bribes him into helping Elizabeth complete her senior thesis so that she can graduate in three weeks. Ironically, it is Elizabeth who filed the grievance against Caulkins when he quoted Ezra Pound, and who has been seen "smooching" with Ballard. After referring to Caulkins's problems with the law and with "sexism, mimes, anti-Semitism," Ballard warns that these are " 'ounces,' but ounces eventually added up to pounds. . . . Even these minor missteps would eventually come to the attention of the president of the board of trustees when they made their annual review of the faculty. Anyone with three possible demerits had a red tag on his dossier and the problems were discussed" (*TBD*, 207). Of course, if Caulkins agrees to help Elizabeth, Ballard will expunge his record. "It was at this point," writes Caulkins, "I was offered a pact with the devil" (*TBD*, 207). As he is helping her during the final session, Elizabeth, who has planned the scenario with her boyfriend Reed and two of her sorority sisters, tries to seduce him. When he stops her and flees back to the living room, her two colluding sorority sisters suddenly appear in the living room and chirp, "as if on cue, 'What have you done to her?' " as Elizabeth begins to "screech and sob" (*TBD*, 213). "At that moment," Caulkins says, "it didn't take any prescience on my part to realize my goose was cooked" (*TBD*, 213).

Thoroughly traumatized and not allowed to teach, Caulkins retreats from the world and spends "five months" in his "darkened apartment except for an occasional hearing." He fakes "normalcy" when his daughter Deirdre calls during what he calls his "frozen period" (*TBD*, 205). After the usual, interminable committee hearings, Caulkins retreats even further when he hears the outcome: "When the bad news finally came in September, I did not emerge until Thanksgiving weekend when Deirdre dragged me into the open air" (*TBD*, 205). Because of her training as a psychiatric social worker in Chicago, Deirdre not only drags Caulkins into the world again but persuades him to spend time on her in-laws' ranch in Arizona (the *here* in Caulkins's initial question about how he got from *here* to *there*). Caulkins's retreat to the Verdugos' ranch, where he can sort out his life and redeem himself, recalls Michael's stay on Dalva's ranch.

"To Be Taken for a Cowboy": Caulkins Recaulks   Although he remains sequestered in his ranch cabin the entire first week, Caulkins gradually reemerges into life's flow to embark on his personal redemption. Just as Dalva, Naomi, Frieda, and old Lundquist help Michael in *Dalva*, the Verdugos—Lillian, J.M., and Lillian's aged mother—help Caulkins transcend his "extended crisis." Out of timidity and fear of reentering the world, he refuses to eat with the Verdugos and lies about being able to cook. Even when he eventually eats lunch with the family and secretly wants to ride in the huge cattle truck to Tucson, he excuses himself under the pretext that he has work to do. When J.M. unthinkingly says, "Oh, I thought they'd let you go," Caulkins bolts from their house, flings himself on his bed, and lies "face down like a distressed girl." Although he gets up to check on the bull just outside his cabin, he confesses, "I thought of lying back down but was fearful that the meltdown that had begun in my brain might continue and that if I dozed off I might awake with a skull full of putty" (*TBD*, 199).

Caulkins's reemerges a bit further when Lillian comes to his cabin, takes him for a walk, and tells him that she will teach him to cook and to drive a standard shift. Pinpointing his depression and crisis, he replies that he is "very good at moping and brooding. Agenbite of inwit" (*TBD*, 205). If Caulkins is to transcend the traumas of his past, he must leave his cabin and learn to cook and drive a standard shift. Significantly, however, after his walk with Lillian, he reneges on a Saturday shopping trip with Lillian and J.M. so that he can drive the Jeep "off for the mountains, or wherever whichever the road took me, with a tremor in my heart rather than a song" (*TBD*, 117). The "wherever whichever" recalls Clare's walk into the cornfield's interior, "wherever that may be."

Like Clare's epiphany in the cornfield, Caulkins's solitary foray into the mountains is a major step in his redemption: "Perhaps in the years to come I will regard that day as the signal day of my life, but for the present I am terribly frightened, if a little thankful" (*TBD*, 217). To underscore his "signal day," he notes that it "beat the hell out of pleasing students, or more particularly Marilyn the last few years of our marriage. Unfaithful wives are great fault finders because it fuels their sense of self-justification" (*TBD*, 217).

Once up the mountain, Caulkins stands on a cliff overlooking an immense valley; when he begins to feel "vertiginous," he sits under an overhang: "It was at this point that everything let go. The insides of my brain and body quaked and shivered and I began to weep. This caused a total loss of equilibrium and I tipped sideways from my sitting position. For a few minutes I could not tell up from down and tears literally flowed. For the first time I understood how a body could be 'racked' by sobs" (*TBD*, 219). He weeps for almost two hours and thinks about throwing away his watch because it reminds him of "those long post-Elizabeth months in the dungeon of his apartment" when he logged "not sunlight or weather or thoughts but the clock" in "dozens of pages" with "strings of inane numbers" (*TBD*, 219). During his weeping purge, he finally understands his suffering:

> It seemed that for half a year I had been trying to ignore what was directly in front of my nose and this had further blinded me: my reality had betrayed me, the reality to which I had devoted my life had disappeared. I no longer had control of the world I live in or a single one of its inhabitants, and I myself was at large. A world that had welcomed me for three decades had shown me the door, and at fifty I owed the world nothing but my contempt, which in itself was too worthless to be indulged. (*TBD*, 219–20)

This scene is crucial for a number of reasons. First, Caulkins learns to operate the Jeep's standard shift; doing so required that he venture outside the cabin's confines, a scene that recalls Deirdre dragging him from the dungeonlike confines of his darkened apartment. Once he is on the cliff, tipping sideways and not knowing "up from down" may suggest his life and world in the "post-Elizabeth months," but his vision, despite his "tremors," is "wide and clear," an image suggesting, as it does in *Dalva* and *The Woman Lit by Fireflies*, a reshaping of the character's perspective. By extension, Caulkins acknowledges the unpleasant facts from which he has been metaphorically hiding in his apartment and the ranch's guest house—reality has betrayed him, his teaching career is over, and his contempt for the world is self-defeating. Moreover, his weeping—the "point" at which "everything let go"—purges him during his time in the wilderness: "Here I was, not in someone's closet but under a rock over-hang, shaking now from cold rather than my torments" (*TBD*, 221). If in *The Woman Lit by Fireflies* Clare's time in the wilderness is about her breaking down and then putting herself back together, then so, too, is Caulkins's time in the mountain wilds.

On returning to the ranch, where he is welcomed back like a "prodi-gal son," Caulkins begins to rejuvenate himself, especially when he bathes and sees his body for the first time since May: "I had looked shriveled, flaccid, ghastly. . . . My God, could this be possible? Of course, there it was. Smaller than life and ready for a coffin. It was difficult to understand how the mind could make the body forget itself" (*TBD*, 223). He begins exercising once he realizes he cannot do one push-up, much less the dozen he could do a year before, and socializes more with the Verdugos, eating meals with them, getting drunk with J.M., and rid-ing in the cattle truck to Tucson. When he sleeps outside for the first time in his life, a "revelation" follows: "I meant to get rid of my person-ality which insisted on maintaining a world that no longer existed. . . . I must reshape myself to fully inhabit the earth rather than dawdle in the sump of my foibles" (*TBD*, 228). A major reshaping occurs when J.M. is short two hands during roundup and Caulkins offers to help, becoming "not so much a cowboy or a cowhand, but a cow helper. Within days J.M. admitted gracefully that I was better than nothing" (*TBD*, 234). More important, the $500 he is paid for work that bruises his body and makes his bones ache, though an "absurdly small" amount, he says, "has thrilled me to no end" (*TBD*, 234–35). Later he adds, "The fact that I was better than nothing is meaningful to me," and he describes the three trips to the Tucson cattle yards in the immense cattle truck as "unalloyed fun" (*TBD*, 235, 238). More to the point, however, "within a few days of the roundup I began to congeal" (*TBD*, 239).

Other incidents mark Caulkins's redemptive process. He destroys his Big Ben electric clock along with his watch, experiencing as he does so the "first full laughter [he] could remember." He discovers nature, since "my excommunication made me quite alone and I have to use what's at hand to keep my soul from evaporating. . . . If there's nothing there worth saving, we'll have to build something new" (*TBD*, 227, 243). He also claims to have had a "technicolor dream" instructing him to "rename the birds of North America" (*TBD*, 246). He renames a brown thrasher the "beige dolorosa," because it is "reminiscent of a musical phrase in Mozart, one that makes your heart pulse with mystery, as does the bird" (*TBD*, 246). Nature and the thrasher not only bring him alive and make him aware of the beauty that surrounds him—a beauty that contrasts with his dark apartment and his post-Elizabeth months—but erase "my occasional urge toward suicide. . . . I suspect it's because this new world is not asking me to hold it together like the other one" (*TBD*, 246).

The most significant redemptive incident occurs as Caulkins is repairing barbed-wire fences up in the hills; he has just received Dean Ballard's letter informing him that his reinstatement hearing has been postponed because of budgetary problems and suggesting that he consider accepting a half-pay disability pension, an offer Caulkins interprets as "paramount to admitting mental incompetence" (*TBD*, 247). Attempting to sublimate Ballard's odious letter by meditating on Keats's ideas about the "vale of soul-making," Caulkins stretches the barbed wire too tight and the wire snaps, slashing his left shoulder and severely gashing his left cheek. When J.M. takes him to a Nogales emergency clinic, the old doctor says that because Caulkins did not come in sooner—he went into shock and fell asleep—a "neat job" will be impossible. Then "he said something that I will cherish forever: 'If you weren't such a worthless old cowboy, I'd send you to a plastic surgeon in Tucson.'. . . It pleased me no end to be taken for a cowboy" (*TBD*, 249, 250). Caulkins's scar, his red cowboy badge, suggests that he has shed the "sump" of his "foibles" as well as his old life and unwittingly reshaped himself in the image of the cowboy. In fact, when he goes to talk to Magdalena, he "walks like a gunslinger," and later not only does he realize that he has supported himself by "rounding up cattle and mending fences," but he even thinks of using his wages for a "down payment on a spiffy 4WD pickup, the kind all cowboys pine for" (*TBD*, 254, 266, 262).

At one point during his rejuvenation, Caulkins admits, "I was an expert on the subject of my mind but was infantile about my emotions" (*TBD*, 261). Caulkins's emotions, however, are tested when Magdalena, Lillian's younger sister—"the sister from hell," according to J.M.—and a *puta*, seduces him, thus complicating his redemptive process. He confesses that, "after my experience with Magdalena I went daft. . . . Making love—a wretched euphemism—to Magdalena was a mistake. Not making love to Magdalena would also have been a mistake" (*TBD*, 246). Magdalena is, however, as greedy as Marilyn and as devious as Elizabeth.

After her boyfriend takes her away, Caulkins is depressed, but Magdalena returns, asking Caulkins for $1,500 for an abortion because he is the "designated father." Although she intimates that if he gives her the money she will "always be ready" for him, she actually wants the money so that she and her boyfriend can buy marijuana, which they trick Caulkins into transporting in hollowed-out statues of the Blessed Virgin Mary. When he realizes that the "pickup load [is] more than enough to use up the rest of [his] life" in prison, he flattens a tire, hitch-hikes to the gas station, and drives happily home in the Jeep, only to run out of gas at the foot of the driveway. As he walks the two miles to his cabin, he says, "There was a small piece of moon to light my way, and my walking meditation was full of pleasant thoughts about my limits." After accepting those limits, he concludes, "The future was acceptable rather than promising. It was certainly my choice" (*TBD*, 275).

Like Harrison's other works, *The Beige Dolorosa* ends cautiously but positively in that Caulkins transcends the dark nights of his soul—his academic and post-Elizabeth traumas and his escapade with Magdalena. Through his newly discovered love of nature and his cowboy image, he has recaulked the broken seams in his being and life. As he says, whatever happens in his future life will be his choice.

Pomp and Circumstances and Academic Satire   In *Dalva*, one target of Harrison's satire is academia. While certainly less humorous than in *Dalva*, the academic satire in *The Beige Dolorosa* is just as trenchant. Greed, which in Harrison's opinion is destroying the nation's life-soul, is what motivates Dean Ballard, who uses causes and people to aggrandize his position. In an obvious attempt to stand well in the administration's graces, for instance, Ballard chairs the "original steering committee" that bans "relations between students and professors and administrators" (*TBD*, 200). In addition, he snoops into faculty lives so that he can red-tag dossiers, a petty tactic about which Caulkins reflects, "We have reached a point where American higher education is beginning to remind one of the articles one reads about Cuba, where everyone is intent upon spying on one another and reporting it to a committee" (*TBD*, 202). Outwardly, Ballard is the dedicated administrator, but under the surface he is egregious and self-serving. More pointedly, Ballard not only has a lengthy affair with Caulkins's wife Marilyn—who will marry him but then leave him after four years—but becomes involved with Elizabeth, for whom he blackmails Caulkins. As Caulkins notes, the "core problem was Elizabeth, who represented the fourth generation of her well-heeled family to attend the college. It should come as no surprise to anyone that the children of families who can fatten the

endowment are catered to" (*TBD*, 206). Compounding Ballard's offi-
cious behavior is a lack of personal and professional ethics: "I was
ashamed to be involved in a mess," admits Caulkins, "which, after the
fact, turned out to be an unprovable triple blackmail engineered by
Reed, with the more tacit cooperation of Ballard, who was saving his
own skin" (*TBD*, 208). In fact, a prominent Pittsburgh lawyer and
member of the college's board of directors senses something is wrong
despite the "circumstantial evidence"; he says, "What a squalid little
place. . . . You have a fine mind. Pick up a law degree and I'll give you a
real job" (*TBD*, 238).

The satiric thrust at students is double-bladed, one light, the other
dark. On the lighter edge, the satire targets students who would rather
party than study and thus includes those students who on Earth Day
turn the college commons into a "massive eco circus" featuring rock
bands, modern dance troupes, costumery, mimes, and "speakers and
poets who were advocates of the American wilderness, recycling and
whatever" (*TBD*, 193); the raucous students who provide the "only discordant note" in the Nogales cantina and whose dates "look like clones
of Barbie dolls" compared with Magdalena; and the University of
Arizona students who pick up Caulkins as he hitchhikes back to the gas
station, on their return from a "Mexican beach vacation they pronounced
'awesome,' a doubtful word for anything they might have experienced"
(*TBD*, 271, 273). Caulkins sadly concludes, "Year after year my informal
surveys of new students in my classes revealed that few if any had read
an appreciable book in the previous year. The worship of the ersatz and
peripheral was the norm" (*TBD*, 261).

The novella's darker satire focuses on Elizabeth and her paramour
Reed, whom Caulkins labels the "nasty little Iago." He manipulates
Elizabeth and even tells her how to dress: "Occasionally Elizabeth will
shed her used-clothing disguise and wear a miniskirt and a soft cotton T-
shirt with no bra, which causes no little confusion. I'm sure it's at Reed's
instigation, as he preens around campus with her, cupping her bottom
and breasts with a satanic leer on his face. All the English faculty have
remarked puzzledly on why our most brilliant students must be our nastiest" (*TBD*, 200). More ominous, once Caulkins casts the deciding vote
to withdraw the department's funding for *Openings*, the literary magazine Reed edits, Reed calls Caulkins a "twit" and begins to plot his
downfall—the triple blackmail and the staged rape at Caulkins's apartment (during which Elizabeth wore, instead of the usual "dowdy out-
fits," a "deep V-neck T-shirt, short skirt, and sandals" [*TBD*, 211]).

According to Caulkins, Elizabeth has an "attention span on the order of a politician's" and is "literally naive." Indeed, when she adamantly insists on titling her senior thesis "Sexism in Yeats" because she believes Yeats's "creepy values are repulsive to today's women," Caulkins cringes: "Of what purpose was it to attack Yeats using values that were unknown to his culture. . . . I tried to lighten the mood by saying, 'This is like attacking Jesus for not flossing,' which passed through her head with the speed of a neutron" (*TBD*, 210). After failing to persuade her to change the title of her thesis, Caulkins admits: "It was at this point that I began to develop a sense of suffocation, as if I were in a dentist's chair to get wisdom teeth pulled. . . . The problem had nothing to do with feminism . . . but with simple stupidity, also the profoundest sense that I was betraying a code of values, a tradition" (*TBD*, 210).

Not only is Elizabeth somewhat vapid, but she is just as dysfunctional as Shelley and Tarah in *Brown Dog*. She huffs out of class after Caulkins quotes Ezra Pound because she "had spent the school year pretending to be Jewish and observing Jewish holidays. The year before, she had become a Native American. Bob said that the black students were cringing over the idea that they might be next on her schedule of adoptions" (*TBD*, 193). In contrast to those students whose merriments are vacuous and harmful only to themselves, Elizabeth is petty and vicious and thus the female equivalent of Dean Ballard. As does he, she uses ethnic causes to aggrandize her stature and deviously becomes involved in the triple blackmail that dupes Ballard and ruins Caulkins's reputation and career. In sum, Ballard, Reed, and Elizabeth, who pervert both the social and human contracts, are among Harrison's least flattering characters.

In their lyrical descriptions of nature, their satire on contemporary life's absurdities, and their modifications of literary conventions and themes, the novellas in *Julip* are linked to Harrison's preceding fiction. While *Julip*, *The Seven-Ounce Man*, and *The Beige Dolorosa* attest to Harrison's artistry at weaving entertaining, thought-provoking narratives, each novella also reaffirms the protagonist's human spirit and desire to reestablish purpose and meaning in life. In the main, all of Harrison's characters create something out of nothing, and they do so by eventually discovering that there is no reason to see life as tragic.

Chapter Eleven

"I Don't Look Very Poetic": Harrison's Poetry

Harrison laughed as he told Eric Siegal, "A lot of people come up and tell me I don't look very poetic. That's a helluva thing to hear when you're a poet" (Siegal, 19). Harrison explained why he turned to poetry as a young man, though he was interested in writing fiction: "I suppose it's because you have so many hormones in your twenties and thirties that you can't sit down for the long haul that's known as writing a novel, yet your feelings are inexpressibly intense at the time, so you take it out on poetry" (Ross, 227). Since making those early remarks, Harrison has written essays, poetry, and fiction; when asked which genre he feels most comfortable with, he answered, "None more than the other. I think if you've messed around as much as I have, you tend to feel fairly comfort able in all of them" (Elliott and Sommerness).

Except for book reviews, cursory references or explications in some critical essays, and overviews like Burkholder's in the *Dictionary of Literary Biography*, Munro's in *Critical Survey of Poetry*, and Mark McCloskey's in *Magill's Literary Annual 1983*, Harrison's poetry has not garnered critical analysis. To begin that analysis, looking at his interpretations of nature and his aesthetic use of autobiography reveals much about his poetic visions and techniques.

Nature Poems

Reviewers and critics generally agree that Harrison's nature poems defy neat labels. Lisel Mueller used quote marks in referring to Harrison's "nature" poems "to forestall any impression of pastoral or rustic verse," but she did believe that he "sees the natural world in a way that is often identified with oriental thought: all is one and one is all; only the manifestations vary."[1] Speaking of Harrison's "preoccupation with nature," Robert Burkholder maintained that there is "much of the romantic poet in Harrison, although it should not be assumed that his romanticism is in any way anachronistic or affected" (267). In reviewing *The Theory and*

Practice of Rivers, Mark Hillringhouse wrote that the new poems are "psychic emblems, a totemic assortment of 'inner states,' poems to herons and loons, bears, horses, and cobras that the author identifies with. They avoid the trap of sentimentality with their zen-like insistence of not imposing any specific idea upon the reader's conscious mind. Along with Barry Lopez and Peter Matthiessen, Harrison is one of our better nature writers. But these are not your typical 'nature' poems. They are openings into the collective unconscious"[2]

"Northern Michigan," a poem in *Plain Song*, describes back-road land that has had "the juice taken out of it." The next five stanzas contain wasteland images: "stump fences surround nothing / worth their tearing down"; by a "deserted filling station" are a "veedol sign" and the "rusted hulk / of a Frazer"; "A barn / with half a tobacco ad"; a "collapsed hen house"; and an "orchard with wild tangled branches." Despite the apparent ruin, however, images of life and light close the poem: in the pasture's far corner is a herd of twenty deer, and three bucks

> are showing off—
> they jump in turn across the fence,
> flanks arch and twist to get higher
> in the twilight
> as the last light filters
> through the woods.

In "Northern Michigan," civilization may have encroached on and despoiled parts of this back-road land, but the natural world and its beauty endure—the deer herd and the three bucks' arching and twisting flanks in the twilight. As John Rohrkemper points out: "Whereas a writer such as Eliot or Hemingway would be inclined to show the pristine beauty of nature first and then nature despoiled, Harrison reverses the order undercutting the potential irony of the scene and suggesting not 'look what we have lost,' but 'look what has always [existed] and still exists despite us.' We end, not with irony, but with the wondrous arc of the leaping bucks" (21). On the other hand, this scene in nature does not inspire Harrison to draw a moral lesson, as a transcendentalist poet might do, but to focus on the transcendent beauty of the moment.

Just as the beauty of the moment in "Northern Michigan" rejuvenates the wasteland images of the opening stanzas, so a transcendent moment rejuvenates the speaker in "Cold August" in *Locations*. "The sun had shrunk to a dime, / passing behind the smallest of clouds," the speaker begins; he then describes the cold in which everything seems to shrink:

> the field was root
> bare—shorthorns had grazed it to leather. August's coldest
> day when the green, unlike
> its former self, returned to earth as metal.

Looking toward the swamp, the speaker sees

> two large shadows floating
> across the river, move up the sloping
> bank, float swiftly as shadows against the field toward where I stood.

As he looks up, two red-tailed hawks pass over him; as they fly off, he says:

> A day born in cold sourness
> suffused me then in its dark,
> brief image of magnificence.

Not only can Harrison distill a landscape's essence, but his word choices reinforce a poem's meaning. In contrast to the sun's cosmic size and brightness when it is replenishing life in spring and summer, it has now shrunk to dime size. Men and animals have harvested the fertile fields that now look like leather. Moreover, the green that once denoted life is now "metal," frozen by frost. While the "large shadows" and the "dark, brief image" complement the poem's opening images, they yield a moment of transcendent magnificence, as images of constriction succumb to images of expansion and the cold's dull hues succumb to the hawks' red-tailed plumage.

The poem "Epithalamium" in *Selected and New Poems* ends in neither a transcendent moment nor an epiphany. As the speaker and his dog wander around the barnyard in "full moonlight" at three in the morning, he says:

> for the first time the wind
> blew straight down from the heavens . . .
> flattening my hair
> against my head; my dog cowered
> between my knees, and the last leaves

of a cold November shot to the ground.
Then the wind slowed and went back to the north.

The speaker ends with, "This happened last night and already at noon /
my faith in it is passing." As with "Northern Michigan" and "Cold
August," "Epithalamium" ends with an unexpected twist. "Epithalamium"
suggests that this rare occurrence—the wind blowing "straight down from
the heavens"—will conclude with an epiphany or a transcendental
moment; instead, the speaker says, "my faith in it is passing."

"Dead Deer" in *Plain Song* depicts nature's crueler, realistic side. The
speaker sees a "rotted" deer, "curled, shaglike," lying "amid pale green
milkweed" and "wild clover." To explain his belief that the deer died
"after a winter so cold / trees split open," the speaker says,

> I think she couldn't keep up with
> the others (they had no place
> to go) and her food,
> frozen grass and twigs,
> wouldn't carry her weight.
>
> Now from bony sockets
> she stares out on this
> cruel luxuriance.

As the green milkweed, wild clover, and luxuriance imply, "Dead Deer"
is about nature's cycles, especially winter and spring, life and death.
Despite the severe winter, spring and its promise of new life soon follows. The dead deer is simply a victim of nature's cycles because the
spring has come too late and thus is a "cruel luxuriance." John
Rohrkemper notes: "Nevertheless, this deer is not victim so much of
man's interference as of the normal timeless rhythms of nature which
might seem cruel to man, but only because of his egotistical need to
anthropomorphize the natural world. If these early poems suggest that
Harrison should be considered in the American romantic tradition, they
also suggest that his vision is closer to that of Melville and the dark
romantics than to that of Emerson and the transcendentalists" (22).
Similarly, "Poem" combines nature's beauty ("The bobcat padding in the
red sumac . . . the pheasant in . . . goldenrod") with nature's life-and-
death moments ("both rise to the flush, / the brief low flutter and catch
in the air"), while the rich, green trees

> yield to conclusions they do not care about
> or watch—the dead, frayed bird,
> the beautiful plumage,
> the spoor of feathers
> and slight, pink bones.

In "Young Bull," also from *Plain Song*, Harrison reveals nature's dangerous side. As the poem opens, the young bull nuzzles the "itch / against a fence post," the fresh wound made by the new bronze ring in its nose. As the bull endures the intense August heat ("pained fluid of August"), the flies, and the chickens scratching about its feet, the speaker pities the bull, but when he brings the animal feed and cold water, it "bellowed and heaved / against the slats wanting to murder me." John Rohrkemper argues that because the speaker mistakenly imagines that the bull will recognize and appreciate human sympathy, nature can be "particularly perilous for those who would embrace its beauty without full awareness of its dangers" (23). In "My Friend the Bear" in *The Theory and Practice of Rivers*, nature blesses the speaker. The speaker has raised this bear for three years, ever since he found her "bawling against the dead carcass of her mother." After keeping her down in the "bone myth of the cellar" in a room "behind the empty fruit jars," he decides to return her to the wilderness. As they head north, her growls become "less friendly as she scents / the forest above the road smell." Although he must jump "free of her snarls and roars" when he frees her, he says she returns each year and they

> embrace ear to ear,
> her huge head on my shoulder,
> her breathing like god's.

In "Counting Birds," the 50-year-old speaker also feels blessed by his life of counting birds. The birds he "became" helped him "escape unfortunate circumstances," and he hopes that on his deathbed he will sing to himself:

> O birds, . . . you've carried
> me along on this bloody voyage,
> carry me . . . into that marvel of this final night.

In *Plain Song*, "Dusk" epitomizes Harrison's ability to describe the sights, sounds, and smells of a lake at dusk. The speaker sees "clouds floating" and "heat lightning / a nightmare behind branches." He smells the ferns and cedars and hears the "long circular / wail of the loon" as it waits, along with the speaker, "for night to come down." The last three lines denote the poem's movement:

> Then it becomes so dark
> and still
> that I shatter the moon with an oar.

The only discordant note is the speaker's oar that shatters the silence and the moon's reflected image. On the other hand, the discordant note at the end of "Lisle's River," also from *Plain Song*, celebrates the speaker's joy at being in the wilderness. "Dust followed our car like a dry brown cloud," the speaker begins, then describes canoeing down the river through cedar swamps and marsh grass, where he and his friends are "at home in a thing that passes." After drinking too much whiskey, they roll a burning stump down the bank that "cast hurling shadows, leaves silvered and darkened, / the crash and hiss woke up a thousand birds." Although a seemingly discordant image, the burning stump's crash and hiss celebrate the speaker's exuberance. As he asks at the end, "Now, tell me, other than lying between some woman's legs / what joy have you had to equal this?" Other Harrison nature poems, like "Morning," "Park at Night," "Sound," and "Lullaby for a Daughter," aptly distill a scene as well. In "Park at Night" are trees

> caged to the waist
> wet statues
> the trickling of water—
> in the fountain
> floating across the lamp
> a leaf
> some cellophane.

In "Lullaby for a Daughter," night is variously defined: as "a bright sun / burned to a black cinder"; "a flower / resting from bees"; "a white moon / riding her mare"; a "star's feast of praise / moon to reign over / her sweet subject, dark."

In *Locations*, "Natural World" details a wantonly despoiled nature. In the first stanza, the speaker circumscribes the natural world:

> The earth is almost round. The seas
> are curved and hug the earth, both
> ends are crowned with ice.

Focusing on a great blue whale swimming near "this ice," the speaker notes that its heart weighs 2,000 pounds, its tongue "weighs twice as much," and the entire whale "weighs one hundred fifty tons." Because so few blue whales are left, this one "often can't find a mate" and "drags his six-foot sex through the icy waters, / flukes spread crashing." The stanza concludes with another fact—the blue whale's brain is "large enough for a man to sleep in." In the last stanza, the speaker obliquely explains why so few blue whales remain:

> On Hawk Mountain in Pennsylvania
> thousands upon thousands
> upon thousands of hawks in migration
> have been slaughtered for pleasure.

The poem ends as the speaker lists other birds of prey "slaughtered for pleasure": merlin, kestrel, peregrine, gyrfalcon, golden eagle, osprey. In his essay "A Sporting Life," Harrison condemns the Oriental belief that ground ivory is an aphrodisiac and the "boggling sexual vanity involved in killing a nine-ton beast for hard-ons" (*JBD*, 150). Similarly, in "Natural World," Harrison condemns the boggling vanity of killing for pleasure not only birds of prey but great blue whales, whose huge heart, tongue, brain, and size should humble man.

Yielding Aesthetic Possibilities

Much of Harrison's poetry originates in autobiography in that he examines and reexamines his life to make sense of it. Munro believed that in *Letters to Yesenin* Harrison struggles with the "ghosts and killing realities of the past and present and tries to arrive at a credible reason for rejecting suicide as a proper response to life's absurdity."[3] Mark McCloskey wrote that the poems comprising *Letters to Yesenin* are "the stage on which the poet considers his most troublesome desires and failures in order to discover where they should lead him—to suicide or to a renewed life."[4] Mark Hillringhouse believed that Harrison's animal poems in *The Theory and Practice of Rivers* are "not so much about those creatures as they are reference points from which the author departs into his meditations. They are different appraisals of the world, his place in it, autobiographical assessments, studies of rural versus urban living, personal failures, frustrations, loves, triumphs, joys and sadness." Hillringhouse argues that the "occasional preachiness" in some of the short poems is integral to what could be called Harrison's "personal

koans": "He is writing homilies for himself. You either get them or you
don't" (158).

In *Plain Song*, "Sketch for a Job Application Blank" is both an autobiographical assessment and a personal homily. This poem was initially
inspired by Harrison's reading of Pablo Neruda in 1960; impressed with
"Neruda's green world, his primary colors and surrealist imagery," he
began a poem to Neruda but quickly abandoned it because "I realized
that the poem was an intellectual exercise, an act of worship, idolatry.
Whitman's introduction to *Leaves of Grass* had made me very sensitive to
derivative art—to this day I cannot bring myself to write about a painting or a statue or another's poem though I often have an impulse to do
so" (*JBD*, 197). Later, however, Harrison exhumed "Sketch for a Job
Application Blank" when he was in Boston and had been unemployed
for a year: "My daily life had become a round of employment offices,
interviews with personnel people who seemed to sense instantly that I
was unsuitable, flatly unemployable. My jacket pocket was filled with
application blanks for all manner of work—I seemed unable to get past
my name and social security number" (*JBD*, 197–98). When he wonders how Neruda would answer the questions on the application blanks,
the "biographical information and other pertinent details" in particular,
Harrison says that "Sketch for a Job Application Blank" took form and
meaning: "I immediately realized that rather than Neruda I had been
attempting to write a poem in praise of myself—to describe what, if any,
were my 'pertinent details'" (*JBD*, 198).

As "Sketch" opens, Harrison refers to those autobiographical details
that uniquely shaped him, like being blind in his left eye, having a large
nose and bucked teeth, being called "pig eye" by his friends, being
described as "loony" by his teachers. He also talks about his personal
fears—the salesman with the display case of glass eyes, the power of "the
great cocked hoof of a Belgian mare," a nest of milk snakes, and machin-
ery like the "pump arm of an oil well / the chop and whirr of a combine
in the sun." Ancestors also shaped his personality. From the Swedes he
inherited the "love of rainy woods, / kegs of herring and neat whiskey";
from his German Mennonite ancestors he inherited "intolerance, an aimless diligence." He also alludes to being saved during a 1951 revival,
being baptized "by immersion in the tank at Williamson," and being
reborn into the world of the flesh:

> I left off the old things of the flesh
> but not for long—one night beside a pond
> she dried my feet with her yellow hair.

In recalling the "pertinent details" that have shaped him as a person, Harrison accepts his personality and life:

> (Now self is the first sacrament
> who loves not the misery and taint
> of the present is lost.
> In strain for a lunar arrogance
>> Light macerates
>> the lamp infects
> warmth, more warmth I cry.)

To accept the "misery and taint of the present"—the interminable job interviews and application blanks—is to lose all significance and meaning in his life. Finally, from his present stasis—being unemployable and at the end of his tether—he will struggle for significance and meaning, or "lunar arrogance." Thus, the poem moves from self-doubt and fear toward an acceptance of self. According to Harrison, "The poem, regardless of its weaknesses, precipitated an explosion of work. I stopped worrying about being unemployable and finished, in addition to 'Sketch,' thirteen poems within a month. . . . I suppose I am fond of it for this reason—it made me function as a poet for the first time, to insist on the act of poetry as perhaps my only viable ability, to construct a complete poem, however short and clumsy" (*JBD*, 198).

Harrison also relies on autobiography in "David," another poem in *Plain Song*. "'David' illustrates another aspect of the autobiographical poem speaking through a 'persona' to insure aesthetic distance. I was unable to say anything about the death of my father directly that wasn't benumbed, cloudy, constricted. When the poem finally began to 'happen' it took shape through the eyes of my younger brother. Though this wasn't a conscious choice, it proved to handle the experience in a much more valid, less literary manner" (*JBD*, 199).

The poem's first line—"He is young. The father is dead"—establishes the aesthetic distance, as well as death as a theme. The next five lines emphasize the distance:

> Outside, a cold November night,
> the mourners' cars are parked upon the lawn,
> beneath the porch light three
> brothers talk to three sons
> and shiver without knowing it.

The poem then telescopes from the night to the cars, to the porch light, to the three uncles and three brothers, to David's mind, which is "all black thickets / and blood." To emphasize the movement in David's mind, the speaker repeats the word *knows*. He "knows" that "flesh slips quietly off the bone"; "he knows" that, "among the profusion of flowers," there will be "no last looks," because "the lid is closed to hide / what no one could bear— / that metal rends the flesh"; finally, "he knows that in the distant talk of brothers, / the father is dead." Technically, the word *distant* emphasizes how David has moved beyond the opening scene, beyond the "profusion of flowers" and the closed casket, and begun to talk to the reality of death. Moreover, while the closing line, "the father is dead," repeats the poem's second sentence, it also emphasizes David's final acceptance of the fact that neither the cold November night, the "distant talk of brothers," nor the "profusion of flowers" can nullify the reality of the father's death.

"A Sequence of Women," also from *Plain Song*, relies on a variation of the technique in "David." "Here the 'lie' is doubly removed, hiding behind the artifice of modified sapphics and a 'mistress' while the true subject was the death of my sister. Though the poem required a great deal of care and close attention I didn't consciously realize it was about my sister until it was finished" (*JBD*, 200).

As the poem opens, the speaker explains that he has "known her too long":

> we devour as two mirrors,
> opposed,
> swallow each other a thousand times at midpoints,
> lost in the black center
> of the other.

In the second section, the speaker describes how she would sit on the bed, watch dust motes float through the air, and talk casually about how her desire to be remembered "as a mare might know / the body of her rider." Abruptly, however, the tone and focus change as he emphasizes in the third section that she has died in childbirth, even though he thinks that "long ago women ceased / dying this way." He realizes:

> But I'm a poor Midas to turn her golden,
> make a Helen, grand whore, of the graceless
> girl; the sparrow that died was only
> a sparrow:

The last stanza underscores death's finality:

> *Though in the dark, she doesn't sleep.*
> *On cushions embraced by silk, no lover*
> *comes to her. In the first light when birds*
> *stir she does not stir or sing. O eyes can't*
> *focus to this dark.*

The siblings "devour" and thus know each other because they are brother and sister and have spent much time together. The reference to "dying in childbirth" underscores the sister's untimely death, and the speaker's inability to write eloquent verse emphasizes those shared moments and experiences that make her life and death far more meaningful than the "sparrow that died." If in "David" the poem's movement is toward acceptance of the father's death, in "A Sequence of Women" the movement is toward acceptance of the sister's death. Indeed, not only do the italics in the last stanza emphasize death, but so does the ironic undercutting of the traditional fairy tale in which a young lover awakens a sleeping maiden with a kiss. Instead, the speaker emphasizes that this "graceless girl" does not "sleep" and will not stir at "first light" because her *"eyes can't focus to this dark."*

Harrison acknowledges that all of his poems "are at least nominally autobiographical, containing events and images drawn from life"; to him, the "unanswered question is why a poet transforms experience, not so much to make it understandable, but to make it yield its aesthetic possibilities" (*JBD*, 200). Harrison's insights about autobiography and "aesthetic possibilities" are evident in "John Severin Walgren, 1874–1962," an elegy to his maternal grandfather and also a poem about death's inevitable process. "Trees die of thirst or cold / or when the limit's reached" are the opening lines, and the next four lines describe an elm's limit as a hole in which the "wood is soft and punky" and "smells of the water of a vase / after the flowers are dumped." In the second stanza, the speaker links "when the limit's reached" to the grandfather who was "so old we could not weep." Abruptly, however, the poem's thrust is about the terror of untimely deaths:

> only the blood of the young,
> those torn off the earth in a night's sickness,
> the daughter lying beside you
> who became nothing so long ago—
> she moves us to terror.

Harrison's "Fair/Boy Christian Takes a Break" from *Plain Song* also plumbs autobiography for its "aesthetic possibilities." As the poem opens, Boy Christian explains that his companion, identified only as "this other," "speaks of bones, blood-wet / and limber, the rock in bodies," and has taken him to the slaughterhouse, where they see "sprawled, as a giant coil of rope, / the bowels of cattle." At the county fair, Boy Christian and "this other" see a hermaphrodite, watch the hidden air tube blow up farm girls' skirts, watch Fantasia do a love dance with a Spaniard, as the "farm boys twitter like birds," and watch the huge Negress do a striptease while "everyone stamps and cheers." Even outside the sideshows, Boy Christian sees the chaste breasts of a farm girl as she leans over to give him a drink of water. In the closing lines, however, Boy Christian confesses:

> Through the evening I sit in the car (the
> other is gone) while my father watches
> the harness race, the 4-H talent show.
> I think of St. Paul's Epistles and pray
> the removal of what my troubled eyes have seen.

"Fair/Boy Christian Takes a Break" recalls Harrison's conversion and eventual reconversion to the world of the flesh, a subject covered in the interviews and in his fiction. Although no reconversion occurs in "Fair/Boy Christian," Boy Christian is initiated into the world of the flesh at the slaughterhouse and especially at the fair's erotic sideshows, then prays for the "removal" of what his "troubled eyes have seen." The reader must decide who "this other" is; there are three possibilities. First, "this other" could be Boy Christian's father, since the boy says that his father has gone ("the other is gone") to watch the harness race and the 4-H talent show. Moreover, in "Memoir of Horse Pulling," Harrison writes about attending local fairs with his father and squandering his "miserably small allowance" before noon, after which he would "pester my father for more change though he was busy judging everything imaginable" (*JBD*, 98).[5] If "this other" is his father, then the poem is about Boy Christian's initiation in one of the rites of manhood, namely, the world of slaughterhouses, sideshow freaks, and eroticism. Whether he twitters like a bird during Fantasia's love dance or "stamps and cheers" during the striptease is a moot point, but the fact is that after his experiences he is troubled about what he has seen.

"This other" could also arguably be one of the speaker's boyhood friends who is as sexually naive and curious about the world of the flesh as Boy Christian is. Unlike Boy Christian, however, the friend, who may have stamped and cheered, simply leaves and is untroubled about St. Paul's Epistles and what his eyes have seen. Knowing that Harrison often deals with the two sides of one brain, however, a third and more dramatic interpretation is that Boy Christian is wrestling with his own two natures: the "Boy" or human nature, and the "Christian" or spiritual nature. In this sense, "Fair/Boy Christian" is another version of the good-versus-evil, or the flesh-versus-spirit conflict. The speaker's boyish nature (the one that "speaks of bones" and the "rock in bodies") goads him into seeing the hermaphrodite, the farm girls' skirts being up-blown, Fantasia dancing, and the Negress stripteasing. As implied in the "farm boys twitter like birds" and "everyone stamps and cheers," Boy Christian enjoys his fall into the world of the flesh, but later his Christian conscience plagues him and he prays for the removal of what his eyes have seen. In this sense, "Fair/Boy Christian" does not end with what Boy Christian has learned from his initiation into the world of the flesh—that is, with his taking "a break" from the Christian world. Instead, the poem concludes by emphasizing the conflict raging in the boy's conscience, about which he can only pray because, while he is a "fair" or average Christian, he is also a "fair" or average boy whose faith has been tested.

Munro accurately observed that Harrison "resists the tendency to write stylized or predictable poetry" (Munro 1992, 1233). And to read Harrison's nature poems, his mainly autobiographical poems, or his longer poems like "Outlyer," "Ghazals," "Letters to Yesenin," and "The Theory and Practice of Rivers" is to become aware of just how varied, layered, and intriguing a poetic voice he has. As the anonymous *Publishers Weekly* reviewer commented:

> Harrison will delight and shock readers who think they already know what a poem is supposed to be. The experience is like coming across a Whitman or Dickinson, a Keats or Rimbaud, after a long diet of formal and classical verse; here is a poet talking to you instead of around himself, while doing absolutely brilliant and outrageous things with language.[6]

Notes and References

Chapter One

1. Kathy Stocking, "Writer Jim Harrison: Work, Booze, the Outdoor Life—and an Absolute Rage for Order," *Detroit Free Press*, 5 June 1977: 20; hereafter cited in text.

2. Jean W. Ross, "*CA* Interview," *Contemporary Authors: New Series*, vol. 8, ed. Ann Evory and Linda Metzgar (Detroit: Gale Research, 1983): 227; hereafter cited in text.

3. Edward C. Reilly, "John Harrison Talks about Jim Harrison," interview, 1 November 1991, Fayetteville, Arkansas; hereafter cited in text as "John Harrison."

4. Edward C. Reilly, "Lake Effect: Talking with Jim Harrison," interview, December 1991, Lake Leelanau, Michigan; hereafter cited in text as "Lake."

5. See Jim Harrison, "The Raw and the Cooked: Ignoring Columbus," *Esquire* 119, no. 4 (August 1991): 32–34. Harrison alludes humorously to his sinus operation. See also Frederick Burger, "Why I Hate TV," *Miami Herald TV*, 13–19 June 1982, 4–6. Harrison affirms, "I've stopped watching baseball and football. Put it this way . . . in the summer they throw the ball, in the fall they kick the ball, in the winter they bounce the ball. We shouldn't let the banality of this escape us."

6. Ric Bohy, "Jim Harrison, The Mad Poet Cools off (a Little)," *Michigan: The Magazine of the Detroit News*, 9 February 1986, 10; hereafter cited in text.

7. Gregory Skwira, "Words from the Woods," *Detroit Free Press*, 25 March 1984, 17; hereafter cited in text.

8. Aloysius Sisyphus, "*The Diddy Wah Diddy* Interview: Jim Harrison," *The Diddy Wah Diddy* (Jackson, Miss.) 6, no. 5 (October 1990): 6; hereafter cited in text.

9. Jim Fergus, "The Art of Fiction CIV: Jim Harrison," *Paris Review* 30, no. 107 (1988): 59; hereafter cited in text.

10. Jim Fergus, "The Sporting Club," *Outside* (March 1989): 43; hereafter cited in text.

11. Robert E. Burkholder, "Jim Harrison," *Dictionary of Literary Biography Yearbook 1982*, ed. Robert Ziegfeld (Detroit: Bruccoli Clark, 1983), 267; hereafter cited in text.

12. Jim Harrison, *Letters to Yesenin and Returning to Earth* (Los Angeles: Sumac Poetry Series Center Publications, 1979), 19; hereafter cited in text as *LY*.

13. Jim Harrison, *Just before Dark: Collected Nonfiction* (Livingston, Mont.: Clark City Press, 1991), 188; hereafter cited in text as *JBD*.

14. Kathleen Stocking, "Hard Cases: Conversation with Jim Harrison and Tom McGuane, Writers of the Purple Rage," *Detroit News Magazine* (17 August 1980): 121; hereafter cited in text.

15. Eric Siegal, "A New Voice from the North Country: Portrait of a Prodigal Poet Who Came Home to Michigan," *Detroit Free Press Magazine* (16 April 1972): 19; hereafter cited in text.

16. Jim Fergus, "Jim Harrison: Today's Hemingway?" *MD* (May 1985): 118; hereafter cited in text.

17. Dexter Westrum, *Tom McGuane* (Boston: Twayne, 1991), 5.

18. Julia Reed, "Books," *Vogue* 179 (September 1989): 510; hereafter cited in text.

19. Kevin Breen, "An Interview with Rick Bass," *Poets and Writers* 21, no. 3 (May-June 1993): 21. Bass writes about the visit he and his wife had with the Harrisons in "Shyness," *Black Warrior Review* 15, no. 2 (1989): 155–59. Harrison visits Roger Welsch in "The Raw and the Cooked: Unmentionable Cuisine," *Esquire* 118, no. 6 (December 1992): 83–84.

20. Jim Harrison, "The Raw and the Cooked: Let's Get Lost," *Esquire* 116, no. 5 (November 1991): 79.

21. Marc Dettman, "Legends of the North," *Grand Rapids* 19, no. 8 (August 1982): 34. This article is also about Dan Gerber and his family.

22. Peter S. Prescott, "The Macho Mystique," *Newsweek* 94 (9 July 1979): 72; hereafter cited in text. In the interview with Kay Bonetti (*Missouri Review* 8, no. 3 [1985]: 83), Harrison says that Prescott, "rather than talking about my book . . . used me as an object lesson in what's wrong with contemporary writing because, he said, I had none of the new feminine sensibility. He's talking about a public movement, a woman's movement, that I don't think has anything to do with the novel. . . . I'm not trying to get out the vote when I write a novel. . . . I don't like to be attacked for reasons anterior to my work."

23. See also Ross, "*CA* Interviews," 228. Harrison says, "I know a lot about Mexican culture, and . . . macho is when you throw a rattlesnake in a baby carriage or bite off your mother's toe—some kind of overpowering violence." In "The Revenge Symposium" (*Esquire* 99, no. 5 [May 1983]: 85), Harrison again defines *macho* and adds, "I prefer the word *nacho*, that delicious little tidbit, to describe my behavior." See Harrison's letter to the *New York Times Book Review* ([19 September 1982]: 37) and his objection to a recent advertisement touting him as a "brawny wordslinger from the Michigan backwoods." In response, Harrison writes: "I resent this tasteless attempt to market me as if I were a John Wayne clone. I have spent 20 years living simply up in the country, trying to perfect my craft and, if the critics will, my art. I am a kind-hearted fool to all but bats and carpenter ants. I cook a great deal and take seven animals on a long daily walk, except for a pet crow who flies in advance to warn us of the press and advertising copywriters."

24.   Ira Elliott and Marty Sommerness, "Jim Harrison: A Good Day for Talking: An Interview with the Author of *Wolf* and *Farmer*," *October Chronicle* (29 October 1976): n.p.; hereafter cited in text.

25.   See also Jean W. Ross, "An Interview with Jim Harrison," *DLB Yearbook* (Detroit: Bruccoli Clark, 1983): 276. Harrison says that a "critic is in the same position as a sports announcer, somebody like Howard Cosell: he has to talk a great deal about something he's not very intimate with." In the *Paris Review*, Harrison says that "getting bad reviews is not nearly as bad as getting no reviews" (67). In "The Revenge Symposium" Harrison candidly admits: "Fifteen years ago in the *New York Times Book Review* [(28 April 1968): 6] I wrote a nasty, cute, snide review of a poet dying of a dread disease, L. E. Sissman. I didn't know he was dying. I probably still wouldn't have liked his poetry, but writing a review should never be an occasion to preen, show off, do vain fandangos at someone's expense. I still mope about my stupidity." See James Mann, "L. E. Sissman," in *DLB*, vol. 5, *American Poets since World War II*, ed. Donald J. Greiner (Detroit: Gale Research, 1980): 241–47. Mann says that Harrison accurately assesses the tone in Sissman's *Dying: An Introduction*.

26.   Jim Harrison, "The Raw and the Cooked: The Morality of Food," *Esquire* 117, no. 3 (March 1992): 78.

Chapter Two

1.   Kay Bonetti, "An Interview with Jim Harrison," *Missouri Review* 8, no. 3 (1985): 65; hereafter cited in text. Harrison talks about meeting Jack Nicholson on *The Missouri Breaks* set: "We got to talking and he asked me if I had one of my novels with me, and I had one. I think it was *Wolf*. He read it and enjoyed it. He told me if I ever got an idea for him, to call him up. Well, I never have any of those ideas. . . . I think he said later that I was the only one he ever told that to who never called" (Fergus 1988, 69).

2.   See "The Raw and the Cooked: Coming to Our Senses," *Esquire* 117, no. 5 (May 1992): 61–62. Harrison writes about falling down a cliff in Hog Canyon while hunting.

3.   Jonathan Yardley, "Also Extravagantly Free-Male," *New York Times Book Review* (12 December 1971): 4; hereafter cited in text.

4.   Joyce Carol Oates, "Going Places," *Partisan Review* 37, no. 3 (Summer 1972): 463; hereafter cited in text.

5.   H. L. van Brunt, *Saturday Review* 154 (25 December 1971): 30.

6.   "First Novelists," *Library Journal* 96 (1 October 1971): 3165.

7.   Jim Harrison, *Wolf: A False Memoir* (New York: Simon & Schuster, 1971; New York: Delta/Seymour Lawrence, 1989): 11; hereafter cited in text as *WFM*.

8.   W. H. Roberson, "A Good Day to Live: The Prose Works of Jim Harrison," *Great Lakes Review* 9, no. 1 (1983): 79, 30; hereafter cited in text.

9.   C. Lynn Munro, "Jim Harrison," in *Critical Survey of Long Fiction*, vol. 4, ed. Frank N. Magill (La Canada, Calif.: Salem Press, 1983), 1288, 1289.

10. John Rohrkemper, "'Natty Bumppo Wants Tobacco': Jim Harrison's Wilderness," *Great Lakes Review* 9, no. 1 (1983): 24; hereafter cited in text.
11. See Harrison's "Memoir of a Horse Pulling" in *Just before Dark*. He reminisces about the intricacies of horse-pulling contests at county fairs.
12. C. Hugh Holman, *A Handbook to Literature* (Indianapolis: Bobbs-Merrill, 1980), 263; hereafter cited in text.

Chapter Three

1. Sara Blackburn, *New York Times Book Review* (9 September 1973): 4, 5; hereafter cited in text.
2. William Crawford Woods, "What a Strange Accomplishment," *Washington Post*, 9 September 1973, 4.
3. *Choice* 10 (February 1974): 1966.
4. Jim Harrison, *A Good Day to Die* (New York: Simon & Schuster, 1973; New York: Delta/Seymour Lawrence, 1981), 42; hereafter cited in text as *AGD*.
5. Francis Haines, *The Nez Perces: Tribesmen of the Columbia Plateau* (Norman: University of Oklahoma Press, 1972), xv.
6. Michael D. Beal, *I Will Fight No More Forever: Chief Joseph and the Nez Perce* (New York: Ballantine, 1975), 23.
7. Harvey Chalmers, *The Last Stand of the Nez Perce: Destruction of a People* (New York: Twayne, 1962), 20; hereafter cited in text.

Chapter Four

1. *New Yorker* 52 (30 August 1976): 90.
2. Parkman Howe, "Two Novels Accent Self-Discovery," *Christian Science Monitor*, 27 January 1977, 23.
3. "Barnyard Love," *Newsweek* 88, no. 9 (30 August 1976): 70.
4. Webster Schott, *New York Times Book Review* (10 October 1976): 32.
5. Wendy Smith, "*PW* Interviews Jim Harrison," *Publishers Weekly* 237, no. 3 (3 August 1990): 60; hereafter cited in text.
6. Jim Harrison, *Farmer* (New York: Viking, 1976; New York: Delta/Seymour Lawrence, 1982), 3; hereafter cited in text as *F*.
7. Jim Harrison, *Selected and New Poems, 1961–1981* (New York: Delacorte/Seymour Lawrence, 1981; New York: Delta/Seymour Lawrence, 1982), 9.

Chapter Five

1. Harrison's inscription in my copy of *Legends of the Fall*.
2. "Life and Letters: 'Legends of the Fall,'" *Atlantic Monthly* 144, no. 3 (September 1979): 92.

3. Vance Bourjaily, "Three Novellas: Violent Means," *New York Times Book Review* (17 June 1979): 14, 27; hereafter cited in text.

4. Keith Opdahl, "Junk Food," *The Nation* 229, no. 1 (7 July 1979): 24.

5. Anne V. Kish, "Fiction: 'Legends of the Fall,'" *Best Sellers* 39, no. 6 (September 1979): 197.

6. "Books: 'Legends of the Fall,'" *New Yorker* 55, no. 24 (30 July 1979): 89.

7. Jim Harrison, *Legends of the Fall* (New York: Delta/Seymour Lawrence, 1979), 34; hereafter cited in the text as *R* (*Revenge*), *TMW* (*The Man Who Gave up His Name*), and *LOF* (*Legends of the Fall*).

8. In Wendy Smith's *PW* interview with Harrison, Harrison jokingly said that Bob Dattila's last name "obviously means 'from Attila'" (60).

9. The word *cociloco* is a typographical error and, according to one source, could be either *cocoloco* or *cochiloco*. When I wrote to Harrison about the matter, he replied: "*Cochiloco*, otherwise known in Latino slang, was a drug assassin, maybe still is. Kilt [sic] a hundred or so" (letter to the author, January 1994).

10. Aleksandra Gruzinska, "E. M. Cioran and *The Man Who Gave up His Name* by Jim Harrison," *Journal of the American Romanian Society of Arts and Sciences* 12 (1989): 85, 92.

11. John Wilson, "*Legends of the Fall*," in *Magill's Literary Annual: Books of 1979* (Englewood Cliffs, N.J.: Salem Press, 1980), 465.

12. *American Heritage History of the Great West* (New York: Simon & Schuster, 1965), reports that Sir George Gore, after a "warm-up venture into present-day Colorado . . . moved north to winter (1855–56) in Yellowstone Valley. To care for and transport his seventy-five sporting rifles, his fifteen shotguns, dozens of pistols, bundles of fishing rods, his special tents, collapsible brass bedstead, and folding tables, he had one hundred and twelve horses, forty men, six wagons, and twenty-one two-wheeled carts, plus Jim Bridger as guide. When he passed through Fort Union . . . on his way home, he boasted to Indian agent Alfred Vaughn that he had killed that spring '105 bears and some 2,000 Buffalo Elk and Deer 1600.' Angrily Vaughn added, 'The Inds have been loud in their complaints.' Bitterly he asked, 'What can I do against so large a number of men coming into a country like this so very remote from civilization. . . . ' And in dejection he answered his own question: 'Nothing'" (318). Gore epitomizes the game violators whom Harrison attacks in his essays and fiction; with his army of men, animals, wagons, and other accoutrements of civilization (especially his pretentious brass bedstead), Gore also symbolizes the encroachment of civilization.

13. Paul H. Lorenz, "Rethinking Machismo: Jim Harrison's *Legends of the Fall*," *Publications of the Arkansas Philological Association* 14, no. 1 (Spring 1989): 41–51.

Chapter Six

1. Paul Stuewe, "Sex in Venice: Essays from Bloomsbury and Uris's 'Jerusalem,'" *Quill and Quire* 48, no. 1 (January 1982): 39.

2. John Buckley, *Saturday Review* 8, no. 10 (October 1981): 76.

3. John D. Casey, "American Settings," *New York Times Book Review* (22 November 1981): 14.

4. George Held, "Outside Man," *American Book Review* 5, no. 4 (May-June 1983): 20.

5. J. D. Reed, "Hick Gumshoe," *Time* 118, no. 19 (9 November 1981): K12.

6. Jim Harrison, *Warlock* (New York: Delta/Seymour Lawrence, 1981), preface; hereafter cited in text as *W*.

7. Elmer M. Blistein, *Comedy in Action* (Durham, N.C.: Duke University Press, 1964), 177.

8. Robert Corrigan, *Comedy: Meaning and Form* (San Francisco: Chandler, 1965), 3.

Chapter Seven

1. Michiko Kakutani, *New York Times*, 21 May 1984, C14.

2. A. C. Greene, "The Man-God of the Michigan Jungles," *New York Times Book Review* (15 July 1984): 14.

3. Richard Deverson, "Call of the Wild," *New Statesman* 110 (23 August 1985): 28.

4. James B. Hemesath, *Library Journal* 109 (1 June 1984): 1144.

5. *Publishers Weekly* 225 (13 April 1984): 52.

6. William Bradley Hooper, *Booklist* 80 (1 June 1984): 1378.

7. "Notes on Current Books," *Virginia Quarterly* 60 (Autumn 1984): 132.

8. Harrison describes going "down this big corridor and up in this elevator about 18 stories, and then we got up on the top of the dam. There weren't any guard rails or anything up, so this engineer goes right over to the edge of the dam. He says, 'Hey, Harrison, come over here,' and I said, 'No!'" ("Lake").

9. Jim Harrison, *Sundog* (New York: E. P. Dutton/Seymour Lawrence, 1984), 119; hereafter cited in text as *S*.

10. Jim Harrison, letter to the author, 28 September 1984. I had written Harrison and mentioned that I was working on a critical article, "Comedy and *Warlock*: A Leap into Faith," and in his reply he wrote: "Frankly I am also curious about your notions concerning *Warlock* and Faith? Strang seems to be my first Christian hero."

11. Harrison provides other interesting insights into *Sundog* in the Bonetti interview: for instance, Harrison's own Upper Peninsula cabin is the model for Strang's cabin, and at two o'clock in the morning Harrison swam down the river outside his cabin at night so he could get the right feeling for describing Strang's swim. Most important, when he was on page 197 of the novel, he realized he was writing about his "alter ego"; "It blew one writing day. It totally terrified me because Strang worked on eleven dams, and I'd written eleven books. I mean it got that bad. And I felt utterly crippled. Just like

Strang's been crippled by his work. I said, 'Oh my God! Can I go on?' Well the energy of the novel had taken over, so it didn't matter" (68–71).

12.　Harrison intended to title the novel *The Foreman*; when I asked him why he decided on *Sundog*, he explained: "I started thinking after [Strang] had that frightening experience as a boy in that house without heat and the frozen woodpile. Then after that it was sort of a celtic notion of a dog following the sun around—that kind of thing" ("Lake").

Chapter Eight

1.　John Clute, "Elegiac Heirs," *Times Literary Supplement* (24 March 1990): 299.
2.　Roz Kaveney, "An Eye for the Regional and Social," *London* 3, no. 3 (June 1989): 16.
3.　Michael C. M. Huey, "Writing and Telling in Harrison's Latest," *Christian Science Monitor*, 13 June 1988, 19.
4.　Jonathan Yardley, "A Lonely Heart in the Heartland," *Washington Post Book World* (6 March 1988): 3.
5.　C. Lynn Munro, "Jim Harrison," in *Critical Survey of Long Fiction*, rev. ed., ed. Frank N. Magill (Englewood Cliffs, N.J.: Salem Press, 1991), 1546. Munro mistakenly identifies Dalva's grandfather and not her great-grandfather as the author of the journals.
6.　Louise Erdrich, *Chicago Tribune*, 20 March 1988, 1.
7.　Jim Harrison, *Dalva* (New York: E. P. Dutton/Seymour Lawrence, 1988; New York: Washington Square Press, 1989), 24; hereafter cited in text as *D*.
8.　Kathleen Stocking, "Heart and Soul," *Detroit Monthly* (September 1988): 178; hereafter cited in the text.
9.　Thomas BeVier, "A Hint of Harrison," *Traverse* (April 1988): 17.

Chapter Nine

1.　Michiko Kakutani, "The Shapes and Textures of Three Lives," *New York Times*, 28 August 1990, C16; hereafter cited in text.
2.　Joseph Coates, "Bedrock Americana," *Chicago Tribune*, 12 August 1990, 1, 4.
3.　John Baron, "The Write Brothers," *Detroit Monthly* (August 1990): 24.
4.　Robert Houston, "Love for the Proper Outlaw," *New York Times Book Review* (16 September 1990): 13.
5.　Judith Freeman, "Women's Intimations," *Los Angeles Times Book Review* (1 August 1990): 1, 5; hereafter cited in text.
6.　Arthur Krystal, "Jim Harrison: Three for the Road," *Book World* (2 September 1990): 7.
7.　Jim Harrison, *The Woman Lit by Fireflies* (New York: Houghton Mifflin, 1990; New York: Washington Square Press, 1991), 3; hereafter cited

in text as *BD* (*Brown Dog*), *SL* (*Sunset Limited*), and *WLF* (*The Woman Lit by Fireflies*).

8. In talking about Robert Bly, Harrison says, "I must confess, I don't understand what's going on in that Wildman-Ironman kind of thing. The people that are obsessed with that come from dysfunctional, totally dysfunctional, families. They are part of the baby boom, now in its forties, and they never had any contact with the countryside or the earth. It's basically urban. I think that's the sociological explanation, but then there is also the disenchantment with success. I think a lot of people are successful, but it doesn't add up. It used to be that somebody would think, if only I could make $25,000, if only I could make fifty, or seventy-five, or whatever it is, a hundred thousand, and everything would be okay. . . . It never stops" ("Lake").

9. Freeman based her comment on the information in *Smart* magazine, where *Sunset Limited* first appeared in the January-February 1990 issue.

Chapter Ten

1. David Lyons, "Endpapers, New Fiction," *Memphis Flyer Literary Supplement* (2–8 June 1994): 1.

2. Werner Trieschmann, "He's a Bankable Archetype If Not a Cult Literary Man," *Arkansas Democrat-Gazette*, 15 May 1994, 8J.

3. David Dawson, "Three Harrison Stories Reveal Subtle Truths," *Memphis Commercial Appeal*, 15 May 1994, G3.

4. Jonis Agee, "The Macho Chronicles," *New York Times Book Review* (22 May 1994): 41; hereafter cited in text.

5. Jim Harrison, *Julip* (New York: Houghton Mifflin/Seymour Lawrence, 1994), 3; hereafter cited in text as *J* (*Julip*), *SOM* (*The Seven-Ounce Man*), and *TBD* (*The Beige Dolorosa*).

6. In "The Macho Chronicles," Agee writes that "in the novella's casual reference to those who have killed themselves after serving as 'house fräuleins, or lust slaves,' we glimpse the dark wreckage that lurks behind the facade of these seemingly happy-go-lucky good ol' boys" (41). None of the "lust slaves" have killed themselves, but three have died over the past 20 years.

7. "Backstage with *Esquire*," *Esquire* 119, no. 3 (March 1993): 38.

8. In *The Seven-Ounce Man*, in an interview for the local TV station about the ancient burial mound, B.D. says, "I was tricked by these Ann Arbor anthropologists, including the famous *wagutz* Shelley Thurman, and then framed for burning one of their tents" (*SOM*, 107). In *Brown Dog*, however, Shelley's last name is Newkirk, not Thurman. Perhaps Homer nodded.

Chapter Eleven

1. Lisel Mueller, "Versions of Reality," *Poetry* 117 (February 1971): 322.

2. Mark Hillringhouse, *Literary Review* 55, no. 1 (Fall 1991): 158.

3. C. Lynn Munro, *Critical Survey of Poetry*, ed. Frank N. Magill (Englewood Cliffs, N.J.: Salem Press, 1992), 1235; hereafter cited in text.

4. Mark McCloskey, *"Selected and New Poems, 1961–1981,"* *Magill's Literary Annual 1983* (Englewood Cliffs, N.J.: Salem Press, 1983), 719.

5. In "Memoir of Horse Pulling," Harrison also writes about seeing a hermaphrodite, a sight that did not "mar" his "young psyche" (*JBD*, 98).

6. *Publishers Weekly* 221, no. 26 (25 June 1982): 114.

Selected Bibliography

PRIMARY SOURCES

Novels

Wolf: A False Memoir. New York: Simon & Schuster, 1971. New York: Strode, 1971. New York: Dell, 1981. New York: Delta/Seymour Lawrence, 1989.

A Good Day to Die. New York: Simon & Schuster, 1973. New York: Delta/Seymour Lawrence, 1981, 1989.

Farmer. New York: Viking Press, 1976. New York: Delta/Seymour Lawrence, 1980, 1989.

Legends of the Fall. New York: Delta/Seymour Lawrence, 1979 (limited signed edition). New York: Delta/Seymour Lawrence, 1979 (regular first edition). New York: Delta/Seymour Lawrence, 1979 (three-volume boxed set). New York: Delta/Seymour Lawrence, 1980, 1982, 1989.

Warlock. New York: Delta/Seymour Lawrence, 1981 (limited signed edition and regular first edition). New York: Delta/Seymour Lawrence, 1982.

Sundog. New York: E. P. Dutton/Seymour Lawrence, 1984. New York: Washington Square Press, 1991.

Dalva. New York: E. P. Dutton/Seymour Lawrence, 1988. New York: Washington Square Press, 1989.

The Woman Lit by Fireflies. New York: Houghton Mifflin, 1990. New York: Washington Square Press, 1990, 1991.

Julip. New York: Houghton Mifflin/Seymour Lawrence, 1994.

Poetry

Plain Song. New York: W. W. Norton. 1965.

Walking. Cambridge, Mass.: Pym Randall Press, 1967 (100 numbered plus 20 signed and lettered copies).

Locations. New York: W. W. Norton, 1968.

Stony Brook Holographs. Stony Brook, N.Y.: Stony Brook Poets Foundation, 1968.

Outlyer and Ghazals. New York: Simon & Schuster, 1971.

Letters to Yesenin. Fremont, Mich.: Sumac Press, 1973 (1,000 softcover, 100 numbered, and 26 lettered hardbound copies).

Returning to Earth. Berkeley, Calif.: Ithaca House, 1977.

Letters to Yesenin and Returning to Earth. Los Angeles: Sumac Poetry Series Center Publications, 1979.

211

Selected and New Poems, 1961–1981. New York: Delacorte/Seymour Lawrence, 1981. New York: Delta/Seymour Lawrence, 1982.

The Theory and Practice of Rivers and Other Poems. Seattle: Winn Books, 1986 (signed limited edition).

The Theory and Practice of Rivers and New Poems. Livingston, Mont.: Clark City Press, 1989, 1990.

Nonfiction

Just before Dark: Collected Nonfiction. Livingston, Mont.: Clark City Press, 1991. New York: Houghton Mifflin, 1992.

Screenplays

Revenge. Coauthored with Jeffrey Fishkin. Columbia Pictures, 1990.
Wolf. Coauthored with Wesley Strick. Sony Pictures, 1994.

Articles and Essays

"Grim Reapers of the Land's Bounty." *Sports Illustrated* 35 (11 October 1971): 38–40ff.
"To Each His Own Chills and Thrills." *Sports Illustrated* 36 (7 February 1972): 30–34.
"Old Faithful and Mysterious." *Sports Illustrated* 36 (14 February 1972): 68–72ff.
"Where the Chase Is the Song of Hound and Horn." *Sports Illustrated* 36 (20 March 1972): 64–69ff.
"Plaster Trout in Worm Heaven." *Sports Illustrated* 34 (10 May 1972): 70–72ff. Reprinted in *Just before Dark*, 55–62.
"Machine with Two Pistons." *Sports Illustrated* 39 (27 August 1973): 36–38ff.
"Guiding Light in the Keys." *Sports Illustrated* 39 (3 December 1973): 78–81ff. Reprinted in *Just before Dark*, 109–19.
"Fishing." *Sports Illustrated* 41 (14 October 1974): 98ff.
"Marching to a Different Drummer." *Sports Illustrated* 41 (4 November 1974): 38–40ff.
"Salvation in the Keys." *Esquire* 85 (June 1976): 152–53.
"A River Never Sleeps." *Esquire* 86 (August 1976): 6.
"Not at All Like up Home in Michigan." *Sports Illustrated* 45 (25 October 1976): 54–56ff.
"Advertisement." *New York Times Book Review* (19 September 1982): 35.
"The Revenge Symposium." *Esquire* 99 (May 1983): 88.
"From the *Dalva* Notebooks, 1985–1987." *Antaeus* 61 (Autumn 1988): 208–14. Reprinted in *Just before Dark*, 283–89.
"Don't Fence Me In." *Condé Nast Traveler* 24, no. 3 (March 1989): 114–25. Reprinted in *Just before Dark*, 184–92.

"Poetry as Survival." *Antaeus* 64 (Spring 1990): 370–80. Reprinted in *Just before Dark*, 294–305.

"Pie in the Sky." *Esquire Sportsman* 2, no. 2 (Fall-Winter 1993): 33–34.

"The Raw and the Cooked." *Esquire*. Harrison's monthly column, especially from 1991 to 1993.

Just before Dark contains Harrison's essays that were published in other magazines, including *Antaeus*, *Smart*, and *Playboy*.

Book Reviews

"California Hybrid." Review of *The Fork* by Richard Duerden, *Against the Silence to Come* by Ron Lowinsohn, *The Process* by David Meltzer, *Out Out* by Lew Welch, and *Hermit Poems* by Lew Welch. *Poetry* 108 (June 1966): 198–201.

Review of *Dying: An Introduction* by L. E. Sissman. *New York Times Book Review* (28 April 1968): 6.

Review of *All My Friends Are Going to Be Strangers* by Larry McMurtry. *New York Times Book Review* (19 March 1972): 5, 26.

"Three Novels: Comic, Cute, Cool." Review of *Geronimo Rex* by Barry Hannah. *New York Times Book Review* (14 May 1972): 4.

"The Main Character in the Cold and the Snow." Review of *The Snow Walker* by Farley Mowat. *New York Times Book Review* (22 February 1976): 4–5. Reprinted in *Just before Dark*, 250 53.

"10,000 Successive Octobers." Review of *The Snow Leopard* by Peter Matthiessen. *The Nation* 227, no. 8 (16 September 1978): 250–51. Reprinted in *Just before Dark*, 253–56.

"Voice in the Wilderness." Review of *Sand River* by Peter Matthiessen. *New York Times Book Review* (17 May 1981): 1, 26.

Audiocassette

"Jim Harrison—Reads *Wolf*, *Legends of the Fall*, *Farmer*, and *Sundog*" (excerpts). Columbia, Mo.: American Audio Prose Library, Box 842, Columbia, Mo. 65205.

SECONDARY SOURCES

Interviews

Bohy, Ric. "Jim Harrison, The Mad Poet Cools off (a Little)." *Michigan: The Magazine of the Detroit News* (9 February 1986): 8–10, 14, 16–18. Both an article about and an interview with Harrison.

Bonetti, Kay. "An Interview with Jim Harrison." *Missouri Review* 8, no. 3 (1985): 65–86. Also available on audiocassette from American Audio Prose Library, P.O. Box 842, Columbia, Mo. 65205.

Brandt, Anthony. "Man of the Moment Jim Harrison: Season of the Wolf."
    Men's Journal (June-July 1994): 96–99. See "Contributors" section in
    which photographer Mary Ellen Mark praises Harrison for his profession-
    alism and greatness.
Dettman, Marc. "Legends of the North." *Grand Rapids* 19, no. 8 (August
    1982): 30–34.
Elliott, Ira, and Marty Sommerness. "Jim Harrison: A Good Day for Talking:
    An Interview with the Author of *Wolf* and *Farmer*." *October Chronicle* (29
    October 1976) [not paginated].
Fergus, Jim. "Jim Harrison: Today's Hemingway?" *MD* (May 1985): 116,
    118–19, 244–46. Both an article about and an interview with Harrison.
————. "The Art of Fiction CIV: Jim Harrison." *Paris Review* 30, no. 107
    (1988): 52–97. Excerpts reprinted in "Jim Harrison," *Contemporary
    Literary Criticism*, vol. 66, edited by Roger Matuz (Detroit: Gale Research,
    1991), 157–61.
Newth, Rebecca. "For Harrison, Writing a Matter of Shifting Gears." *Arkansas
    Democrat-Gazette*, 15 May 1994, 8J.
Nuwer, Hank. "The Man Whose Soul Is Not for Sale: Jim Harrison."
    Rendezvous: Journal of Arts and Letters 21, no. 1 (Fall 1985): 26–42.
Ross, Jean W. "An Interview with Jim Harrison." In *Dictionary of Literary
    Biography Yearbook*, edited by Richard Ziegfeld. Detroit: Gale
    Research/Bruccoli Clark, 1983), 275–76.
————. "*CA* Interview." In *Contemporary Authors: New Series*, vol. 8, edited by
    Ann Evory and Deborah A. Straub (Detroit: Gale Research, 1983),
    227–29.
Siegal, Eric. "A New Voice from the North Country: A Portrait of the Prodigal
    Poet Who Came Home to Michigan." *Detroit Free Press Magazine* (16
    April 1972): 18–20. Both an article about and interview with Harrison.
Sisyphus, Aloysius. "The *Diddy Wah Diddy* Interview: Jim Harrison." *Diddy
    Wah Diddy* [Jackson, Miss.] 6, no. 5 (October 1990): 6–7.
Skwira, Gregory. "Words from the Woods." *Detroit* (25 March 1984): 8–9, 11,
    13–15, 16, 18–19. Both an article about and interview with Harrison.
Smith, Wendy. "*PW* Interviews Jim Harrison." *Publishers Weekly* 237, no. 3 (3
    August 1990): 59–60. Both an article about and interview with
    Harrison.
Stocking, Kathleen. "Hard Cases: Conversation with Jim Harrison and Tom
    McGuane, Riders of the Purple Rage." *Detroit News Magazine* (12 August
    1980): 14–15ff. Both an article about and interview with Harrison.
Stocking, Kathy. "Writer Jim Harrison: Work, Booze, the Outdoor Life—And
    an Absolute Rage for Order." *Detroit Free Press*, 5 June 1977, 21–22,
    24–26. Both an article about and interview with Harrison.

BIBLIOGRAPHY

Colonnese, Tom. "Jim Harrison: A Checklist." *Bulletin of Bibliography* 39, no. 3 (September 1982): 132–35.

Critical Articles, Books, Essays

Aubrey, Bryan. "*Dalva*." In *Magill's Literary Annual 1989*, edited by Frank N. Magill (Englewood Cliffs, N.J.: Salem Press, 1989), 212–15. Critical analysis of *Dalva*.

"Backstage with *Esquire*: Rewards of Revenge." *Esquire* 91, no. 9 (8 May 1979): 5. Biographical information and two interesting Harrison comments.

Bass, Rick. "Shyness." *Black Warrior Review* 15, no. 2 (1989): 155–59. Bass and his wife Elizabeth visit Harrison and Dan Gerber at Jamie Harrison Potenberg's home in Montana.

BeVier, Thomas. "A Hint of Harrison." *Traverse* (April 1988): 17. About *Dalva* with comments by Harrison.

Biskin, Peter. "Who's Afraid of the Big Bad Wolf?" *Premiere* 7, no. 7 (March 1994): 56–63. Mainly about Mike Nichols and Jack Nicholson, but Harrison comments about his lycanthropic experience in the U.P., Douglas Wick, and the origin for the movie *Wolf*.

Bourjaily, Vance. "Three Novellas: Violent Means." *New York Times Book Review* (17 June 1979): 14. Perceptive insights into *Legends of the Fall*.

Breen, Kevin. "An Interview with Rick Bass." *Poets and Writers* 21, no. 3 (May-June 1993): 18–25. Bass explains the influence of Harrison and *Legends of the Fall* on his own literary career.

Burkholder, Robert E. "Jim Harrison." In *Dictionary of Literary Biography Yearbook 1982*, edited by Richard Ziegfeld (Detroit: Gale Research/Bruccoli Clark, 1983), 266–76. Informative overview of Harrison's life and writings.

Chatham, Russell. *Silent Seasons: Twenty-One Fishing Stories*. Livingston, Mont.: Clark City Press, 1988. Includes Harrison's comments about fishing's therapeutic values plus his essays: "A Plaster Trout in Worm Heaven," "A Sporting Life," and "Ice Fishing: The Moronic Sport," all of which appear in *Just before Dark*.

———. *Dark Waters: Essays, Stories and Articles*. Livingston, Mont.: Clark City Press, 1991. Some pictures of and information about Harrison and McGuane.

Collins, Nancy. "Wolf, Man, Jack." *Vanity Fair* 57, no. 4 (April 1994): 118–24, 166–70. Although mainly about Jack Nicholson, Harrison comments about his own lycanthropic experience that became the basis for the film *Wolf*.

Eckstein, Barbara J. "On Being Male in America; Or, The Dancer in the
    Dance." *Southern Review* 19, no. 1 (March 1986): 76–88. Perceptive
    insights about *Farmer*.
Fergus, Jim. "The Sporting Club." *Outside* (March 1989): 40–44, 112–17.
    Essential for understanding the friendships between Harrison, McGuane,
    Chatham, and Valdene.
Gilligan, Thomas Mahler. "Myth and Reality in Jim Harrison's *Warlock*."
    Critique 25, no. 3 (Spring 1984): 147–53. Insights about midlife crisis,
    myth, and reality.
Gruzinska, Aleksandra. "E. M. Cioran and *The Man Who Gave up His Name* by
    Jim Harrison." *Journal of the American Romanian Society of Arts and Sciences*
    12 (1989): 83–93. Excellent analysis of this novella, its conflicts, themes,
    and their relation to Cioran's works.
Iyer, Pico. "Romancing the Home." *The Nation* 238 (23 June 1984): 767–70.
    Reviews *Sundog* while emphasizing Harrison's relationship with Emerson,
    Thoreau, and transcendentalism.
Lorenz, Paul H. "Rethinking Machismo: Jim Harrison's *Legends of the Fall*."
    Publications of the Arkansas Philological Association 15, no. 1 (Spring 1989):
    41–51. Cogent discussion refuting the assertion that Harrison's novellas
    are macho.
McDowell, Terry. "Russell Chatham: A Complicated Sense of Place." *Smart* 11
    (July-August 1990): 58–60. Informative background about Chatham,
    his life and art.
Morice, Laura. "Drama: *Wolf*." *US* (June 1994): 75. About the movie *Wolf*;
    Harrison talks about his lycanthropic experience in the U.P.
Munro, C. Lynn. "Jim Harrison." In *Critical Survey of Long Fiction*, vol. 4, edited
    by Frank N. Magill (La Canada, Calif.: Salem Press, 1983), 1286–95.
    Biographical overview plus literary analysis of Harrison's novels from
    Wolf through *Warlock*.
———. "Jim Harrison." In *Critical Survey of Long Fiction*, rev. ed., edited by
    Frank N. Magill (Englewood Cliffs, N.J.: Salem Press, 1991), 1534–49.
    Biographical overview plus updated analysis of Harrison's novels and
    novellas, including *Legends of the Fall*, *Sundog*, *Dalva*, *The Woman Lit by
    Fireflies*; Munro mistakenly identifies Dalva's grandfather (instead of her
    great-grandfather) as the writer of the journals.
———. "Jim Harrison." In *Critical Survey of Poetry*, edited by Frank N. Magill
    (Englewood Cliffs, N.J.: Salem Press, 1992). Biographical information
    plus analysis of Harrison's poetry.
Potter, Jeff. "A Drink with Jim Harrison." *Out Your Backdoor: A Magazine of
    Informal Adventure* 3 (Spring 1991): 12–13. Account of Potter's meeting
    with Harrison and Harrison's comments.
Prescott, Peter S. "The Macho Mystique." *Newsweek* 94 (9 July 1979): 72. The
    article that initiated the war between Harrison and critics who label him
    a macho writer.

Ravo, Nick. "Will Write for Food." *New York Times*, 17 April 1994, 8V. A visit with Harrison in Sonoita, Arizona, at his favorite restaurant, Er Pastaro, and his comments.

Reed, Julia. "Books." *Vogue* 179 (September 1989): 502, 506, 510. Biographical information plus remarks by Harrison.

Reilly, Edward C. "Cervantes' *Don Quixote* and Harrison's *Warlock*: Some Similarities and Differences." *Notes on Contemporary Literature* 15, no. 3 (May 1985): 3. Analysis of Harrison's borrowing but changing details from *Don Quixote*.

————. "The Tragedy and the Folly: Harrison's *A Good Day to Die*—An Earlier Vision." *Publications of the Mississippi Philological Association* (1986): 23–33. Contrasts the courage and purpose of the Nez Perce with Harrison's characters as wanderers without purpose.

Roberson, William H. "A Good Day to Live: The Prose Works of Jim Harrison." *Great Lakes Review* 9, no. 1 (1983): 29–37. Seminal examination of Harrison's characters, themes, and conflicts from *Wolf* through *Warlock*.

————. "The Macho Mistake: The Misrepresentation of Jim Harrison's Fiction." *Critique* 29, no. 4 (Summer 1988): 233–44. Insightful discussion arguing that Harrison does not write macho fiction.

Rohrkemper, John. "'Natty Bumppo Wants Tobacco': Jim Harrison's Wilderness." *Great Lakes Review* 9, no. 1 (1983): 20–28. Seminal analysis of Harrison's *Wolf*, *Warlock*, and *The Man Who Gave up His Name* and some of his poems.

Stocking, Kathleen. "Heart and Soul." *Detroit Monthly* (September 1988): 178, 180. About *Dalva*; Harrison also comments about life and work.

Wilson, John. "Legends of the Fall." In *Magill's Literary Annual: Books of 1979*, edited by Frank N. Magill (Englewood Cliffs, N.J.: Salem Press, 1980), 462–66. Critical analysis of *Legends of the Fall*.

Index

The Author

Edward C. Reilly is associate professor of English at Arkansas State University and author of *William Kennedy* in the Twayne U.S. Authors Series.

The Editor

Frank Day is a professor of English and head of the English Department at Clemson University. He is the author of *Sir William Empson: An Annotated Bibliography* (1984) and *Arthur Koestler: A Guide to Research* (1985). He was a Fulbright lecturer in American literature in Romania (1980–81) and in Bangladesh (1986–87).